David Thomson

Handy Book of Fruit Culture under Glass

David Thomson

Handy Book of Fruit Culture under Glass

ISBN/EAN: 9783743313446

Manufactured in Europe, USA, Canada, Australia, Japa

Cover: Foto ©Lupo / pixelio.de

Manufactured and distributed by brebook publishing software (www.brebook.com)

David Thomson

Handy Book of Fruit Culture under Glass

HANDY BOOK

OF

FRUIT CULTURE UNDER GLASS

HANDY BOOK

OF

FRUIT CULTURE UNDER GLASS

BY

DAVID THOMSON

AUTHOR OF 'HANDY BOOK OF THE FLOWER-GARDEN,' 'A PRACTICAL
TREATISE ON THE CULTURE OF THE PINE-APPLE,' ETC.

SECOND EDITION, REVISED AND ENLARGED

WILLIAM BLACKWOOD AND SONS
EDINBURGH AND LONDON
MDCCCLXXXI

PREFACE.

The culture under glass of the fruits treated on in this book, has, in some instances, been included in larger and more compendious works on horticulture in general; and on the other hand, various smaller works have appeared, each occupied exclusively by one fruit.

But there is not, so far as I am aware, any book of moderate size in which the forcing and general culture of these fruits collectively is discussed. The present Handy Book has been written with a view to supplying this want; and the Author indulges the hope that, compact as it is, it will be found to contain every necessary detail with regard to such culture.

In writing it, he has kept specially in view the requirements of inexperienced amateurs who wish to superintend their own fruit-houses, and of young gardeners entering on the study of their profession.

All the fruits which are most generally cultivated under glass have been included among the subjects discussed; and the systems on which they are recommended to be grown are those which it is considered yield the most speedy and certain return with a minimum of labour and cost.

DAVID THOMSON.

Drumlanrig Gardens.

CONTENTS.

	PAGE
THE PINE-APPLE,	1
Pineries,	2
Varieties of pines,	9
Soil,	13
Propagation,	15
Suckers,	16
Succession plants—spring treatment,	20
Succession plants—summer and autumn treatment,	27
Fruiting plants,	35
Retarding and keeping pine-apples after they are ripe,	40
How to keep up a constant succession of ripe fruit all the year,	42
Plants that miss fruiting,	45
The planting-out system,	46
Insects to which the pine is subject,	47
THE GRAPE VINE,	50
Site for vineries,	52
Vinery for early forcing,	53
Vinery for late grapes,	56
Drainage,	59
Borders—their composition,	61
Varieties of grapes,	68
Selecting vines for planting,	70
Preparing young vines for planting,	71
Time and manner of planting vines,	77
Treatment the season they are planted,	81
Management of vines the second season,	86
Management of vines the third and fruiting year,	90
Weight of crop, thinning, disbudding, &c.,	96

Spur-pruning for next season's crop, ... 98
Training, ... 100
Keeping grapes through the winter, ... 101
General management of borders, ... 102
Renovating exhausted vines, ... 105
The pot-culture of grapes, ... 107
Inarching vines, ... 108
Setting up grapes for exhibition, ... 110
Packing grapes, ... 112
Insects to which vines are subject, ... 114
Diseases to which vines are subject, ... 130

THE PEACH AND NECTARINE, ... 136
Peach-house for early forcing, ... 138
Peach-house when ripe peaches are not required before July, . 139
Drainage, depth, and width of border, ... 143
Soil, ... 144
Varieties for early forcing, ... 146
Propagation and selection of trees, ... 147
Planting, ... 151
Pruning and training, ... 152
Disbudding, or summer pruning, ... 159
Thinning the fruit, ... 161
Root-pruning, ... 162
Forcing and general management, ... 163
Dressing the trees and borders, ... 164
Temperature, ... 165
Ventilation, ... 167
Moisture in the air and syringing, ... 168
Setting the fruit, ... 169
Watering, ... 170
Ripening and gathering the fruit, ... 171
Packing peaches to be sent to a distance, ... 172
Insects, ... 173
Diseases, ... 174

THE FIG, ... 176
Fig-house, ... 180
Soil and formation of border, ... 181
Varieties of figs, ... 183
Propagation, ... 184
Time and manner of planting, ... 189
Training and general management the first year, . . . 191
Pruning and pinching, ... 193

Figs in pots,	197
Forcing and general management,	200
Temperature, watering, &c.,	201
Ripening the fruit,	203
Second crop,	204
Insects and diseases,	205
Packing figs,	206
THE MELON,	207
Growing melons in dung-beds or pits,	210
Sowing the seed, and management of young plants,	211
Training and stopping,	213
Soil and planting, &c.,	214
Moulding up—temperature,	216
Impregnation, watering, &c.,	217
Culture in melon-houses trained on wires near the glass—form of house, depth of soil, &c.,	220
Preparing the plants, planting, &c.,	223
Watering, &c.,	224
Temperature and syringing,	225
Ventilation,	226
Impregnation, training, and stopping,	226
Very early forcing,	227
Varieties,	229
Insects and diseases,	229
THE STRAWBERRY,	231
The best runners,	232
Preparing runners for their fruiting-pots,	233
Soil and potting, &c.,	234
Strawberry-house,	239
Forcing,	240
Setting and thinning the fruit, &c.,	242
Insects to which they are subject,	245
Strawberries in a greenhouse or pit,	245
Tying up the fruit-stalks, &c.,	246
Packing ripe strawberries for carrying,	247
Preparing fruit for exhibition,	248
Varieties for forcing,	249
THE CUCUMBER,	251
The seed-bed,	252
Sowing the seeds, and treatment of the young plants,	253
Fruiting-pits, planting-out, &c.,	257

PREFACE.

The culture under glass of the fruits treated on in this book, has, in some instances, been included in larger and more compendious works on horticulture in general; and on the other hand, various smaller works have appeared, each occupied exclusively by one fruit.

But there is not, so far as I am aware, any book of moderate size in which the forcing and general culture of these fruits collectively is discussed. The present Handy Book has been written with a view to supplying this want; and the Author indulges the hope that, compact as it is, it will be found to contain every necessary detail with regard to such culture.

In writing it, he has kept specially in view the requirements of inexperienced amateurs who wish to superintend their own fruit-houses, and of young gardeners entering on the study of their profession.

348917

All the fruits which are most generally cultivated under glass have been included among the subjects discussed; and the systems on which they are recommended to be grown are those which it is considered yield the most speedy and certain return with a minimum of labour and cost.

DAVID THOMSON.

DRUMLANRIG GARDENS.

CONTENTS.

	PAGE
THE PINE-APPLE,	1
Pineries,	2
Varieties of pines,	9
Soil,	13
Propagation,	15
Suckers,	16
Succession plants—spring treatment,	20
Succession plants—summer and autumn treatment,	27
Fruiting plants,	35
Retarding and keeping pine-apples after they are ripe,	40
How to keep up a constant succession of ripe fruit all the year,	42
Plants that miss fruiting,	45
The planting-out system,	46
Insects to which the pine is subject,	47
THE GRAPE VINE,	50
Site for vineries,	52
Vinery for early forcing,	53
Vinery for late grapes,	56
Drainage,	59
Borders—their composition,	61
Varieties of grapes,	68
Selecting vines for planting,	70
Preparing young vines for planting,	71
Time and manner of planting vines,	77
Treatment the season they are planted,	81
Management of vines the second season,	86
Management of vines the third and fruiting year,	90
Weight of crop, thinning, disbudding, &c.,	96

CONTENTS.

Spur-pruning for next season's crop,	98
Training,	100
Keeping grapes through the winter,	101
General management of borders,	102
Renovating exhausted vines,	105
The pot-culture of grapes,	107
Inarching vines,	108
Setting up grapes for exhibition,	110
Packing grapes,	112
Insects to which vines are subject,	114
Diseases to which vines are subject,	130
THE PEACH AND NECTARINE,	136
Peach-house for early forcing,	138
Peach-house when ripe peaches are not required before July,	139
Drainage, depth, and width of border,	143
Soil,	144
Varieties for early forcing,	146
Propagation and selection of trees,	147
Planting,	151
Pruning and training,	152
Disbudding, or summer pruning,	159
Thinning the fruit,	161
Root-pruning,	162
Forcing and general management,	163
Dressing the trees and borders,	164
Temperature,	165
Ventilation,	167
Moisture in the air and syringing,	168
Setting the fruit,	169
Watering,	170
Ripening and gathering the fruit,	171
Packing peaches to be sent to a distance,	172
Insects,	173
Diseases,	174
THE FIG,	176
Fig-house,	180
Soil and formation of border,	181
Varieties of figs,	183
Propagation,	184
Time and manner of planting,	189
Training and general management the first year,	191
Pruning and pinching,	193

Figs in pots,	197
Forcing and general management,	200
Temperature, watering, &c.,	201
Ripening the fruit,	203
Second crop,	204
Insects and diseases,	205
Packing figs,	206
THE MELON,	207
Growing melons in dung-beds or pits,	210
Sowing the seed, and management of young plants,	211
Training and stopping,	213
Soil and planting, &c.,	214
Moulding up—temperature,	216
Impregnation, watering, &c.,	217
Culture in melon-houses trained on wires near the glass—form of house, depth of soil, &c.,	220
Preparing the plants, planting, &c.,	223
Watering, &c.,	224
Temperature and syringing,	225
Ventilation,	226
Impregnation, training, and stopping,	226
Very early forcing,	227
Varieties,	229
Insects and diseases,	229
THE STRAWBERRY,	231
The best runners,	232
Preparing runners for their fruiting-pots,	233
Soil and potting, &c.,	234
Strawberry-house,	239
Forcing,	240
Setting and thinning the fruit, &c.,	242
Insects to which they are subject,	245
Strawberries in a greenhouse or pit,	245
Tying up the fruit-stalks, &c.,	246
Packing ripe strawberries for carrying,	247
Preparing fruit for exhibition,	248
Varieties for forcing,	249
THE CUCUMBER,	251
The seed-bed,	252
Sowing the seeds, and treatment of the young plants,	253
Fruiting-pits, planting-out, &c.,	257

CONTENTS.

Preparing the pit for the plants, soil, &c., ... 258
Management after planting in the fruiting-pit, . . . 259
Watering and stopping, &c., ... 261
Winter cucumbers, ... 263
Cucumber-houses, ... 264
Soil, &c., ... 265
Planting, temperature, &c., ... 266
Insects, ... 268
Diseases, ... 268
Varieties, ... 269

THE CALENDAR, ... 270
   January, ... 270
   February, ... 274
   March, ... 277
   April, ... 281
   May, ... 285
   June, ... 289
   July, ... 292
   August, ... 296
   September, ... 299
   October, ... 303
   November, ... 306
   December, ... 309

A FEW OBSERVATIONS ON HEATING BY HOT WATER, . . 313

INDEX, ... 319

HANDY BOOK

OF

FRUIT CULTURE UNDER GLASS.

THE PINE-APPLE.

This noble fruit has derived the name of pine-apple from its striking resemblance in shape to the cones of some of the pine-trees. It is probably the most rich and luscious of fruits. "Three hundred years ago it was described by Jean de Levy, a Huguenot priest, as being of such excellence that the gods might luxuriate upon it, and that it should only be gathered by the hands of a Venus."

Some say that it is a native of Brazil, and found its way from that country to the East. It is, however, not very clearly determined to what part of the world we are indebted for the pine-apple; and there is little doubt that it is also a native of the West Indies, for many of its varieties are found growing wild on the continent and islands of the West. It was first brought into Europe by a Dutch merchant, and introduced into this country from Holland in 1690; and first cultivated for the dessert by Mr Bentinck, ancestor to the present ducal family of Portland.

FRUIT CULTURE UNDER GLASS.

The superior cultivation of the pine-apple has always been regarded as one of the greatest triumphs of horticulturists. Improved practice is perhaps as much apparent in pine-culture as in any branch of horticulture. Superior results are now attained in eighteen months to what it required twice that time to produce in the recollection of the writer. To Mr James Barnes, late gardener at Bicton Park, Devonshire, we are indebted for exposing and discontinuing the erroneous practice of annually disrooting pine plants, and subjecting them to too high a soil temperature. This was the first step in contracting the period considered necessary to bring the pine-apple to maturity. And of more recent date is the very general cultivation of the pine-apple in much smaller pots than were used some thirty-five years ago: and where the pot system is practised, the use of smaller pots makes them more easily managed, and at less expense.

PINERIES.

That which naturally claims attention first in treating on the cultivation of the pine-apple is, the description of houses or pineries which afford the greatest convenience and facilities for first-rate cultivation, their situation, and the exposure which they should occupy. The situation should be one well sheltered from cutting winds, and having a full south aspect. There is nothing that necessitates hard firing to keep up a given temperature more than exposure to high winds; and the atmosphere will be the more conducive to healthy growth the less firing is required to maintain the heat. Therefore, shelter from north, east, and west should be taken into consideration in the erection of

THE PINE-APPLE.

pineries, especially if the situation is naturally exposed to high winds. It must, however, be borne in mind, that whatever the sheltering objects, they must not be allowed to interfere with full exposure to sunshine at all seasons of the year.

During by far the greater portion of the year, pines cannot possibly have more light and sun than are necessary to produce a stocky fruitful growth in the dull atmosphere which so much prevails in this country. Pineries should therefore be constructed so as to admit and diffuse as much light and sunshine as can be had. In the few months when at times the sun may be more scorching than is desirable, a slight shading can easily be applied. When the sash-and-rafter principle is adopted, I would advise that the sashes should not be less than 6 feet wide, and divided into five openings or panes of glass.

For summer growth I would give the preference to

FIG. 1.

span-roofed houses, running north and south (fig. 1). In the morning and afternoon they receive the full sun; and for a period in the middle of the day, when the sun is in meridian, the pines are, in such houses, partially shaded from the scorching rays of the sun, while at the same time they are exposed to a great diffusion of light. Such houses are decidedly the best for summer growth; but, for six months of the year, they do not, from their position, embrace so much direct sunshine as a lean-to house facing due south. Moreover, from the greater amount of glass as a radiating surface in span-roofed houses, they require more fire-heat to keep up the temperature. In these respects the lean-to gives advantages over the span-roofed pinery, in whatever position the latter is placed. For starting pines in December and the two following months, as well as for swelling off fruit during winter and early spring, I recommend lean-to houses, as represented by fig. 2.

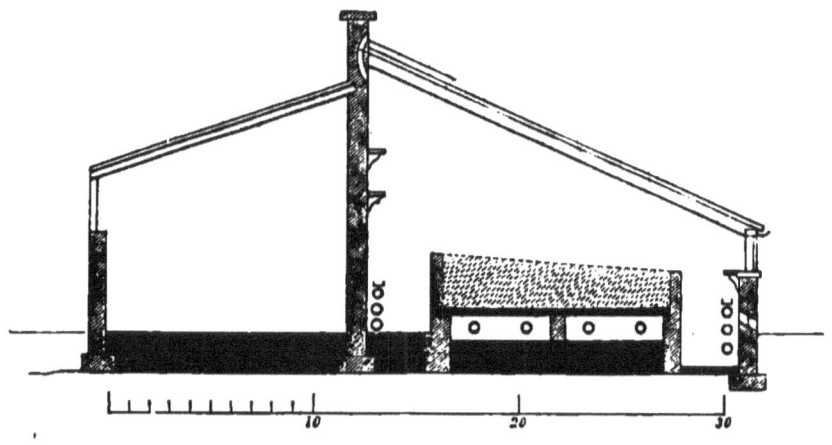

FIG. 2.

The dimensions of the two pineries represented by the woodcuts, are 40 feet by 18 feet, which give a house of handsome proportions. But as the extent of the pineries must be guided entirely by the supply required, I will not enter further into this question. Suffice it to say, that it is more desirable to have several structures of moderate size than a less number of larger ones. A constant succession of ripe fruit is much more easily kept up by having a number of compartments.

For suckers, a common lean-to pit, as represented by fig. 3, is very well adapted, as the young plants can be kept near the glass, and well exposed to light. Where expense is not an object, and for the sake of convenience, this pit may be wider, and have a path along the back, in which case another row of pipes will be necessary. But as the woodcuts given will explain more correctly than words the description of pineries recommended, I will not extend my remarks under this heading. It will be observed that the accommodation which I prefer and recommend is partly span-roofed and partly lean-to.

Fig. 3.

In the formation of the pine ground, the lean-to or early houses should be on the north of the space selected, so that the back affords the shelter from the north which is so desirable; the span-roofed structures to stand north and south, or at right angles with the early lean-to houses, and at a sufficient distance from them not to obstruct sunshine. The early house is thus nearest the boiler in the back shed, and forms the very best shelter to the span-roofed or succession pits, which should not be very high. I am aware, indeed, from experience, that such houses and arrangements are not absolutely necessary for the production of first-rate pines; but they afford great advantages and convenience, and I recommend them as admirably adapted for the culture of this noble fruit.

The pine-apple being a fruit which requires a high temperature, particularly in some of its stages of growth, there should be a good command of heat both for top and bottom. It is not only a false economy to stint the amount of pipes employed, but a larger heating surface moderately heated is much more conducive to the health of plants than a smaller surface kept at scorching heat. I therefore recommend, as shown in the sections given, a liberal amount of pipes and plenty of boiler-power. Besides this I feel fully persuaded, from my experience, that coverings applied to the glass, particularly in the case of fruit swelling off during the colder months of the year, are an immense advantage. A high and steady temperature can be much more easily and economically maintained, and without a parched atmosphere, which in the case of hard forcing in winter requires so much and such constant counteracting.

I have a decided objection to flat-roofed pineries. They are dark, and very productive of drip in winter—conditions the most undesirable in the culture of most plants, and especially so in that of the pineapple. Ventilation should be amply provided for at the apex of the roof; and, particularly in fruiting-houses, there should also be ventilators at intervals along the front, so placed as to cause the air to pass inward in contact with the hot-water pipes. Front ventilation is not to be recommended as a rule; but it is well to provide for it in the erection of pineries, so that in very hot calm days it can be applied, especially in the case of fruit that are colouring.

All pineries and pits should be provided with a steadily-acting steaming apparatus, which can be used or not according as circumstances demand.

A great many methods of supplying moisture to the atmosphere of hothouses have been adopted—such as zinc troughs placed on the pipes, troughs cast on the pipes themselves, a flow of water running in an open gutter, rising out of the flow-pipe at one end of the house and dropping into the return at the other. I have tried all these ways, and more besides, and consider them all inferior to that represented by fig. 4. This is a flat-bottomed open gutter or trough, 6 inches wide, and 2½ inches deep, running the whole length of the house. In the centre and along the whole length of the trough is fixed a rain-water or lead pipe, 2½ inches in diameter. This, as will be seen, is connected with the flow-pipe as it leaves the boiler, and with the return-pipe at the other end of the house. At the middle of the house a tap is fitted into the 2½-inch pipe; a flow of water from the tap can be so adjusted as to let water sufficient trickle into the

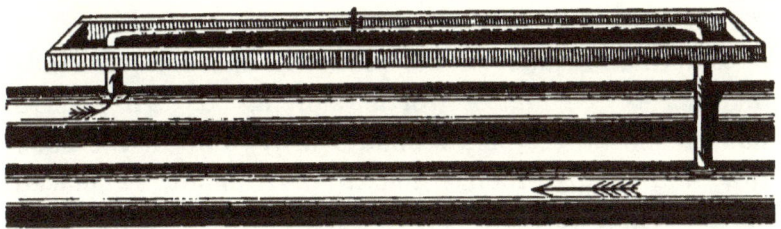

Fig. 4.

trough to keep it full and the small pipe nearly immersed in water. The supply to the boiler being by ball-cock, the small quantity of water that escapes from the tap is constantly supplied. This apparatus requires next to no attention, and heats regularly the whole length of the house. In open gutters without this small pipe, we have always found too much steam at one end of the house and next to none at the other, especially in long houses. The arrangement we recommend is quite equal in heating power to a row of 4-inch pipe. When atmospheric moisture is not required, the water can be dried up out of the trough by simply turning the tap. This system of supplying moisture is applicable in the case of forcing the other fruits treated of in this volume. The pipes should also be so arranged that, by means of stop-cocks, the bottom-heat can be shut off, and applied and regulated according to the amount recommended for the different stages of the growth of the pine.

In all pine-stoves where there is not a supply of soft water from lake or stream, there should be a tank into which to conduct the rain-water from the roof, and passing through the tank a coil of hot-water pipe to warm it. This, in cases where pines are grown extensively, saves a vast amount of trouble in warming water, or in drawing it from the heating apparatus, which latter, for several reasons, is not desirable.

The arrangement of the plants in the various kinds of pineries is a matter worth referring to. In lean-to houses the tallest plants should always be in the back row, and in span-roofed houses they should be placed in the centre row, so that in each case the plants form a sloping bank of foliage all fully exposed to the sun. Where the plants are of very equal growth, the centre of the bed in span-roofed houses should be a little higher.

As I intend to refer to the management of the leaf-and-tan bed in the cultural directions to be given, I will not here enter on that question. I may just state that, apart from the increased labour and liability to violent heating, I have a warm side for the tan-and-leaf bed for pine-growing. I consider the heat derived from this old-fashioned source second to none other for the production of fine pines. Yet I would never prefer it to hot water, because it entails more labour and much more watchfulness, which, in these high-pressure days, is a powerful argument in favour of deriving all the heat from hot water, by which means it can be easily applied and regulated to a degree. Nevertheless, I intend to speak of the management that I adopt in the case of pines grown on a bed of leaves and tan for the supply of bottom-heat. To derive top-heat from fermenting material is a thing which, I believe, is now rarely thought of, and is, to say the least of it, an expensive and cumbrous system.

VARIETIES OF PINES.

In making a selection of varieties, it is not necessary to have many in order to keep up a constant supply of first-rate pines. I believe I am correct in saying that nearly all pine-growers have discontinued the practice of growing so many varieties as were commonly grown many years ago, and will not, therefore, give an extended list, but will enumerate and shortly describe those which are considered the best, and indispensable in pine-growing establishments of ordinary dimensions.

THE QUEEN.—This old and well-known variety still holds its position as one of the best for ripening from May till the end of October. It is a free grower, dwarf and compact in habit, a very certain fruiter, comes quickly to maturity, is very handsome in shape, and of a rich golden colour. Its flavour, as a summer and autumn pine, is not excelled by any other, and it keeps in good condition for three weeks after being ripe. It propagates itself freely by suckers. From May till the end of October there is no pine to surpass it for general excellence; but it will not swell freely in winter, and, as a winter pine, is generally wanting in juiciness and flavour. The Ripley and Moscow Queens are distinct varieties of this, and both good.

SMOOTH-LEAVED CAYENNE.—Taken as a whole, this is the finest pine I know for supplying ripe fruit from October till May, and is the most generally useful variety in cultivation. It swells more freely, and is more juicy in winter, than any other pine that I have grown, and its flavour is excellent. The habit of the plant is somewhat taller than the Queen, and more spreading, with very broad, brittle, dark-green leaves. It is a large and handsome fruit, and, when well swelled, weighs a pound for every pip in depth. Colour a rich yellow, shape slightly conical; when swelled to its best it is rather barrel-shaped. This splendid pine has taken a high position in most collections. For some time spurious smooth-leaved varieties were thrown on the market for this one, and in consequence it fell into considerable disrepute; but it has now fairly established its deservedly high position among pines. It should be in all collections.

BLACK JAMAICA.—Tall and erect in growth, a certain fruiter, medium size, with large flat pips, rather dull in colour, very high flavoured, probably the highest flavoured winter pine in cultivation; but some object to its hardness of flesh, and prefer the Smooth Cayenne on account of the melting juiciness of the latter. Still there can be no doubt of the excellence of the flavour of this variety, and a few of it should be cultivated wherever winter pines are esteemed.

WHITE PROVIDENCE.—A strong and tall-growing variety. Leaves very broad, and covered with down. It yields the largest fruit of any variety in cultivation. Globular in form, with very large flat pips. Flavour quite second-rate. It is an easily-grown and free-fruiting pine; but unless where there is plenty of room it is not to be recommended, and a few plants are sufficient in the largest collection.

CHARLOTTE ROTHSCHILD.—Resembles the Smooth Cayenne in size and habit of plant, but its leaves are studded with strong spines; fruit large, flavour good; is a splendid winter pine—in this respect almost equal to the Cayenne; is a certain fruiter, and grows to a large size. I have ripened it in 11-inch pots, weighing 11 lb. It should be in every collection.

PRINCE ALBERT.—A tall but very compact grower, can be grown in the same space as a Queen. Fruit large, conical, very showy; crown small. Swells well in winter. Flesh soft, very juicy and well flavoured. Free fruiter. It has the fault of not keeping many days after it is ripe, and often large fruits of it begin to decay at their base before they are coloured to the top. A few only should be grown.

LAMBTON CASTLE SEEDLING.—This splendid variety was put into commerce in 1878, and it fully maintains its good character. Remarkable for its free-fruiting habit and large fruit. We believe it is capable of being grown to 12 lb. weight. Fig. 5 is an engraving from a photograph of a fruit ripened in midwinter at Lambton Castle on a plant 19 months old. The fruit measured 12 inches high and 20 inches in circumference, and weighed over 10 lb.; and including the crown, the height from the surface of the pot did not exceed 30 inches. Colour of fruit high orange. Foliage robust, and thinly furnished with unusually strong spines. Keeps well after being ripe, and is exceedingly juicy and well flavoured.

There are a great many more varieties which I might describe, such as different varieties of the Queen, Black

12 FRUIT CULTURE UNDER GLASS.

Prince, Enville, Prickly Cayenne, Globe, Antigua, and Blood-red, &c.; but though they are all distinct, they have characteristics which depreciate them; and unless in large establishments where they are grown for the

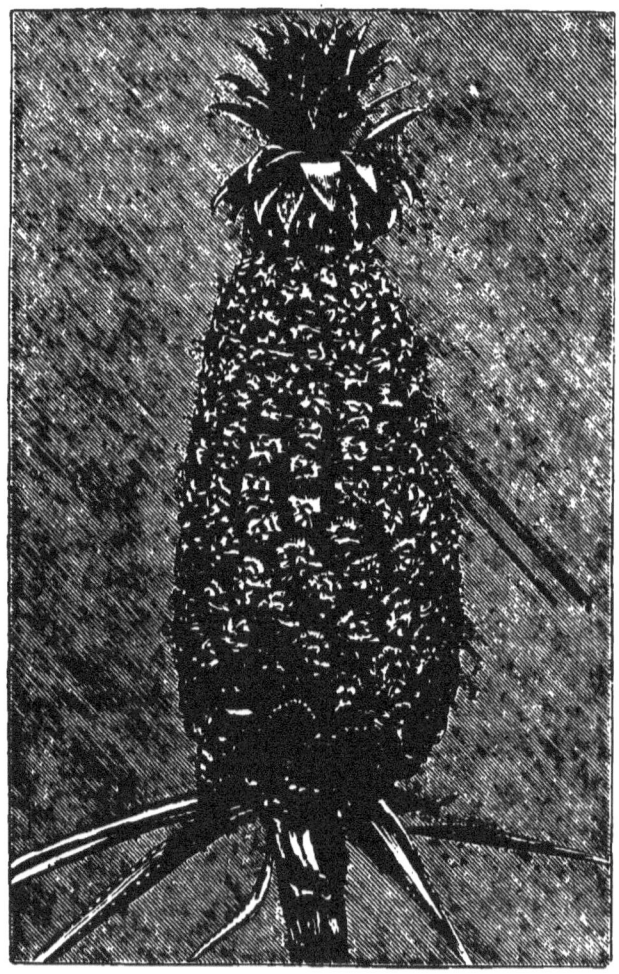

Fig. 5.

sake of mere variety, they have no claims upon the space at the disposal of pine-growers in general; and as I prefer to occupy space with cultural directions, as being the more useful, I will not describe any of these varieties that I cannot recommend. In my own practice, I have found the Queen, Smooth Cayenne, Charlotte Rothschild, and Prince Albert the best and freest-fruiting.

SOIL.

Dr Lindley, in his 'Theory of Horticulture,' says,— "We are informed by Beyrick, that the pine-apple in its wild state is found near the sea-shore—the sand accumulated there in downs serving for its growth as well as for that of most of the species of the same family. The place where the best pine-apples are cultivated is of a similar nature. In the sandy plains, Praya Velha and Praya Grande, formed by the receding of the sea, and in which few other plants will thrive, are the spots where the pine-apple grows best." Although the soil in which the pine-apple is found growing in its native or wild state cannot be taken as an absolute guide, still the fact that sand is its native choice would of itself serve to teach the cultivator that a heavy clayey soil, having a strong attraction for water, is not likely to be the most suitable for the healthy growth of pine-apples. I believe that practice has set its seal to this; at least my experience leads me to recommend a fibry calcareous loam in preference to that which all gardeners know as a heavy and tenacious loam. That in which I have grown the best pines was taken from the surface of a rocky crag, and was very full of fibre. It should be collected and stacked for twelve months before it is used; and a few months before being required for potting, put into a dry airy shed, breaking it up or teasing it with the hands—not separating a particle of the fibre, but rather sifting or shaking a portion of the mouldy particles from it. It thus forms a soil with much more fibre in it than is generally used for pines, and one which the soft, rather fleshy roots of the pine seem wonderfully to enjoy.

This soil is used without any addition of manure consisting of animal excrement. I consider it very undesirable to use anything that has a tendency to produce a pasty, retentive tendency in the loam, or that would rapidly hasten the decomposition of the fibrous part of it. Animal excrement has a tendency to do both, and on that account I never use it for the pine: all that is added to or mixed with the loam is an 8-inch potful of half-inch bones, and the same quantity of soot, to each barrowful of the loam. These mixtures are highly manurial, have a beneficial mechanical effect on the soil, and offer no inducement to the inroads of worms, but the contrary.

I have always observed that the most vigorous of the roots are found in the most fibry part of the ball. Besides, turfy loam, free from all slimy matter, is regarded as the best medium for supplying nourishment in a liquid state, as will be found recommended further on in this treatise. I would therefore recommend a friable loam, with all the verdure that grows on it—such as the top three, or at most four, inches of an old pasture, where such can be had; and should such not be attainable, and the cultivator therefore be obliged to use a heavier soil, I would recommend that a portion of sand, pounded oyster-shells, charcoal, old plaster, or mortar-rubbish be mixed with it, to prevent its ever becoming compressed or puttied —a condition which is most injurious.

PROPAGATION.

Generally there is little trouble in propagating and keeping up a stock of young plants, as the majority of varieties propagate themselves freely by suckers and crowns. The latter I never use, except in the case of some varieties which are very shy in producing suckers—such, for instance, as the Smooth-leaved Cayenne, and C. Rothschild. Suckers are much more desirable, and grow into strong plants more rapidly than crowns. Those varieties that do not produce suckers in sufficient abundance I always find easily enough increased by preserving the old plants from which the fruit is cut, stripping all the leaves off them, and placing them entire in shallow boxes, covering them to the depth of an inch with light rich soil, in a bottom-heat of $90°$. In this way every latent bud on the stems bursts into growth; and as soon as they begin to emit roots, they are twisted carefully from the old stem, and potted in 6-inch pots. The stems may also be split up through the middle, cut into pieces according to the number of buds, potted singly in small pots, and plunged in bottom-heat. This plan gives more labour and requires more room, and sometimes the pieces rot before the buds start. However, either way can be practised with success.

By this mode of propagation a clean stock can be produced from plants infested with scale. In this case the stems should be well scrubbed with soap and water before being placed in boxes or pots. In this way a perfectly clean set of plants have frequently been produced from stock which had been overrun with insects.

SUCKERS.

Suppose a quantity of suckers to come under treatment from the beginning of August to the middle of September—the time when suckers are generally in a fit state to be taken from plants that have produced the summer supply of fruit: let them be carefully detached from the parent plants, cut their rugged base smoothly off with the knife, and remove with the hand the short scaly leaves which cluster round their base, and under which appear the young roots. The leaves should not be removed any higher up than where these young roots assume a brownish hue. As this operation is proceeded with, the suckers, for convenience, should be classed into two lots, the smaller and the larger being placed by themselves. The larger set, presuming that they are strong and healthy, are to be potted in 8-inch, and the smaller in 6-inch pots. The pots, if not new, should be well washed both outside and inside. The crocking should be efficiently performed, using rather finely broken crocks with all dust sifted out of them. They should be arranged in the bottom of the pots to the depth of one and a half inch in the 6-inch, and two inches in the 8-inch pots. Over the crocks should be placed a thin layer of dry moss or the most fibry part of the loam, and over all a sprinkling of fresh soot, which acts as a barrier to worms and affords a stimulant to the plants.

In potting the suckers, place them sufficiently deep in the pots to keep them steadily in their places; press the soil firmly about them with a blunt-pointed piece of wood, and leave it about three-quarters of an inch from the rim of the pots, that there may be no difficulty in watering them when necessary. It being presumed that a pit was previously made ready for their reception, they should be plunged at once to the rim of the pot; and should the bottom-heat be derived from leaves or tan, or both, and not likely to exceed 90°, the plunging material may be placed firmly round the pots; but if the heat is likely to exceed 90°, let the material be placed lightly and openly round them. Let the plants be arranged as previously directed according to the structure of the pinery, and in doing so avoid crowding them together, the consequence of which is to draw the young plants up weakly—and to make good plants of them afterwards is almost impracticable.

They must now be shaded from the sun during the brightest part of the day for ten or fourteen days, or, in fact, till it be found that they are making roots. In the afternoon, when the shading is removed, they should have a gentle dewing overhead through a very fine rose. The shading and dewing must not be abruptly discontinued, but by degrees; and entirely given up whenever the young roots are two or three inches long. Then they should have a watering with water at 85° sufficient to moisten the whole ball. After this they soon begin to grow freely, and air should be given early in the day when fine. A good supply of air, as much light as possible, and a moderately moist atmosphere, with a very sparing use of the syringe only in hot weather, will prevent them from making a weakly drawn growth.

From the time the suckers are potted, the great object is to obtain a compact sturdy growth as one of the principal points of future success, which will enable the plants to go through the rigours of winter with impunity. This is dependent chiefly upon free

B

exposure to light, a good supply of air without draught, and a moderate amount of heat and moisture both at the roots and in the air.

The night temperature for September should range from 65° to 70°, with 10° to 15° more for a while when shut up in the afternoon with sun-heat. After the middle of October the heat should be 5° less, and it should gradually decrease till, by the middle of November, it is 55° to 60° at night according to the weather, with 5° more by day. During October the bottom-heat should not range higher than 85°; and for the three following months I consider 75° quite sufficient to keep the roots healthy through these dull months. In olden times, when every sucker potted in autumn was deprived of its black and lifeless roots in spring, it was considered that pines lost all their previous year's roots in the common course of nature. But there is no doubt whatever that the real cause of the evil arose from the common rule of renewing the beds in which the pines were plunged at the fall of the leaf, the consequence of which was a degree of bottom-heat which pine-roots cannot bear and live. The good pine-grower of the present time is not satisfied if, when September-potted suckers are shifted in early spring, their roots are not white and full of life, instead of black and shrivelled.

Under ordinary circumstances I would recommend that the suckers now being treated of should be kept quiet from the middle of November till the middle of February, and not encouraged to grow. To rest them thus, a temperature of 55° is preferable to 60°, unless during very mild weather, but 60° should never be exceeded. The atmosphere should be dry rather than otherwise; and I have very rarely found that, when grown on a bed of leaves and tan, during these months they ever require any water at the root. The tan in which the pots are plunged is generally moist enough for the maintenance of pine-roots in a healthy condition, and the soil in the pots is regulated as to moisture at this season by the state of the plunging material. Where the bottom-heat is supplied with hot-water pipes in air chambers or tanks, the plants may require an occasional watering; but with the bottom-heat that I have named, the waterings required will be very few indeed. Young stock is in very little danger of fruiting prematurely from being kept rather dry, if all else be right; and in all other respects it is much the best practice.

When the thermometer rises to 65° a little air should be put on, always at the highest point of the pit or house. But, unless during a continuance of dull damp weather, the temperature should not be purposely raised in order to admit of giving air. In most pineries there is a sufficient amount of circulation going on in the atmosphere through the laps of the glass and other chinks to render systematic air-giving, with the low temperature and dry atmosphere that I have recommended, unnecessary. It is therefore only during sunny days, when the heat is raised, that air-giving must be carefully attended to during the season of rest.

Under ordinary circumstances this is the winter treatment to be recommended as that which will give succession plants in the most robust and healthy condition in spring, and that can be grown into the very best fruiting stock by the following autumn. Scarcity of intermediate plants may, however, in certain cases, render it desirable to considerably increase the size of the plants in order to gain time. When such is the case they should be kept gently on the move all winter, by keeping the temperature at from 60° to 65°, with a little more moisture at the root than has been recommended. The highest temperature named should be given during the brightest and calmest weather, when it can be secured without anything like violent firing; and during weather the reverse of this, the lowest is much the safest. This winter growth can only be pursued with success when the pineries are light and fully exposed to every ray of sunshine that can possibly be had. Otherwise the plants will become drawn and weakly, a condition which will more surely than any other defeat the object in view. It is only when there is a scarcity of good succession plants that I would advise these autumn suckers to be pushed on, with the view of resting them in April and May, in order to start them for supplying fruit in autumn.

SUCCESSION PLANTS—SPRING TREATMENT.

This is the distinguishing term which is applied in spring to the suckers of the previous autumn, and it is as succession plants that I will now treat of their spring and summer culture.

Except in the case of plants which may have been kept in a growing condition all winter, it rarely occurs that September - potted suckers require a shift into larger pots before the middle of February; more especially if at first they are potted into 6-inch and 8-inch pots as recommended. In my own practice I am, however, never regulated by dates, but by the condition of the plants. Succession pine plants in a proper condition for shifting I would describe as those which have moderately filled their pots with roots in a white and healthy state of preservation. They should not be shifted till roots have formed themselves round the ball of soil sufficient to keep it together. On the other hand, they should not be allowed to stand unshifted till they become anything like pot-bound. If the former condition is not arrived at before the middle or end of February, the operation of shifting should be deferred, and the plants gently excited into action by increasing the night temperature to 60° when cold, and 65° when mild, with 10° more with sun-heat by day. Keep the bottom-heat at 85°, and increase the moisture both in the soil and air, till their roots are in the condition I have named. Should they have become pot-bound, which sometimes occurs in the case of strong suckers, especially when in the smaller-sized pots, the balls should be partially broken up with the hand, and the roots disentangled as much as possible. Plants with hard matted balls seldom start freely into growth, and are liable to start prematurely into fruit. The best way is to keep a watchful eye on young stock and shift them the first opportunity after they are sufficiently rooted.

About a week before the shifting is performed, the plants should be carefully examined, and all those that are dry should be watered, so that at shifting time the soil may be moderately moist. If shifted with their balls dry it is difficult to properly moisten them afterwards, particularly as it is not desirable to water them immediately after being shifted. The other preliminaries of getting the necessary amount of soil prepared and placed in some place to warm it, and the pots cleansed, crocked, and arranged in convenient readiness, should be all seen to before the day on which the pines are to be repotted. Hurry and confusion will thus be prevented in taking advantage of the first mild day for shifting and rearranging the succession stock. In draining the pots it must be borne in mind that the plants are to remain in them till they have perfected their fruit and a crop of suckers for another season's stock, and the drainage should be efficiently performed, as directed when treating of suckers, only the depth of crocks should be a little greater in the case of the pots recommended for fruiting in.

The house or pit intended for the reception of the plants after they are shifted should be thoroughly cleansed. The glass and wood-work should be all washed, and the walls whitewashed with hot-lime, so that there may be admitted and diffused as much light as possible, which for a stocky and fruitful growth early in the season is one of the most important conditions in the cultivation of the pine-apple. In the case of those who are dependent on fermenting material for bottom-heat, all that may be necessary in relation to that will be to add about six or eight inches of fresh tan, well mixing it with a foot of the surface of the old bed. But should the leaves have been several years in the pit, and the heat much declined, it will then be necessary either to take out the tan and mix in some fresh leaves with the old, or to add a greater proportion of fresh tan without interfering with the leaves at all. In the latter case the old tan should be sifted, preserving the roughest part of it. There is not an operation connected with the growth of the pine-apple that I dread more than entirely renewing the leaves and tan in pine-pits; and rather than run the risk of sudden and violent fits of bottom-heat, I have allowed the leaves in the bottom of pits to remain undisturbed for six or seven years at a time. I have always found, where tan is easily got, that the safest and best way is to sift the tan once a-year, and mix in with the old a few inches of fresh tan, which raises a steady and sufficient amount of bottom-heat. A bed so managed is far more under control than when the leaves and tan are annually or even biennially renewed entirely. All this labour in preparing beds is dispensed with where the bottom-heat is supplied by a well-regulated system of hot water—and the labour connected with the shifting and arranging of pines in spring or any other season is much lessened and simplified.

Supposing that I am now treating of Queens that are required to fruit early in the following year, to supply ripe fruit in May and June—little more than eighteen months from the time they were taken as suckers from their parent plants—I prefer shifting them into their fruiting-pots at once, instead of giving them two small shifts. Indeed, the size of pots into which they have been potted as suckers, and those into which I shift them for fruiting, admit only of one shift without reducing the balls. The strongest plants in 8-inch are shifted into pots 12 inches wide and as many deep, and those in 6-inch into 11-inch pots. These sizes are sufficient for the production of the very finest pines. Fine fruit is not dependent on size of pot so much as on other points of culture. I have had fine crops in 9-inch pots, but they require more attention in watering. And what is of no small consequence, especially to those who have a regular supply of fruit to keep up from limited accommodation, it is found that pine plants grown in comparatively small pots are much more manageable in the way of getting them to start than when grown in larger pots. From this it will be observed that all that I recommend in the way of repotting pines, in their progress from the sucker state to their yielding and ripening their fruit, is simply one shift.

Before turning the plants out of their pots, a few of the short sucker leaves round their collars should be stripped off. When turned out of their pots, all inert soil on the surface of the ball should be removed with the hand, and the crocks taken from the bottom part, taking care not to injure the roots. The ball should then have a gentle tap or two with the palm of the hand, and the outside roots be disentangled a little without breaking up the ball. This is what is recommended in the case of plants that have the soil and roots in a thoroughly satisfactory condition—having fine healthy white roots, with a moderately matted ball, and the soil in a healthy condition. When, as may occur in individual plants, the soil is either over dry or soured with wet from having stood in a drip, it is best to shake out the plants either more freely than I have directed, or entirely, according as the condition named may exist to a limited or extreme extent. The pots should be filled firmly up with soil, so that the plants when placed in them may be from two to three inches deeper in the pot than they were before. Being an advocate for very firm potting, I recommend that the soil should be rammed firmly round the ball with a blunt-pointed piece of wood. Be it remembered that the soil I have recommended to be thus acted upon is not a damp mixture of heavy soil and animal excrement, but a light turfy loam through which water passes freely; and the more firmly it is put into the pot the less water it holds in suspension, a point of no small importance in the growth of so succulent a plant as the pine. I never remember seeing really healthy pines or fine fruit in a rich puttied soil, holding a superabundance of water about the roots. The soil should be made thus firm all round the ball and about the collar of the plants up to within an inch of the rim of the pot.

When the whole are shifted they should be plunged in their growing quarters at once. And should there for the time be a scarcity of room for the desired number, with the prospect of more room in the course of a few weeks by getting rid of others that are fruiting off, they may be arranged rather thicker than is proper for them to make their summer growth. But if at once they can have the necessary amount of room —namely, two feet from plant to plant in and between the rows—all the better; for there is nothing more to be deprecated in pine-growing than overcrowding.

Particular attention must now be paid to the bottom-heat; 85° to 90° should be aimed at. And, where the heat is derived from tan and leaves, should it exceed 90°, the pots should be moved from side to side, so as to leave an opening round their sides. Although there may not be absolute danger of burning the roots while they have not reached the sides of the pots, yet too much bottom-heat causes an over-rapid growth at too early a season, which, in the absence of longer days and brighter sunshine, is exceedingly undesirable. During the month of March the atmospheric heat should range during cold dull weather from 60° to 65° at night. I am not particular as to a few degrees, but much prefer being guided by the outside temperature. During bright sunshiny days, when the pinery can be shut up in the afternoons with sun-heat, the temperature at 8 P.M. may be 70°, allowing it to sink to 65° by morning.

For a few days after being shifted keep them rather close, and the atmosphere moist, till they begin to lay hold of the fresh soil. Then give a little air daily as soon as the temperature exceeds 70°; and with steady sunshine the amount of air may be gradually increased till 2 P.M., when it should be gradually diminished according to the character of the day, and shut up so as to run the heat up to 80° for a short time before dark. There should not be any attempt at causing a rapid growth till the days get longer and the light more intense. The plants will root freely into the fresh soil, from the increased bottom-heat and the healthy irritable state of the roots, without much perceptible top-growth for a time.

There will not be any necessity for water at the root for some time—not, certainly, till the early part or middle of April, and even then water should not be over liberally supplied. The experienced can tell by the very appearance of the plants when they require it; but the inexperienced should examine the soil occasionally and apply water when it becomes dry a few inches from the surface of the ball. Rain-water is of course the best, and it should be heated to not less than 80°, nor more than 85°. At this season it is much safer to err on the side of giving a moderate amount of water than to keep the soil too wet while it is yet unoccupied with roots. The perspiratory organs of the pine are not very active at any season; and as the plant partakes so much of a succulent nature, a little extra moisture in the air is a much safer way of preventing injury from drought than by applying much water at the roots so early in the season.

It is often found, in the case of those who have next to no experience in pine-culture, that young pines after they are shifted are kept far too wet. I have taken the soil out of the pots and squeezed the water out of it. No more fatal course can be pursued at any stage of their growth, but particularly in spring when newly shifted.

SUCCESSION PLANTS—SUMMER AND AUTUMN TREATMENT.

Raise the night temperature by the end of April to 70° when the weather is dull, but when the pineries can be shut up with sun-heat the thermometer may range to 75° at 10 P.M. with advantage, falling to 70° towards morning. With a proportionate amount of atmospheric moisture the plants will now begin to grow freely. The increase of light and sun-heat will render a less amount of fire-heat sufficient, and, as a general rule, the state of the weather admits of a more liberal supply of air being given. This enables the cultivator to push forward his early plants without the danger of drawing them, which exists at an earlier period of the year.

In order to keep up the temperature with as little fire-heat as possible, air should be given early in the morning, almost as soon as the sun strikes the glass, and increased as formerly directed, so that the shutting up may take place at an earlier hour than is usual. This allows of the maximum temperature while there is yet a strong light, and husbands the heat of the sun for the evening. The steaming-troughs should be filled up every day when the pinery is shut up, and at the same time the paths and walls damped with the syringe. Without a moist atmosphere at this season the growth will be deficient in broadness, texture, and that dark-green hue which indicates that all is going on well. I disapprove of heavily syringing young growing pines, and much prefer the moisture to be applied by evaporation. On the afternoons of very bright days an occasional syringing overhead through a fine rose is beneficial, and keeps the plants clean; but regular heavy syringings have a tendency to keep the soil in a puddled state, as the leaves conduct all the water that falls on them into the pot, and this has a tendency to produce a soft unfruitful growth.

With increased air, light, and heat, and the very moderate syringings recommended, the state of the soil as to moisture must be carefully watched. An equal and healthy amount of moisture must be maintained. No amount of attention should be considered too much to prevent the soil from becoming dusty-dry on the one hand, or over-wet on the other, otherwise a check may be given and an amount of mischief produced that no after-treatment can retrieve. It is a great mistake to suppose that a check is not as likely to arise from plants being kept too dry as from the opposite extreme.

When bottom-heat depends on leaves and tan, it not unfrequently occurs, although the heat may be just right in March and April, that the hotter sun of May causes an increase of heat just at a time when the young roots are reaching the sides of the pot and are most susceptible of injury. The safest way is to have a thermometer in the bed, and as soon as the heat exceeds 90°, to shake the pots from side to side and leave an opening all round them for the heat to escape. After the heat subsides, the tan can be pressed to the sides of the pots again. Of course, when bottom-heat is derived from hot water, it can be easily regulated without these precautionary measures, which apply only to fermenting materials.

The temperature should now be carefully regulated, and fire-heat applied in the evening just in time to prevent the heat from sinking below 70° at 10 P.M. And when the morning gives signs of a bright day, the fires should be damped down the first thing, and kept low all day. There is nothing more injurious than to have hot pipes, and a bright sun, with a maximum supply of air on. Such a state of things creates currents of scorching dry air, very trying to the plants, and robs the pineries too much of moisture. By the middle of May the plants will be growing freely, and moisture and air must be increased in proportion to the progress they make. The house should be damped the first thing in the morning as well as at shutting-up time. And after being shut up close for four or five hours, when the weather is calm and very warm, a little "chink" of air should be left on all night. A little more air should be put on at 7 A.M., and gradually increased with the rising of the sun, till at twelve o'clock there is sufficient to create a circulation among the plants. Air should be given at the back or highest part of the house or pit; but, unless when the weather is close and sultry, none should be given at the front. With the increase of heat, light, and air, they will make rapid progress, and consequently more water at the root will be required, and it should always be about the same temperature as the bottom-heat. I have found Peruvian guano the best and most convenient stimulant for mixing with the water—not in strong doses now and then, but simply to well colour the water with it every time the pines are watered: an ordinary handful to four gallons of water is sufficient.

In some localities, and with fine summer weather, after midsummer the temperature can often be kept up sufficiently without the aid of fire-heat. In a close structure there will be no difficulty in doing so, especially when early air-giving and shutting up is practised. The heat can thus be husbanded so as to keep the thermometer at 75°; and when this can be accomplished without the aid of fire-heat, so much the better in all respects. This is, I am aware, not applicable either to all localities or all seasons; for many climates, even in favourable summers, will render the use of the fires necessary the whole season.

Although very much opposed to shading pines in a general way, it is sometimes necessary, when they are growing rapidly and the weather becomes suddenly very bright after a continuance of dull weather. The shading should never be heavy nor long continued. Tiffany or hexagon netting I have always found sufficient, and that only during the brightest part of the day. If all is going on right at the roots, and a moist atmosphere is steadily kept up, I have never found a necessity for more shading than this. At the same time, it is most undesirable that pines should become browned and wiry; and slight shade and more frequent gentle dewing at shutting-up time should be resorted to as soon as signs of this appear. Of two evils, the browning of the leaves is not so injurious as a weak watery growth—the result of too much shade and a close atmosphere. I find the Smooth-leaved Cayenne much more impatient of sudden bursts of

THE PINE-APPLE. 31

bright sun than Queens or other varieties; and to grow it to perfection it should never be allowed to become much browned. In the case of this fine variety I have in bright warm seasons fixed a single ply of hexagon netting over the pits, and allowed it to remain for a couple of the hottest months. This simply breaks the power of the sun a little. In order to prevent this wiry, browned condition during summer, care should be taken that the plants are never once allowed to go too long without being watered, and a uniformly moderate moist state of the soil must be maintained.

Should any of the plants throw up young suckers from the axils of the lower leaves, they should be removed at once. The best way of doing this is to have a long-handled pair of broad-mouthed pincers, with which the suckers can be easily twisted out as soon as they are observed. Where much syringing overhead is practised, suckers frequently show themselves in abundance, in the case of Queens particularly. This is one of the many evils which result from the too liberal use of the syringe. It often occurs during the season of rapid growth that some of the centre leaves adhere closely to each other for a longer time than is good for them: they should be separated either with the hand, or with a slight touch of a stick where the hand cannot reach them.

As the stock of which I am now treating consists principally of plants that are selected to start into fruit for the early supply of next season, the plants should always have their pots well filled with roots, and be of a stocky well-matured growth, by the end of August, otherwise there is little certainty of their being got to start in time to be ripe in May and June.

If grown on the shady, large-pot, and wet-at-the-root system, they will not be in a fit state for the purpose now named; and even with the best of management to induce them to start without first making a growth in January and February, it is necessary that they should complete their growth early under the influence of plenty of light and air, or they will make a fresh growth when the temperature is raised with the object of starting them, instead of coming up at once into fruit. True, those which make a growth first, I have always found, throw the finest fruit; but where an early summer supply of fruit is required, it must be had from those which start without any growth. In properly preparing plants for this purpose, there are two things which must be guarded against. The one is that of having the plants pot-bound too early, and subjected to a high temperature too long in autumn. In this case the fruit comes up slowly late in autumn, or in winter, a hardened knot like a thimble, and is worthless, especially in the case of Queens. The other is a watery immature growth, from which it is impossible to get early fruit.

In September water must be judiciously and very sparingly applied. No more should be given than is just sufficient to prevent the plants from suffering either from aridity of atmosphere or dryness of soil. Give a liberal supply of air on fine days. Towards the end of September they should be as completely at rest as a comparatively low temperature, a dry atmosphere, and a proportionately dry state of the soil in which they grow, can place them. I have frequently allowed Queens in this stage to remain without a drop of water at the root from the first week in October till January, and found the plants so treated in the very best condition. To start pines into fruit at any given time, and more especially very early in the year, it is necessary to their doing so satisfactorily, that they have a period of rest previous to their being subjected to the treatment required to start them. Such as have completed their growth as I have described early in the season, can have from ten to twelve weeks' rest, and be started in time to ripen their fruit in the end of May and June. From the beginning or middle of October, onwards to the end of December, it rarely occurs that pines intended to start thus early are the better for a drop of water, when grown on a bed of fermenting material. And when the bottom-heat is supplied with pipes, it is much the safer way to keep the plunging material moderately moist than to water the pines often.

The night temperature should drop gradually to 60° by the middle of October. In November, and until the time they are to be started, I prefer the temperature at 55° at night during cold windy weather, and 60° when mild. The bottom-heat should be proportionately low, just enough to maintain the roots in a white healthy condition, and 80° is quite enough for that. When with sun-heat during the day, which may occur during clear frosty weather, the temperature exceeds 65°, air should be given. With such weather as this it is sometimes necessary to fire sharply at night to keep up the required temperature; in which case the fires should be checked the first thing in the morning, especially when a cold night is succeeded by a bright day. Where it can be so arranged that covering can be used over the glass during cold weather, it prevents radiation, and the atmosphere

C

can be kept in a condition much more congenial to pines than when more fire-heat is necessary. For although a damp atmosphere, which leads to an accumulation of moisture and to drip, is by all means to be avoided at this season, yet a parchingly dry atmosphere produced by highly-heated pipes is very prejudicial, and cannot well be counteracted in winter without producing the opposite evil. Hence the benefit of covering the glass at night. When, however, it becomes necessary to apply moisture to counteract the too drying effects of hard firing, the best way is to sprinkle the paths instead of the pipes, because the moisture will be carried more gradually into the atmosphere, and is therefore not so likely to accumulate and drop into the centres of the plants, which, as all pine-growers have doubtless found out, is attended with spotted leaves, and not unfrequently deformed fruit.

Winter treatment the reverse of what I have here recommended—a high temperature and more water at the root and in the air—causes the plants to grow all winter; and from want of light and air they become drawn and weakly—in fact, worthless,—or probably some of them may start at the dead of winter, when, particularly in the case of Queens, there is very little chance of their blooming and setting properly, and will either way be worthless. An instance of such treatment once came under my notice, when, instead of a low temperature, 75° of heat was kept up during the whole resting season, with moisture in abundance. The consequence was, that when the time for starting them came round they were tall, tender, and only fit for the waste-heap.

Pine plants arrived at the stage I have been now

treating of are termed fruiting plants, and under that heading I will speak of their further treatment.

FRUITING PLANTS.

Ripe pines being required in the early part of June, it will be necessary to set a quantity of Queens in motion by the first of January, to succeed those which are generally termed winter and spring fruiters, and which will be treated of by-and-by. Queens are by far the best variety to start at this season, with the view of getting ripe fruit from them quickly to keep up the succession after the winter fruiting varieties. Yet for the sake of variety, and also to keep up as long a succession as possible from the same lot of plants, it is desirable to start a few of the later varieties at the same time; but Queens should form the great majority.

Where bottom-heat is derived from leaves and tan, the bed in the fruiting pinery should have fresh material added to it, as formerly directed, to increase the heat to from 85° to 90°; but in doing this, very particular attention must be paid to the state of the bed, as over-much bottom-heat at this stage would prove fatal to anything like success. The principal part of the roots being at the bottom and round the sides of the pots, they are now more than ever particularly liable to suffer from too much heat, and great caution is necessary. Should there be any fear about the over-heating of the bed after it is prepared, it will be much safer to only half plunge the pots at first, till it be certain that the heat will not exceed 90°.

Those who have the more desirable and superior

appliance of hot-water pipes or tanks for bottom-heat, will be spared the trouble and anxiety which is attached to the otherwise by no means inefficient, when well managed, fermenting bed. They can regulate the bottom-heat with much more ease and safety.

In selecting the plants for starting at this early season, those only should be taken which are most likely to start without making a growth. I will therefore suppose that the cultivator has a hundred plants of those treated of as "succession plants," and that from these it is desired to have a supply of ripe fruit from the first of June till October, and recommend that fifty of those most likely to start at once should be selected. In doing so the experienced eye will fix upon those with the thickest collars, and that have the greatest number of short sharp-pointed leaves, thickly set together in their centres. These are the most likely to send up their fruit without making a fresh growth, although some of them may disappoint even the most experienced; still, in a general way, when prepared the previous autumn and winter as I have described, they will not disappoint.

In arranging and plunging these plants, a few of the bottom leaves should be stripped off, all the loose soil on the surface removed, and a top-dressing of loam put on, pressing it firmly to the collars of the plant and the sides of the pot. In moving these plants it is a common practice to tie the leaves up for the sake of convenience; but I would here say that it is a practice that is injurious at any stage of the pine's growth, and particularly when the plants are full grown, and should have stubby, short, thick leaves that will not bear being squeezed into a bundle without considerable injury. I seldom tie pines up at any stage when working amongst them. Those who shift and plunge the strong prickly varieties can easily protect their hands from being torn by wearing a pair of gloves. In plunging them they should not be put thicker than two feet from centre to centre, and that side of the plant which has been to the sun all the growing season should be placed so still. Indeed, very strong plants require more room.

As soon as they are all plunged, if they are dry, water them with guano-water at 80°, giving them sufficient to moisten the whole ball, but be careful not to splash it about the leaves. The atmospheric temperature for January should be 65° at night, and 70° by day without sun; with sun, 80° will be sufficient, and air should be given when it exceeds that. The moisture in the air must also be proportionately increased, and should be done by sprinkling the paths and walls with tepid water two or three times a-day, instead of steaming the pipes for the present. A watchful eye must be kept on the state of the soil, and no more water given than is sufficient to keep it moist, but not wet. With too much water, and the degree of top and bottom heat now necessary, the tendency of pines to make growth at this season and miss starting for the time being is increased. With these conditions the plants having a mass of healthy roots in an irritable state will soon show signs of motion, and all the more surely in proportion as the heat and moisture are steadily administered.

In February the heat must be advanced to 70° at night, and 75° by day, and air put on when it exceeds 80° with sun, shutting up the house early in the afternoon so as to husband sun-heat. The moisture in the air must not be much more than in January, and the same cautious application of water to the roots must be observed till the fruit makes its appearance. Most of the plants will show fruit before the last week of February. The centres of the plants will be observed to open by degrees, and on examining them the young fruit will be found emerging from the centre. Whenever this is observed, the plants, if inclining to the dry side, should have a watering sufficient to thoroughly moisten the whole ball, and the bottom-heat already named should be steadily kept up.

Supposing all the plants to have shown fruit, the night temperature for March should not range under 70° nor over 75° with the mildest weather. There being generally great fluctuations of weather during this month, the temperatures I have named should be aimed at accordingly. The moisture in the air must be sparingly applied till the fruit is out of flower, and air admitted on all fine days, putting it on early in the morning, and shutting it off early in the afternoon. Water at the root will be more frequently required, especially when they are plunged over a hot-air chamber. But avoid, as one of the greatest possible evils, a wet sloppy state of the soil. As soon as they are out of flower, sprinkle them overhead every fine afternoon with clear water at a temperature of 80°. As the season advances, with longer days and shorter nights, early shutting up with sun-heat must be practised; but, except with sun-heat, I do not recommend in April any increase of night temperature over that recommended for March, even though it be required to ripen the fruit with as much speed as possible. The forcing should be accelerated by day with sun-heat. Shut up soon after three o'clock, giving them a gentle dewing overhead, filling up the steaming-trays, sprinkling the surface of the plunging material and about the collars or bottom leaves of the plants. The temperature may then be run up to from 85° to 90° for an hour or two. The fires, which should now be low through the day, should be quickened in time to keep the heat from falling below the proper night temperature at 10 P.M.

Under this treatment the fruit will swell rapidly, and careful attention must be paid to watering. The great thing to be aimed at being to keep the soil in a healthy growth-giving state—moist, but not wet—it is a common practice to give occasional strong waterings with guano, sheep, or deers' dung. Instead of this, I prefer, as already directed for succession plants, to water every time with a weaker solution of these manures, and I prefer guano to any other; and during the rapid growing season, I always put a little of it into the evaporating pans once or twice a-week, and find it gives that fine dark-green hue and thickness of texture so desirable to see in pines. They should be gone over as soon as the suckers appear, and where there are more than two to a plant remove them. When suckers or gills appear on the stems or under the base of the fruit, they should be removed immediately they are discovered.

The month of May generally brings comparatively warm sunny weather, and vegetation gets into full play; and I am not sure but what May is the very best month in the whole year for swelling off pines. It is not generally so hot and scorching as the succeeding three months; less air is therefore needed. The pineries can be shut up earlier, so that less evaporation goes on, and the swelling fruit can have a longer period of sun-heat and moisture in the afternoon than when the sun is more powerful, and when it is not safe to damp and shut up before four o'clock. Advantage should therefore be taken of these circumstances, and the fruit pushed on, when it is an object to get them ripe as soon as possible. Under these circumstances, the heat may be run up to from 90° to 100° for an hour or two, and the air loaded with moisture. Syringing must not, however, be to excess, or the result will be large crowns and an undue growth of suckers, to the detriment of the size and appearance of the fruit.

When the fruit begins to change colour, which, if the plants have been set agoing in January, will be in the end of May or early in June, it is necessary, in order to get highly-flavoured fruit, to increase the amount of air, and decrease the moisture both in the air and the soil. Indeed, as soon as the fruit is half coloured, no more water should be given than is necessary to keep the plants from suffering, and the moisture of the atmosphere should be gradually withdrawn. At the same time, avoid starving them into maturity.

RETARDING AND KEEPING PINE-APPLES AFTER THEY ARE RIPE.

When a greater number of pines begin to ripen at any given time than is necessary to supply the demand, it then becomes desirable that a portion of them should be retarded to form a succession of fruit in good condition. In the absence of a compartment specially for the purpose, I have frequently placed them in a vinery where grapes were nearly ripe, and where the temperature was comparatively cool, with a circulation of dry air. In such a place, pines that have begun to colour ripen slowly, and they are excellent in flavour. The cool dry air of the vinery, and the shade of the vines, are good retarding conditions; and this is as good a way, apart from having a place for the purpose, as any that I have tried. I have also removed them to a cool dry room when about half coloured, and kept them there a month or six weeks, and found them in excellent condition. This treatment, of course, applies to summer fruit. Later in the season I have kept Smooth-leaved Cayennes in a room for six weeks after they were quite ripe. In this way a succession of fruit can be very much extended as compared to keeping them in a warm pinery.

When the fruit is all cut from a pit or houseful of plants, the suckers should be carefully attended to. The comparatively dry condition of the air and soil which is necessary to good flavour is not favourable to the suckers at this hot season of the year; consequently, when the suckers are strong, I frequently detach them from the plant as soon as the fruit begins to colour. If the suckers are small when the fruit is cut, they should be left on the parent plant; then the soil should have a good watering to encourage them to make further growth. It rarely occurs that they are not quite large enough to be potted about the time the fruit begins to ripen. I may here remark, that the practice of allowing the suckers to lie in a cool dry place, with the object of what is called drying them, is one for which I never could see any reason, or any good end that could be gained by it. On the contrary, in my opinion, the practice is injurious to the progress of the young plants. To say the least of it, it is attended with a loss of time. When it is desirable to have the fruiting plants of which I am now treating to ripen earlier than the beginning of June, they must, of course, have heat applied to them in December instead of January; and with properly constructed and heated pineries there is nothing to prevent this. But where the houses are not light, tight, and well heated, it is a matter of no small difficulty, and it is much safer to wait for the "turn of the day." The other half of the set of fruiting plants of which I have been treating should be kept quiet till the end of February. Introduced into heat, and managed in the same way as the early half, they will come in as a succession lot. And, as is always likely, a good many of them which the experienced eye rejected while selecting the earliest, make a growth before starting, and in that way still further lengthen out the succession of ripe fruit from this portion of the stock. For this purpose Queens are most useful in all respects, and can be had in good order from May till November.

I have considered it the best way to follow out the treatment of this one set of plants, without mixing up with their management that of different sets of plants necessary to supply ripe fruit in winter and spring. Of these latter I will now speak.

HOW TO KEEP UP A CONSTANT SUCCESSION OF RIPE FRUIT ALL THE YEAR.

Where a regular supply of fruit has to be kept up with the least possible intermission all the year round, it is more certainly accomplished by potting a quantity of suckers at frequent intervals. Supposing that a number of suckers are potted August 1880, these will give the earliest fruit for 1881. And those that ripen in September and October, give the suckers that will succeed the earliest lot, so that these two sets supply fruit for six months of the twelve. The other six months of winter and spring—particularly spring —are those in which pines are most valued, as other fruits are then scarce. March and April are the most difficult months of the whole year in which to have ripe pines.

In June and July I always endeavour to start a quantity of the Smooth-leaved Cayenne and Charlotte Rothschild. These are noble pines when well grown, being unsurpassed for appearance and long keeping after they are ripe, and swell better after October than any other pines I know. Smooth Cayenne I consider the better of the two. The Black Jamaica is also a most useful pine for winter swelling, and probably is unsurpassed for flavour at the dullest season of the year. The Queen is comparatively worthless as a winter pine compared to these two; it does not swell kindly, and is always dry and juiceless compared to them.

There should be two sets of these winter sorts, as recommended in the case of Queens and other early sorts for summer and autumn fruit. The Smooth-leaved Cayenne is so very shy in making suckers that I always endeavour to save as many crowns as I can, and take all the suckers that can be got in October from the fruiting plants, whether the fruit be ripe or not. These suckers and crowns are potted generally into 6-inch pots, and shifted in spring as soon as sufficiently rooted, as described in the former part of this treatise. They are shifted into 11-inch pots, and grown on in the usual way, only that they are not kept so dry in autumn and winter as is desirable for early starting plants. The temperature, too, is kept five degrees higher than for Queens at rest; the object being not to mature the growth of these so as to predispose them to start in spring. The heat is quickened, both top and bottom, in February, and they make a spring growth; are rested in May and June by being kept drier and cooler; and then, with increased heat and moisture, I rarely ever fail in starting them all in June and July. Care must be taken that they never get too dry at the root, particularly in spring, as that would be likely to start them before they are required. This applies with the same force to Jamaicas and Charlotte Rothschilds. These will keep up the supply of fruit till the end of the year.

It is necessary to have a later lot of these varieties to come in for spring, and this I find rather difficult in the case of the Smooth Cayenne. It makes suckers still more tardily from late plants. The method I generally adopt is to save the old stems of those that ripen their fruit through the winter, and place them in strong bottom-heat to spring the latent buds. These grow into nice plants, ready to shift into 8-inch pots in September, and I shift these into their fruiting-pots in March, and by pushing them on they start in September and October, and succeed those started in June and July. For this purpose I most decidedly give the preference to the Cayenne; and from plants of it so managed, I have had very fine fruit in the spring months. They are kept on at a temperature of from 60° to 65° all winter, with a steady bottom-heat of 85°. I have frequently had ripe fruit from 4 to 6 lb. in 9-inch pots from last year's suckers.

There is nothing peculiar in the management of these

winter fruiting sorts, except it be that I never keep them so dry and so completely at rest in winter as those intended to start early. This is with the view of their not resting and maturing themselves so thoroughly in autumn and winter as would cause them to start when excited in spring. The Smooth Cayenne requires more moisture at the root when growing than is good for most other sorts. It is also more impatient of bright sun early in the season than any I know, more especially if kept gently on the move all winter. And rather than allow the foliage to become bronzed, shade should be applied for a time, as already directed. When swelling off in winter, water at the root will of course not require to be so frequently given as in summer, and there should be no syringing. The evaporating trays will keep the air sufficiently moist. Air must be put on for a short time in the middle of every fine day.

PLANTS THAT MISS FRUITING.

It not unfrequently occurs that a few plants miss starting into fruit along with the others, but continue to grow, in spite of every effort to make them fruit. The common practice is to throw these away. When I have room to conveniently operate on these, I cut the plants over at the surface of the soil, and strip a few of the leaves off them, and pot them deeply and very firmly in fruiting-pots. They are slightly shaded for ten days, by which time, with a brisk bottom-heat, they begin to send out wonderfully strong roots, and then the shading is discontinued, and they are watered. In this way they are transformed into *dwarf* strong plants, and I always find that they start into fruit very soon after, and swell off fine fruit. When I have found a set of pines that have been drawn and are not likely to be got to fruit satisfactorily, I have treated them in this way instead of throwing them away, as is often done in such circumstances.

THE PLANTING-OUT SYSTEM.

Although I have given a good deal of attention to the planting-out system of pine-culture, and made myself acquainted with the most successful instances of its adoption, I have very seldom adopted it. Not that I suppose fine fruit are not produced by it: facts prove the contrary. But with the space at my command I have decided that, to keep up the supply which I have produced nearly every week in the year, I could more certainly do so on the pot system than by having the plants planted out in beds. Plants in pots are entirely under control at all times, for being moved or removed to force forward or retard the ripening of fruit as circumstances demand. This is of vast importance where the space in pine-beds is small in proportion to the demand for fruit, and in this respect pines in pots give an advantage over the open bed. Neither do I consider it necessary to have finer fruit than can be produced from 9, 11, and 12 inch pots. In fact, it is not the size of pot, nor the greater range that the planting-out system gives to the roots, that are the principal points of good pine-culture.

The planting-out system may be practised either over a bed of leaves or with hot water for bottom-heat. The best example of this system that I have ever seen was at the Royal Gardens, Frogmore; and there, a bed of leaves for bottom-heat is preferred to hot-water pipes. The suckers are not potted, but planted at once into beds of soil over a bed of leaves about two or three feet deep. From the sucker pits they are transplanted into the succession pits, and from the latter into the fruiting pits, where they are planted two feet apart in the rows. In other respects the treatment is the same as for plants in pots.

Others again, where the bottom-heat is derived from hot water, do not have recourse to regular transplanting, but either move the stools as the fruit are cut, and put in a little fresh soil and another plant; or they adopt the "Hamiltonian system" of leaving a sucker, and sometimes two, merely cutting down the old plant to the sucker and putting some fresh soil round it. The system can of course be modified as circumstances will allow; but from all that I have seen of it, it is my opinion that as fine fruit are produced in pots; and for rapid and certain fruiting, and where the most is to be made of space in keeping up a supply, the pot system is the best. At all events, any one who makes himself master of pine-apple culture in pots can have no difficulty in growing them in open beds of soil. The same points must be aimed at in both systems. And for beginners, any errors or mistakes in management can be more easily retrieved, I should say, in the pot than in the planting-out system.

INSECTS TO WHICH THE PINE IS SUBJECT.

White Scale.—This is the most destructive and formidable insect which the pine-grower has to dread; and in forming a collection of pines, every possible precaution should be taken to avoid getting plants infested with white scale. A very few of it will soon overrun a whole collection, and cause a great deal of trouble and expense in getting rid of it. It is an oval-shaped insect, grey, speckled with brown, and adheres closely to the surface of the leaves, and preys upon the juices of the plants, rendering them very unsightly, and weakening them with great rapidity. It increases with amazing rapidity, and yields only to the most severe and laborious treatment. I have known collections which have soon been rendered all but useless through the introduction of a single plant with a breed of this scale in it.

I am glad to say that I have been fortunate hitherto to escape having anything to do with it, and have so far the want of experience in destroying it. Many are the remedies which have been recommended for its destruction; while some have looked upon it with despair, and have got rid of it only by getting a clean stock of plants, after having destroyed the infected ones, and thoroughly cleansed their pineries.

Brown Scale.—This insect sometimes affects pines, but it is not nearly so difficult to deal with as the white scale. I know from experience that syringing with clean water, heated to 140°, completely kills it without injuring the plants.

Mealy Bug.—This is also a most formidable insect to get rid of when it is established on pine plants. The white dusty material with which it surrounds itself completely protects it from the influence of hot water applied through the syringe, and it is second in its destructive effects and difficulty of being eradicated only to the white scale itself. If allowed to go on, it affects every part of the plant—the fruit, leaves, and roots. Consequently, the first appearance of it should be dealt with as a serious evil, to be checked and eradicated at once.

The most effectual remedy for all these insects is to mix four wine-glassfuls of paraffin-oil with four gallons of water, keep the whole well mixed, and apply it to the plants with a common garden syringe. Allow each plant to stand a few minutes, and then syringe freely with clean water. This destroys the insects without injuring the plants.

THE GRAPE VINE.

WITH two exceptions the grape vine (*Vitis vinifera*) is the earliest fruit-bearing plant of which there is any record. From earliest ages it has occupied a prominent and very important position amongst the fruits of the earth. There is strong presumptive evidence that it was cultivated by the antediluvians; and it is specially referred to as having occupied the attention of Noah as soon as the waters of the flood had subsided from the face of the earth. When Moses sent the heads of the children of Israel to spy the land of Canaan, and to bring back word whether it was "fat or lean," they brought back an example of the grape to prove that it was worthy of their promised possession. Through the long ages that have elapsed since then, with their ever-varying tastes and habits, the luscious grape has been an important product of cultivation; and it has lost none of its early popularity. At the present time it is more extensively cultivated under glass than ever it was at any period of the world's history; and in this country hothouse grapes are now an article of commerce to a much greater extent than ever they were, with every likelihood of their becoming increasingly important. It is much to be regretted that a destructive parasite (*Phylloxera vastatrix*) has become a formidable destroyer of the vine, both in the vineyards of the Continent and in the vineries of Britain. The French Government has offered a premium of £12,000 to any one who will provide a remedy that will destroy the insect without injuring the vine. I wrote to the French Minister of Agriculture, expressing my conviction that no such remedy was likely to be discovered, and recommending that the affected vines should be simultaneously destroyed and the ground cropped with cereals for a year or two. Up to this date no remedy has been discovered, and the ravages of the insect are increasing to an alarming extent.

It must be regarded as somewhat strange that the native country of the grape vine has not been definitely settled by botanists. It can be safely assumed that it is indigenous to a great part of Asia, the climate of which is suited to its growth. From Asia it was no doubt introduced into Egypt and Greece, and from these parts found its way into France, Spain, and other Continental countries, where it has so long held a position of much importance. It is supposed that its cultivation in France dates as far back as the second century. Its introduction into Britain has been attributed to the Phœnicians, as early as the days of Solomon, when trading for tin to the southern coast of England; others ascribe its entrance into this country to a short time after the Christian era, when the Romans had full possession of the country.

There is no doubt that it was at one time cultivated in the south of England for wine-making with very considerable success. It is authentically recorded that at Arundel Castle, in Norfolk, great quantities of wine were made from the produce of a vineyard there, and that in 1763 there were 70 pipes of wine in the castle cellars, all produced from grapes grown in the Arundel vineyard. The first mention of artificial heat being applied to the vine is in 1718, when the Duke of Rutland, at Belvoir Castle, forced it by means of heated walls. In Switzer's 'Practical Fruit-grower' there is to be found the first plan of a vinery, with directions for forcing grapes under glass. As a branch of horticulture, grape-growing under glass has certainly more than kept pace with any other, both in its general diffusion and its improvement, until it may be looked upon as of national importance.

SITE FOR VINERIES.

There are two extremes of circumstances which are inimical to the most successful culture of the grape vine, and these are considerably dependent on the site where vineries are erected. A low damp position, into which the water in its immediate vicinity finds its way, and from which it cannot be drained to the depth of at least 3 feet, should be avoided; for stagnant water is ruinous to vines, and such a site may be regarded as the very worst. An elevated, excessively dry site, with a gravelly subsoil which suffers very soon and severely from drought, should also be avoided if possible, as excessive drought is also very unfavourable to the production of fine grapes. A site sloping gently to the south, from which water can be effectually drained, is the best, and should always be chosen when available. Shelter from north and east winds is also of importance. But the sheltering objects should never be so near the vinery as to prove injurious by their shade. When vine-borders have from necessity to be made near large growing trees, an effectual barrier—such as a brick and cement wall—should be provided against the inroads of the tree-roots.

VINERY FOR EARLY FORCING.

What I intend to be understood by the term "early forcing," is that which produces ripe grapes in April and May, and which necessitates the commencement of forcing in November and December respectively. The forcing thus extends over a period during which the days are short, sunless, and cold — conditions which, it need scarcely be said, are adverse to vegetation of every kind. Even the most ignorant of the art of forcing through such a season will at once conclude that the production of good grapes in early spring, in this ever-changing climate, must be one of the most difficult tasks of the horticulturist. Whatever structure it is that insures the greatest possible amount of light, and is at the same time the most easily heated to and maintained at the necessary temperature, must of necessity be the best for early forcing. Very little consideration will serve to convince any one that the form of vinery which presents almost its entire surface of glass to the south, so as to catch every gleam of sunshine, must be the best.

The "lean-to" as represented by fig. 6 is beyond all doubt the best for early forcing. Indeed it is a good form for producing grapes at any season of the year, but especially at the time now under consideration. The wood-work should not be any heavier than gives sufficient strength, and it should be glazed in large panes with 22-ounce British sheet-glass. The

54 FRUIT CULTURE UNDER GLASS.

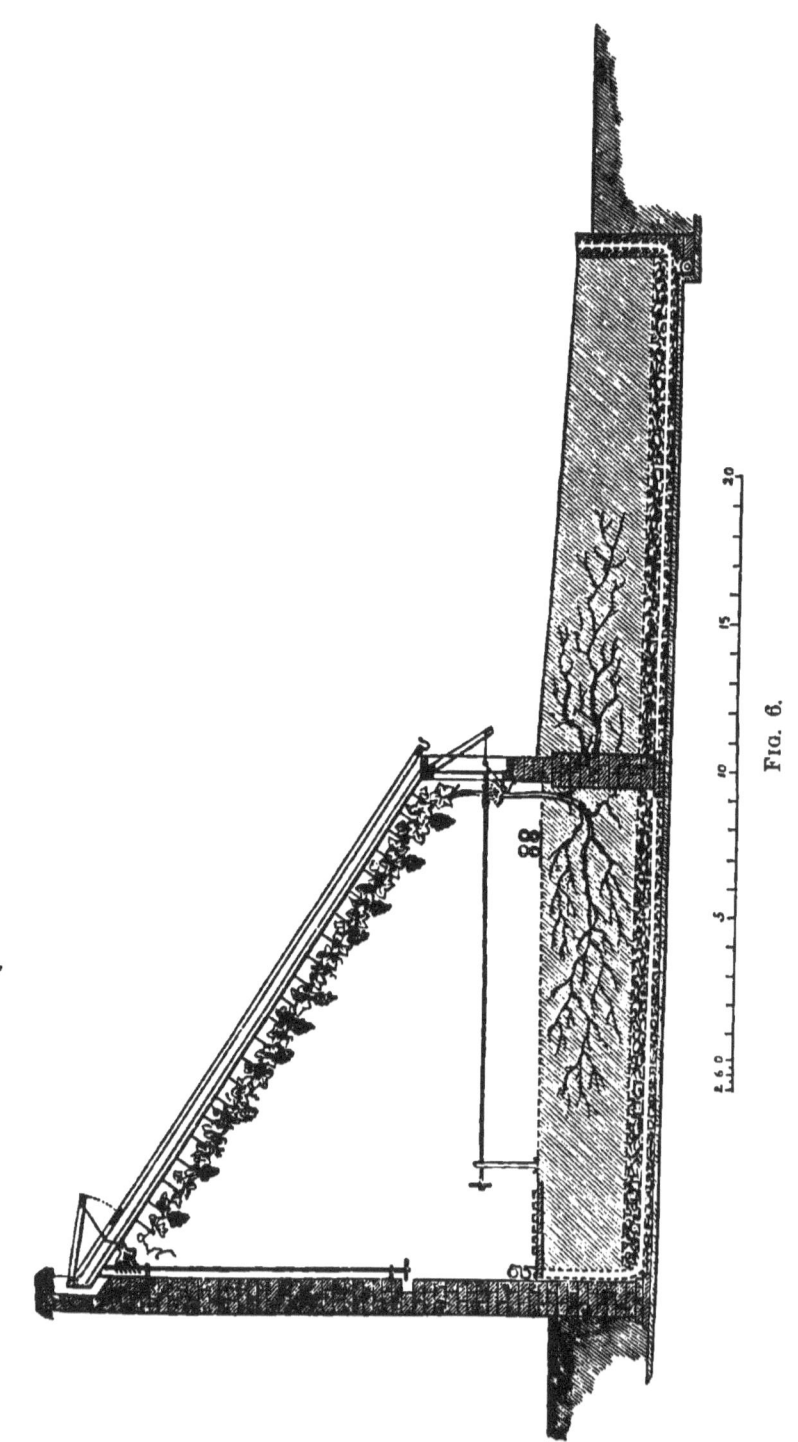

Fig. 6.

amount of pipes for heating it should not be less than six rows of 4-inch pipes the whole length of the house and round both ends, besides a steaming-tray. The whole of the inside wood-work and back wall should be white, so as to reflect as much light as possible on the tender growths of the vine. Reference to the engraving shows the arrangement of the drainage and depth of soil as referred to under the head of "Border-making."

In forcing that has to commence in any of the winter months, there can be no doubt that artificial heat judiciously applied by hot-water pipes to the soil from beneath is a great advantage. · In arranging for this the pipes should be immediately over the concrete, and covered over in a shallow chamber by pavement, and the drainage placed over the pavement; or the pipes may be surrounded with an open or honey-combed brickwork drain, which drain can be connected with similar open drains running right and left among the open rubble, of which the drainage is composed. A border 24 feet wide should have four rows of hot-water pipes running underneath it.

The ventilation, especially of vineries where early forcing is carried on, is of very great importance; for it is, especially in these days of large panes of glass and close laps, highly desirable to keep the air fresh, and constantly renewed. The ingress of cold currents of air is most objectionable; it is therefore necessary to heat it before it enters the body of the vinery and plays on the tender foliage and fruit. Many ways have been recommended to effect this end; but the best way is that invented by William Thomson, and illustrated by him in his 'Treatise on the Vine.' It is termed the "hot-air ventilator," and consists of a sheath of "copper placed over or incasing a row of the front pipes. The diameter of the sheath is one inch more than the hot pipe it encloses, consequently there is an open space of half an inch all round the pipe inside the sheath. This cavity is fed with fresh air from the exterior of the house, by a pipe 5 inches in diameter, which springs from the lower surface of·the sheath and passes through the front wall of the house to the external air. There is a valve in this feed-pipe to modify the supply of fresh air at pleasure. In the upper surface of the sheath is a double row of holes, so that the moment the cold air comes into the chamber round the pipe and gets hot, expanded, and lighter, it makes its exit through these holes into the general atmosphere of the house."

VINERY FOR LATE GRAPES.

Having shown that a lean-to vinery facing due south is the best form for early forcing, under this head I have no hesitation in saying that for the same reasons that I have recommended the lean-to for winter forcing, when the sun is only a short time above the horizon, the span-roofed vinery running north and south is best for the ripening of grapes, say after the middle of July, excepting Muscat of Alexandria, which, north of York at any rate, should be in lean-to vineries. A span-roofed house in this position gets the benefit of sunshine longer in summer than does the lean-to. The east side gets the morning sun, at noon the whole roof is exposed to it, and on till late in the evening the west side is exposed to the sun, when it would merely be shining on the end of a lean-to. Besides this, a span-roofed house, from 20 to 24 feet wide, encloses a larger vol-

THE GRAPE VINE. 57

ume of air than a lean-to of the same width, and this is of much importance in vine-culture. In large airy houses grapes are better flavoured, are more fleshy, and consequently hang better through the winter. After considerable experience in grape-growing in lean-to houses, ranging from 6 feet wide to what may be termed large airy vineries, I unhesitatingly recommend that they be built large and roomy. Besides the reasons already named, large vineries can be fired to a given temperature more steadily than small ones, because a large volume of air is not so easily influenced by external variations of temperature, just the same as a thin wedge of iron is sooner heated and sooner cooled than a thick one. Fig. 7 represents a span-roofed vinery of the dimensions I recommend for ripening grapes late in summer and autumn to hang through the winter. It will be observed that a drain runs in the draining material from the front to the back of the border in fig. 6, terminating in an upright shaft just below the hot-water pipes at the back of the vinery and at the front of the outside border, thus communicating with the external atmosphere and that of the vinery.

These drains should be constructed 6 feet apart the whole length of the border, and be open jointed, so that the air from them can find its way right and left among the open rubble, which should form the lower stratum of the drainage. This is for the purpose of what has been termed aeration, which means the exposure of the soil to the air from under-currents. No doubt, for summer forcing, it is beneficial, especially in wet climates, to open the mouths of the upright shafts in hot sunny weather, thus admitting warm air underneath the border.

It is a very common error to fix the wires to which

58 FRUIT CULTURE UNDER GLASS.

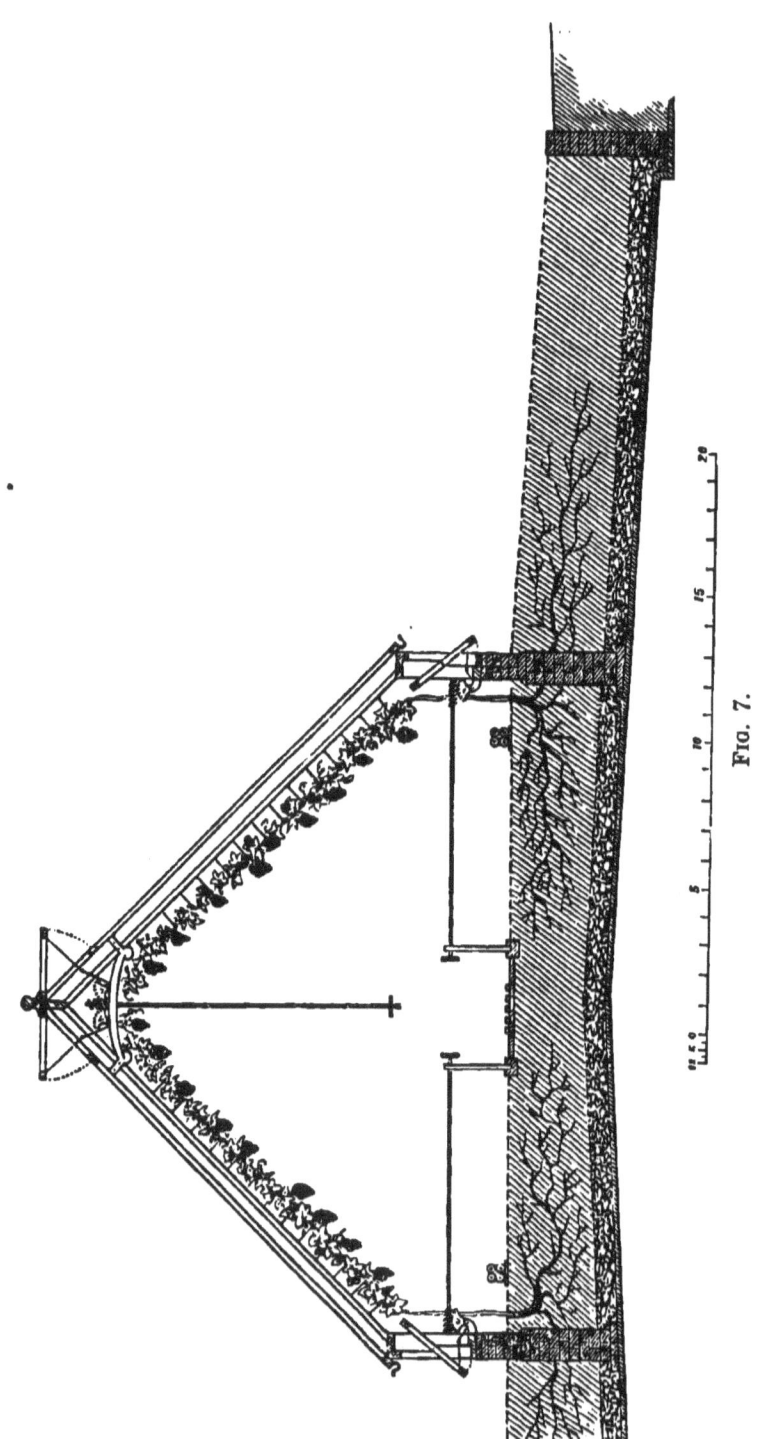

Fig. 7.

the vines are tied too near the glass; they should be not less than 16 inches from the glass, to allow a free circulation of air between it and the foliage. It is scarcely necessary to point out the evil of having the foliage in close contact with the glass. The wires should be fixed at 1 foot apart. Moisture in the atmosphere should be provided for in all vineries. See page 7, where there is described, in connection with pineries, the method I think best.

DRAINAGE.

The first thing that should be thought of and most effectively secured in the making of borders is drainage; for however great the skill otherwise brought to bear on the after-management of the vine, first-rate results need not be looked for if the roots are subject to stagnant water. One of the most important points in successful grape-growing, is the preservation in winter of the young roots made in summer, which is impossible if the border is subject to stagnant water. Of course the extent and character of the drainage necessary have to be determined by the position of the vinery, the nature of the subsoil, and to some extent by the average amount of rain which is peculiar to the district. The amount of drainage necessary on the retentive clay of such as Middlesex, or in the lower ward of Lanarkshire, the Dumfries or Argyle coasts, where so much rain falls, would be superfluous on the rocks of some parts of Somerset, or on the generally dry soils of East Lothian. By these conditions should also be decided to what extent borders should be elevated above the natural ground-level.

In preparing the site and drainage on damp retentive subsoils, let all the natural soil be excavated to the depth of 4 feet from the bottom of the arches or lintels at the front of the vinery, and, supposing that the outside border is to be 20 feet wide, give it a slope of 18 inches to the extremity of the border. The site for the inside border should be sloped to the same extent, upwards in the case of lean-to house, to the back wall. Lay down a layer of concrete, 3 to 4 inches thick, over the whole site of the border. Run a main drain parallel with the border at its extreme front, and 6 inches below the lowest level of the concrete. In order to make sure of the most perfect drainage, lay tile-drains at right angles with this main drain, up to the back of the vinery, at every 8 feet. Over the whole surface of the concrete, and covering the tile-drains, spread a layer of broken bricks, road-metal, or round gravel with all sand sifted out of it, to the depth of 8 inches. Finish off with a sprinkling of smaller gravel, and a turf, grassy side downwards, over the whole surface. The site is thus ready for the border. The slope of the site, and soil, drains, &c., can be seen at a glance in fig. 7.

On what may be termed healthy gravelly subsoils in dry localities, where water neither stands nor rises, such extra care in drainage is not absolutely necessary. But where there is the least chance of there not being a ready and immediate escape for water, no hesitation should ever be allowed as to the necessity of draining as has been directed. I have never seen vines do well in wet, and as a consequence cold borders, and know of instances where wet and unproductive borders have been rendered fruitful by perfect drainage. Although the vine in a growing state requires much moisture, it will not put up with stagnant water at any season.

BORDERS—THEIR COMPOSITION.

In forming borders for the cultivation of grapes, greater regard should be directed towards the maintenance of vines in such a condition as is likely to yield satisfactory crops for a lengthened period of time, than to the production of larger bunches with perhaps less certainty for a few years, to be followed by a general and rapid decline in the constitution of the vines, and, as a necessary consequence, in the amount and quality of the crops they bear. That such different results are to a very great extent indeed dependent on the mechanical and manurial state of the soil, is a fact that cannot fail to have become perfectly obvious to those who have studied the growth of the vine in borders of opposite characters and composition. That the vine will continue in a healthy bearing state for a greater length of time under favourable circumstances than almost any other fruit-bearing plant or tree, is abundantly proved by the fact that of many of the same varieties that are cultivated in this country, there are in France and Italy whole vineyards, now in full bearing, which were in the same condition three centuries ago. And in this country there are instances of vines now bearing well in vineries that were planted some eighty, and others more than a hundred, years ago. I have inspected excellent crops of grapes on vines at Dumfries House, in Ayrshire, which, I was told, can be traced back one hundred and forty-five years. At Speddoch, in Dumfriesshire, the seat of Gilchrist Clark, Esq., there is a splendid Black Hamburg vine, entirely filling a house 70 feet by 22 feet, which annually bears heavy crops of magnificent grapes. Such vines are found growing in calcareous and not over-retentive soils, and many of the old vines on the Continent in an argillaceous gravelly soil, and some on the mere debris of rocks.

While referring to these facts, it is not forgotten that there are other circumstances and important points in cultivation, connected more especially with the early forcing of grapes under glass in this country, which are of necessity adverse to the constitution and longevity of the vines. But these references show more forcibly what is invariably observed in practice —viz., that deep, retentive, over-rich moist borders are not those from which vines with good sound constitutions and fine grapes are to be reared for a long series of years. And I would therefore urge on the inexperienced to avoid, on every consideration, the formation of borders of retentive soils with large infusions of manure. It is scarcely necessary now to warn them against carrion-borders. These have, we believe, long ago been abandoned as next to poison for vines.

The result of rich retentive borders for the first few years, as long as the fibry or organic matter is decomposing, is a strong, rank, long-jointed growth, having a decided tendency to be unfruitful if the season be dull and wet. The bunches most frequently produced from such a growth are long in the stocks—a sort of production between a tendril and a bunch—such as are most frequently attacked with shanking, and at last, when dished, show a disagreeable amount of long weak stalks. The roots formed in such pasty borders never ripen, and die back in winter to the thick inactive roots.

When such borders settle down, and the turfy part has vanished, there is left a close adhesive, damp, rich mass of matter, most unfavourable to the thick fleshy roots of the vine. After a while the vines become less excitable. The grapes regularly shank, and do not colour; and if the border is examined in winter, all the roots that can be found in it are entirely destitute of the fibry parts formed the previous season, the preservation of which is of great importance.

The most successful grape-growers are now very unanimous in choosing a calcareous turfy loam, taken to the depth of 6 or 7 inches from the surface of an old pasture-field, as being the best for the fruitfulness and lengthened wellbeing of the vine. Such a soil, pure and simple, contains in itself all the elements of successful grape-growing for a good many years. It contains a large amount of fibre or organic matter, which in its slow decomposition supplies the elements of fertility. In choosing such a soil, that which is sandy and spongy should be avoided. This is what is generally termed "light sandy loam." It continues to grow vigorous vines, which bear fine grapes, while the fibry part of it lasts and is decomposing; but when the fibre has ceased to be in it, there is not stamina sufficient left for vines. A loam with what is generally termed more " body " in it should be selected — avoiding, of course, that which has too much clay in it, and which, when its organic matter has decayed, becomes solid, impervious to air, and too retentive of water. The medium between these two soils is the best for grape-growing,—that which may be described as having enough of sand or silicious matter in it to make it friable and prevent its ever becoming adhesive, in combination with as much clay or alumina as gives it body, constituting it a rather strong but friable loam. In all my observations and experience I have invariably found the most robust and fruitful vines growing in borders composed of soils of this description, especially when taken from the red sandstone formation. Although such a soil as this contains nearly all that is necessary for the production of first-rate grapes for some years, regard must be had to the time when the turfy organic matter in it has decomposed and changed into mould, leaving the border destitute of its primitive fertility, and less porous than is desirable; and substances that will retain their manurial and organic character beyond this time must be added to it as shall now be directed.

In taking the top spit of such old pasture-soil as I have described, the verdure and soil should be taken to the depth of half a spit, or about six or seven inches. It is very often found to be much infested with wire-worm, an insect which, when introduced into vine-borders, preys upon the young roots of vines. In time of severe frost these pests retreat downwards, and it is therefore best, if possible, to collect the soil when it is frozen. The turf should be stacked in the compost-yard for some months before it is used. I have, however, frequently carted it in when in a dry state, and prepared and mixed it immediately. When this has to be done, the grass should be cut closely off with a scythe before the ground is touched. In the process of chopping and mixing the turf, it should, if possible, be protected from wet; and where there is not shed-room sufficient to hold it, it can be covered with wooden shutters or tarpauling.

The loam should first be chopped up, but not too finely, mixing the fibry portion of it regularly with the finer. Then to six parts of loam add one part of old lime-rubbish taken from old buildings, and one part charcoal. To every 6 cubic yards put 1 cwt. of rough bone-meal, and 2 cwt. of half-inch bones. When lime-rubbish can be more easily had than charcoal, and *vice versâ*, the one can be substituted for the other. When a heavier soil than is desirable has to be taken, then add more lime-rubbish and charcoal; and when the soil is lighter, use less of these substances. In the absence of either lime-rubbish or charcoal, old brickbats pounded down to the size of road-metal can be substituted as the next best. I have used burned clay with good effect when other open material could not conveniently be secured. These porous materials, especially charcoal, have the power of absorbing carbonic acid gas and ammonia from the air, besides being conservative of moisture in time of drought, and absorb manurial applications, to be gradually given off to the roots of plants. We do not recommend that any animal manures, such as horse-droppings, be mixed with this compost. These should be applied as top-dressings when the state of the vines demands them.

When the nature of the soil is essentially clayey, although the most turfy portion be taken, it never fails in after-years to revert to a clayey adhesive body; a larger proportion, therefore, of the open materials named should be used, and the border need not be so deep. I would strongly urge that no more manure be used than the comparatively small proportion named. A border composed as has been directed, forms a body of soil of the best possible description for conveying to the roots in after-years nourishment from rich top-dressings and waterings without becoming soured and unhealthy. When these materials have been all put together, turn the heap over at least twice before wheeling it into its place. As it should be dry, it may be firmly beaten with the back of a fork, or even gently trodden with the feet. But it should never be either mixed or wheeled when in a wet sodden state. To allow for its subsiding, it may be filled in 6 inches higher than the ultimate level.

Being well aware that there are many who may be desirous of growing grapes who cannot possibly get the top spit from an old pasture, and although this is recommended as the best soil, I am far from wishing to convey the impression that such is indispensable to the production of very fair crops of grapes. Wherever ordinarily good garden-soil is at command, there is no reason why grape-growing should not be attempted and attended with considerable success. Let it be supposed that the bulk of the border has to be composed of ordinary garden-soil, tolerably rich with *humus*, or vegetable matter in a state of decay, common to most garden-soils where vegetables have been grown. Take six parts of this as the base of the composition, add one part half-decayed stable-litter, mixing it well with the soil, and forming the whole into a ridge to lie for a few months. Meantime, if possible, collect as much of the tough turfy vegetation which generally abounds by the sides of old highways and roads—on to which the road-drift or scrapings have been washed for years—as will form about the fourth of the bulk required for the border. Such accumulations are generally one mass of vegetable fibre, an element so much wanting in old garden-soil. This should also be thrown into ridges to lie and partially decompose for a few months. Then it can be chopped with the spade and thoroughly mixed with the heap of garden-soil and stable-manure. To this add the same proportions of lime-rubbish, charcoal, and bones recommended in the case of the top spit from old pasture. This will make a compost in which vines will grow vigorously and bear well, and one which will for many years be a good medium for feeding the vines with waterings of manure-water and top-dressings of manure.

I have superintended the making of borders where the soil chiefly consisted of weeds or rack gathered off farm-fields and allowed to lie till it was half decomposed or fully more, and then added the other constituents named to it, and a portion of soil burned, or rather charred, in the usual way, and the result for years has been most satisfactory.

In forming these composts into vine-borders, the too common practice of making the whole of a wide border the first year is not a good one. The fact that a great proportion of the border must lie unoccupied with roots while the fibry and best part of it is undergoing decomposition without being of any service to the vines, is argument sufficiently strong against making the border the whole width the first, and in favour of extending the completion of it over several years. Eight feet outside the house is quite sufficient for the first year, and an addition of 5 feet for two successive years will complete a border 18 feet wide. By this method an opportunity is afforded of seeing that the extremities of the roots are not running over-deep, and an upward direction can be given to them; and the vines are afforded the stimulus of fresh soil to feed in for the first few years, which is of much importance. If the surrounding soil is of a character decidedly unfavourable, it is desirable to confine the roots within the limits of the artificial border. This can be done by a brick-and-cement wall. Where the natural soil is favourable, this is of less importance for late grapes; but for grapes that have to be ripened not later than June, it is desirable to have all the roots in the made border, and thus under control.

VARIETIES OF GRAPES.

The varieties of grapes cultivated in this country have increased considerably of late, both by the introduction of Continental varieties and by the distribution of seedlings raised in Britain; consequently the inexperienced have greater difficulty than ever in making selections to meet their wants. The following are the varieties I recommend for early forcing in, say, a 40-feet vinery admitting of 13 rods:—

6 Black Hamburg.
3 Duke of Buccleuch.
1 Buckland's Sweetwater.
1 White Frontignac. } Grafted on Muscat
1 Grizzly Frontignac. } of Alexandria.
1 Foster's White Seedling.

Late grapes for using throughout the winter months:—

3 Lady Downes Seedling.
4 Muscat of Alexandria. } At hottest end of
1 Alnwick Seedling.   } house.
1 Alicante.
2 Gros Colemar.
1 Golden Queen.
1 Raisin de Calabria.

When a long succession is required from one house, and early forcing is not practised :—

4 Black Hamburg.
2 Duke of Buccleuch.
1 Muscat Hamburg — grafted on Muscat or Black Hamburg.
1 Duchess of Buccleuch.
1 Gros Colemar.
2 Lady Downes Seedling.
2 Muscat of Alexandria.

For forcing early in pots :—

7 Black Hamburg.
2 Duke of Buccleuch.
1 Foster's White Seedling.
1 White Frontignac.
1 Duchess of Buccleuch.
1 Madresfield Court.

For growing in a cool vinery :—

4 Black Hamburg.
3 Esperion.
2 Reeves's Muscadine.
1 Foster's Seedling.
2 Buckland's Sweetwater.
1 Black Prince.

In gardens where the vineries are numerous enough to admit of classing the Muscat, Frontignac, and others that require a high temperature together, it is always best to do so. And the late-keeping varieties, such as Alicante, Gros Colemar, Lady Downes, and Alnwick Seedling, should also be classed together.

Those who have a fancy for very large bunches can grow the Syrian and Barbarossa.

SELECTING VINES FOR PLANTING.

The speedy and permanent well-doing of vines depends very much on the condition in which they are when planted. There are two descriptions of vines to which I have a decided objection. These are such as are raised by layers from old vines, and those that are more than one year old from the eye. The former method is not much practised now—the latter is common enough. These, I have invariably observed, never start into growth so satisfactorily, nor do they ever make such vigorous and fruitful vines, in a given time, as those that are only one year old, provided that they have been properly grown and ripened. The one-year-old vine is what I consider the best and most desirable for general planting, especially in the case of inexperienced cultivators. At the same time, it is a matter somewhat difficult to decide whether a plant raised from an eye in spring, and planted when 2 or 3 feet high in May or June, will not equal, if it do not actually outrun in the race of success, the year-old plant. For my own part, in the case of vineries such as have been recommended admitting of the vines being planted inside, I would have some difficulty in making a choice between a well-ripened and well-rooted one-year-old plant and one raised from an eye the same spring. The results from both descriptions of plants are so nearly alike that it is of little moment upon which the choice should fall. But, as has been already said, the one-year-old plant is safer in the hands of the inexperienced; and directions for rearing and planting both these descriptions of plants will be given.

THE GRAPE VINE.

PREPARING YOUNG VINES FOR PLANTING.

To prepare one-year-old vines for planting, about the middle of January select the necessary number of strong prominent buds from vines that have thoroughly well and early ripened their wood. Cut away the wood to within a quarter of an inch on the upper side of the bud, and that on the under side to within an inch—making clean cuts with a sharp knife. The buds are thus ready for insertion. Take the required number of 4-inch pots, drain them well, and fill them up rather firmly with three parts light fibry loam, and one part of finely-sifted, well-decomposed leaf-mould. Make a hole in the centre of each to receive the buds, into which they are to be inserted, and surrounded with a little propagating sand. Cover them to the very tips of the buds. When they are put in, place them in a house slightly warmer than a common greenhouse; and if the soil is moist, do not water them for a week. The first week of February remove them to some house or pit where they can be plunged near the glass in a bottom-heat of 80° to 85°, with a night temperature of 55° to 60°. Keep them steadily and moderately moist, and they will soon burst their buds; and as they begin to develop their leaves, raise the temperature 5°, and let it run up 10° more with sun-heat by day before giving air. The process of leaf-development and the formation of roots will be nearly simultaneous, although generally leaves slightly precede the roots. Consequently, after they have formed two or three small leaves, they halt in growth till the roots have fairly commenced their work. At this stage see that they do not become over dry. Just keep the soil moist, but not wet, and, always with water at a temperature of 80°. As soon as the young roots reach the sides of the pots and down to the drainage, raise them by degrees out of the plunging material, and place them on its surface. Range the night temperature at 65° at night, with 10° or 15° more by day with sun. As soon as they have pretty well filled their pots with roots, and begun to grow away freely with stronger and more transparent-like growth, shift them into larger pots: 7 and 8 inch pots are large enough for growing vines into an excellent condition for planting; for far more depends on the character of the roots they make, and the ripeness and soundness of the canes, than on mere bulk of growth.

There is nothing that so much influences the character of the roots that young vines make after this stage as the nature of the soil, and the position in which they are grown. Take one of these young vines now ready for a shift out of a 4-inch pot; let an 8 or 10 inch pot be drained, as is so often the case, with a few large pieces of broken tiles or even bricks put into the bottom of the pot in a careless manner: pot it in a soil of rather tenacious character, and add a large proportion of rotten manure; then plunge in bottom-heat, and grow it crowded together with others far from the glass, and what is the result? The soil, instead of being thoroughly filled with well-ripened fibry roots at the end of the season, is only occupied by a comparatively few long fleshy roots, which never ripen properly, and die in the winter. The cane itself is not of that compact, short-jointed, well-ripened stamp which alone is a sure indication that all is right. When such a vine is shaken out in spring to be planted, it is found comparatively rootless, and in every way inferior.

Take the same young vine and shift it into a well and carefully drained pot not larger than 8 inches, in a compost composed of a good, sound, rather light loam, having a fourth part of thoroughly decomposed manure, and a sprinkling of bone-meal and sand mixed with it. Pot firmly, and place it on the surface of the plunging material, or even on a shelf or the floor of a light house, and grow it the whole time without bottom-heat, and the result is a potful of beautiful well-ripened fibrous roots, that keep fresh through the winter in such quantity that when they are shaken out of the soil for planting in spring, the pot appears to have been full of roots and nothing else. There is no comparison between these two descriptions of vines for planting. All is in favour of the latter, of course. Avoid, therefore, in growing young vines, badly-drained pots, a close retentive soil, and bottom-heat after they are well rooted.

All summer they should be grown on at an average temperature of 70° at night, with from 10° to 20° more by sun-heat in the afternoon for a while when shut up. No check for lack of water should ever be risked while in a growing state; for besides other evils, they will, if not well supplied with water both at the root and in the atmosphere, be very subject to the ravages of red-spider. Of light, the grand consolidating and ripening agent, they should have as much as possible. All vines grown in the shade of other vines, or anything else, should be avoided. The lateral growth should be kept regularly stopped to one bud, and the vines stopped at 5 feet. They are often allowed to grow longer, but it is a mistake, inasmuch as the buds lower down the vine, where the permanent growths generally start, are never so strong and plump as when stopped shorter. The finest planting vines I ever grew were in 6 and 7 inch pots, and stopped at 3 feet. They were ready to burst their pots with finely-ripened fibry roots, and their tops stood stiff and erect like hazel-rods, studded with prominent buds. It would save nurserymen much space and labour if planters would accept smaller vines of a concentrated and well-ripened growth. Much could also be saved in packing and carriage, and the article would be in most instances of a far better character.

After the growths are thoroughly browned, and there is no danger of the main buds starting, the laterals should be entirely removed; but do everything to preserve the foliage on the main growth intact to the last. Should the foliage suffer from any cause, in that case leave the lateral leaves. Give plenty of air in all stages of their growth, or they will be liable to get crippled from excrescences forming on the under sides of the leaves, an affection which is brought on by a too damp atmosphere with too little air. As the ripening process goes on, expose them to a free circulation of dry warm air. After they have shed their leaves, place them for the winter where neither their stems nor roots are exposed to more than a very few degrees of frost. Care should be taken that the roots are never allowed to become mealy dry. Too much wet must also be avoided. A cool shed where the pots can be plunged in decayed tan or leaves free from worms will winter them very well.

To grow such plants into strong fruitful vines for fruiting in pots the following year, it is only necessary to shift them on into 11-inch pots, grow them to from 6 to 7 feet in the full blaze of the sun, and in all other respects to treat them like those for planting.

THE GRAPE VINE.

When the pots are well filled with roots in both cases, water them three times weekly with weak guano and dung water alternately.

An excellent system of preparing young vines, both when they are intended to be struck from eyes and planted the same season, and when to be grown in pots for either planting or fruiting in pots the following spring, was adopted for the first time by Mr Thomson of Tweed Vineyard when he planted the immense graperies there. It is described by him as follows :—

" I indicated that I considered the present system of preparing young vines for planting had a good deal to do with the early declension of the fruitfulness of the vine, and I now proceed to give a sketch of the method I adopted in the spring of last year for preparing something like 1500 young vines, half of which were intended for my own planting. On the 7th of last February I placed a layer of very fibry turf over the pavement of a pine-pit, under which were pipes for giving bottom-heat. On this turf I laid 4 inches of fine turfy loam; made small holes in it at about 6 inches apart—these were filled with white sand—and a vine eye was placed in each, so as to be just covered. They started in the usual way, and grew rapidly, throwing out strong roots from the eye. When these roots had begun to interlace each other, and the vines were from 6 inches to 9 inches high, they were cut round by a strong knife, so that each vine was isolated on its own piece of turf. The points of their roots being cut, they flagged for a few days, but soon threw out scores of small active roots from every large one that was cut. When this had taken place, a small trowel was run under each square, and the plants lifted and placed on a similar bed of turf, but this time from 9 inches to 12 inches apart, and filled in round about with soil of the same character as at first, avoiding manure of any sort. Here they soon began to grow rapidly again; and when they had attained the height of 3 feet, and the borders were ready for them, they were cut round as in the first instance, and allowed to stand till a fresh set of young roots were just started, when they were raised on a spade, with ball quite entire, and placed in their new borders. This operation was easily performed, and they received not the smallest check, but grew rapidly at once; and when cut back—some to 10 feet and others to 3 feet—just eleven months from the day the eyes were placed in the sand, their average girth is from 2 to 3 inches; and they are ripe, close-jointed, and solid as hazel-sticks to the apex of the houses—some 22 feet. Those that were not required for planting were potted; and for this purpose I can as strongly recommend the system as for planting. When vines prepared thus come to be turned out of their pots in the process of planting, there is no occasion for breaking up the ball, for there are no coiled roots in it to disentangle—they are more like those of a box or privet bush than a vine, as usually seen; and when planted, they begin by taking their work before them, instead of running away out of the border.

" So much for the vines. And now as to what may be done with a view to retaining this tendency to a multiplication of small active roots across the border. Just make up 3 feet of it inside and 3 feet outside the house the first year. In April or May of the second year, fork down 1 or 2 inches of the face of this bank of soil, both inside and outside the house; and against the roots that will there be found, some of them taking the lead, place a section of sharp river or pit sand, or gravel, at least 4 inches thick. As soon as the roots enter this poor sharp material, they will branch into a thousand small active roots, and enter the layer of new soil that has been subsequently laid against this sand or gravel. This may be repeated at every addition to the border, and the result will be that, instead of a few long, straight, naked roots, the whole border will be full of a class of active woody roots, that survive the cold and wet of winter infinitely better than those great snake-like ones formed in rich soil. These perpendicular sections of sand or gravel have the additional advantage of acting as drains to draw off superfluous water."

TIME AND MANNER OF PLANTING VINES.

To fix a given day or week, irrespective of circumstances, for the performance of gardening operations, is now very much a thing of the past. In the planting of vines this is especially applicable; they may be planted from February to August, according to circumstances. In order, however, to get the best possible growth the first year, spring and early summer are the best seasons to plant. It is only where vineries and borders cannot be got ready in time, or where a crop has to be cut the same season from the house to be planted, that later planting should be practised. The exact time in the early part of the year should be decided by several considerations, such as the character of the season, the state of the vines themselves, and whether the vines are intended for being forced early or for late crops. Just as the vines, in the case of one-year-old plants, are bursting their buds in a cool place, is the condition, all other things being equal, in which they are ready to make a vigorous start. The exact time when this takes place depends considerably on the time they ripened and shed their foliage in autumn. When kept in a cool airy place, they are at this stage, in ordinary seasons, about the end of March or beginning of April, which is a good time to plant. When intended for early forcing, I recommend their being planted about the middle of February, when, in the case of early varieties, they can be easily excited into growth by fire-heat. It is an established fact, that being started early one season, they are the more susceptible of early excitement the next; and consequently they can be brought sooner into an early forcing condition when planted and started somewhat early. Late varieties intended for late grapes should, on the other hand, be planted just as they begin to burst their buds in a cool place, which is generally in April.

For a vigorous start and growth, April and May are the best months to start young and newly-planted vines. Except in the case of those required for early forcing, it is best to wait for long days, bright sun, and the natural impulse of the plant, before applying much fire-heat.

In the case of vines struck from eyes the same spring, the end of May is a good time, just as the plants have attained to about 2 feet in height, and their roots have been prepared according to the Tweed Vineyard practice. I have, however, planted them at various times from May to July with very similar success. In one case where I had to ripen a crop of grapes, in the same house I planted vines about 4 feet high at the middle of July, putting a supernumerary to every light, from which I cut ripe grapes the following July, thus not losing a year's crop.

Manner of Planting.—How to plant is of more importance than when to plant, for the success of after-years depends more upon it. Let it be supposed that the border is in readiness for the plants. Here there is a mass of soil, and one of the chief objects aimed at in planting should be how best to do it, so as to cause the roots to take the most equable and thorough possession of it in their progress of growth. If the vines be turned out of their pot without breaking their balls or "shaking them out," nine out of every ten will not form a fresh growth from the old roots, but will stand still until there are young roots pushed out from the stem above the old roots, immediately under the surface of the soil. These roots will of necessity be few in number, but strong, and will push away into the border without branching much for a time. This, of course, is undesirable. If the roots are thoroughly divested of the soil and spread carefully out, and if at the same time 1 foot or 18 inches of the stem is laid in the soil, they will in this case also stand still, until the stem throws out a whorl of strong roots near the surface of the soil, and the vines will entirely forsake the old roots. This will more especially be the case if the old roots are, as sometimes happens, laid out into the cold outside border, and the stem emerges from the border inside, where it is subject to the influence of the hot-water pipes. These two ways of planting are consequently objectionable.

The best way is to thoroughly divest the roots of all the soil, wash them clean in tepid water, and disentangle them carefully. Should any of them be much stronger and longer than the others, cut these back, and dash a handful or two of dry sand about the roots, and give them a shake. Root-pruning, however, is rarely necessary when vines are grown as has been directed. The vine is thus ready for planting. Remove the soil to the depth of 9 inches, and to a width sufficient to take in the extended roots. In this space carefully place the vine, spreading out the roots and keeping the stem 6 inches off the front wall. Cover up the lower roots with some of the finest of the soil, making sure that every root stretches regularly out from the stem all round. Pack the soil firmly about them with the hand, and lay down each layer of roots with soil in between and about them, till those nearest the surface are covered 3 or 4 inches deep. Fix a stake in the soil at the back of the vine, tying the top of it to the first wire, and tie the vine neatly to it, so that as it grows and strengthens the stem may be straight and neat. Settle the soil about the roots with water through a fine rose at a temperature of about 100°; then cover the surface of the soil with a layer of old mushroom-bed manure, to prevent evaporation and the necessity for frequent watering. This is especially necessary if the roots are near the pipes. Supposing that the lights are 6 feet wide, let a permanent vine, to be brought away with two rods each, be planted to each rafter. This will give a rod to every 3 feet run of the vinery. Vines should never be thicker, and in many cases 6 inches or a foot more will be to the advantage of the vine, though many begrudge the room. In the centre of each light plant a vine to be trained with one stem, for the purpose of being fruited the following season, half-way up the roof; and where as many grapes as possible are, as is usually the case, an object, plant a set of vines every 6 feet along the centre of the house to crop the top half of the vinery. This double set applies to wide vineries, one set being enough for vineries not more than 14 or 15 feet wide. These temporary sets of vines can be grown the first year and fruited the second without any detriment to the permanent vines, and when the temporary vines have fruited one or two years they can be removed. I refer to the quotation at p. 75 for the manner of planting spring-struck vines prepared on the Tweed Vineyard principle, and which, as will there be seen, is as simple as planting a strawberry plant—the aim of the whole of the excellent method of root-pruning and planting there described being to get the vines to start into growth from the very stem with a great quantity of fibry, instead of a few strong fleshy, roots. When this method of root-pruning and growing the young vines without their ever being potted cannot be adopted, they should be grown in flat shallow trays, and the vines planted before the roots get cramped and begin to twist and coil. Vines may be planted quite well when 1 foot high. I once planted a quantity when about 8 inches high, and put a bell-glass over them for two or three days, because the roots had been disentangled and laid carefully out; but there can be no doubt about the superiority of the root-pruning and non-potting system. When planted in outside borders, place some dry litter over the roots, removing it on sunny days, but putting it on at nights to retain heat.

TREATMENT THE SEASON THEY ARE PLANTED.

Under this heading I begin by stating that I consider the point to be aimed at is the largest possible amount of well-ripened wood and roots. On the attainment of this depends to a very great extent the production of vines the second season that will yield first-class grapes the third year of their growth. Presuming that the vines are planted and started into growth with fire-heat in April, as soon as the buds are burst half an inch or so, rub them all off, in the case of the temporary vines to be fruited next year, down to near the top of the front sash. After they advance a little more, and a good strong bud can be selected a few inches below the top of the front light, remove all except it and another in the meantime, in case any accident should occur to one of them. In the case of the permanent vines at each rafter, rub them all off down to the bottom of the rafter. From thence let one bud come away as a leader, and ultimately leave just other two, one on each side of the stem, starting from half a foot or so below the leader. These three shoots, with their lateral growths, and the temporary vines, will be enough to cover the whole roof with foliage without crowding any of the leaders.

Raise the night temperature to 60°, and admit air in the morning as soon as the thermometer rises above 75° with sun, increasing the air as the heat increases. Apply fire-heat sparingly the greater part of the day with sunshine. Keep the atmosphere moderately moist, and gently syringe the vines and sprinkle the floor with tepid water when the house is shut up in the afternoon. After the plants that have been raised from eyes the previous season make some 8 or 9 inches of growth, they generally stand still for eight or ten days; and I have known the inexperienced have great impatience, and fear lest something serious was amiss as the cause of an almost total cessation of top-growth. This pause is consequent on the growth having been so far supported by the stored-up sap in the stem and roots of the vine, which when exhausted brings the growth to a standstill, till the roots get into action and send up a fresh supply of sap. During this cessation, if the weather be bright and a good deal of air has to be admitted, they may droop a little in the middle of the day, in which case it is advisable to shade them slightly for a few hours, keeping the air moist, and to syringe the young growths at shutting-up time till the roots begin to grow. The first indications of this are easily noticed in the production of stronger tendrils than formerly, and in the fresh expansion of tender-looking leaves. These are sure signs that the last year's fibres have sent out young rootlets; and if one of the vines were lifted at this stage, the young whitey-green roots would be found starting at innumerable points. When they begin to grow freely, range the night temperature from 65° to 70°, with a rise of from 10° to 15° by day with sun-heat. Keep the steaming apparatus full of water, and the surface of the border sprinkled in the morning, and again at shutting-up time when the weather is bright. A corresponding decrease of moisture must take place in the absence of sun, and only syringe the foliage occasionally on the afternoons of bright days after the vinery is shut up. Very soon after they make the fresh start alluded to, they will grow with gradually increasing rapidity and vigour. They should be carefully looked to every second day, and have the fresh growths fastened loosely to the wires with soft matting, the tendrils pinched off, and the lateral growths regulated—not pinched back to a single leaf, as is sometimes practised. The whole of the roof should be furnished, but not crowded, with foliage, and the pinching and tying of the lateral growths regulated with this end in view. In proportion to the extent of foliage will be the extent of the roots formed in the border. This treatment of course applies to the permanent vines, from which no fruit is to be taken the following year; and all the growth and expansion that the roof affords them without shading the temporary vines should be allowed them. When they reach the top of the house they may be trained down the back wall. In the case of those planted with the intention of their bearing a crop of fruit the following year, a more restricted growth is desirable. The laterals should be regularly stopped when they form two leaves, and the leading shoots stopped when they reach little more than half-way up the roof; and those planted for cropping the upper portion of the house should be stopped when they reach past the top wire. These being restricted, and their energies, so to speak, concentrated, they form better-developed buds on the main stems, from which the crop of next season is produced. Care, however, must be exercised in stopping with the same pertinacity after the leader is stopped, for there is a danger of the main buds bursting if the laterals are then too closely pinched; so that it is better to allow them to grow more for a time near the top, where some few of the main buds generally push after the stopping; and these, too, should be allowed to grow a little till the stem gets firmer, and there is no danger of the buds bursting lower down.

Watering must be attended to after the vines have started into rapid growth, and sufficient applied at intervals to keep the inside border moist. In the middle of summer, and before the roof gets so covered with foliage as to protect it from the sun, examine the soil at least every week, and water it when necessary. Should the season be very dry, the outside portion of the border will be the better for a slight mulching of half-decayed litter, which will prevent the necessity for watering so much. The inside border, after the roots have penetrated into it, will also be the better of a similar mulching, but only to a slight extent. Avoid applying water that has not stood in the vinery cisterns for some time to get warmed a little.

I am not favourable to syringing much, but it does more good and less harm to young fruitless vines than under other circumstances, and it is a preventive of red-spider. As the season advances, and the sun gets powerful, leave air on to a small extent all night after syringing the foliage, and it should be increased as early as 6 A.M., in order to get the foliage dry before the sun acts powerfully on the glass, otherwise the foliage may suffer under the clear glass now used.

The night temperature during the summer months may range from 70° to 75°, when the necessity for fire-heat is at its minimum. With the increase of light, air, and heat, atmospheric moisture should be increased, and *vice versâ;* but by all means avoid at any time a close, stagnant, damp atmosphere. As soon as the wood begins to ripen, admit more air, causing a circulation among the foliage by opening the front lights more freely, and gradually decrease the amount of moisture. Examine the foliage, and if there be any red-spider on it, give a few vigorous syringings, and take every means of keeping the foliage in a healthy state, till the vines have matured it, and throw it off in a natural way. When the wood gets dark brown and well solidified, open all the ventilators to their full extent, except in times of high winds, which might injure the leaves, it being indispensable to the proper maturing of the roots and wood that the foliage should remain its natural period on the vines.

MANAGEMENT OF VINES THE SECOND SEASON.

Pruning.—When the vines have rested about three weeks after they have shed their leaves, pruning should not be delayed any longer. Cut down the permanent vines at each rafter to about 1 foot below the top of the front light or bottom of the rafter. The general practice is to cut them down exactly to the bottom of the rafter; but as they are to be trained with two fruit-bearing and permanent rods, I prefer cutting them lower down, both because the two permanent rods can be more easily trained into their proper place, and because the first few buds formed at the base of long young rods are never so prominent, and do not break and show fruit, or come away into strong lateral growths, so well as those further up the rod. By cutting them below the angle, these weaker buds are formed where they are not so important for fruit-bearing the following season. Shorten back those that have been grown with a single rod, to bear fruit for a year or two, to about 8 feet. The day after they are cut, dress the wounds over with styptic, to prevent any possibility of their bleeding in spring when the sap begins to move. Young strong vines are more apt to bleed than older ones. Wash the wood-work and glass, and otherwise thoroughly clean the house. If there has been any red-spider about the vines the previous year, wash them with a soft brush and soapy water.

Then fix the vines in their proper places to the wires, remove the dry soil which is loose in the surface of the inside border, and fork the surface to the depth of two inches, or as far down as there is no danger of interfering with the young roots. Put as much fresh soil over the surface as has been removed, and the house is ready for starting when required in spring. During the course of winter or early spring an eke of fresh soil should be put to the borders, presuming that only a portion of them was made the first season. Any protection from rain during winter that has been put over the outside border should not be removed till the vines are starting in spring.

Throughout the whole spring keep the house cool and well aired, applying no more fire-heat than is just sufficient to exclude frost. Vines intended for the supply of late grapes should be allowed to break into growth without the aid of fire-heat. This in ordinary seasons they will do from the middle to the end of April. In the case of vines intended for early forcing, shut up the house on the 1st February, and apply fire-heat to keep the temperature from falling below 45°, to be increased to 50° at night by the beginning of March, and 60° as soon as the vines have pushed their buds a quarter of an inch—the temperature to be increased and regulated as directed for the first season's growth, and as shall again be referred to in treating of the fruiting year and forcing the vine. The vines will this season grow with rapidity, and, having their growth concentrated into two rods, with great strength. Throughout every stage of their growth up till the ripening period, the inside border must be regularly watered, so that there be no chance of a check from over-dryness at the root. It is impossible to say exactly when water should be applied; it must be applied before the soil gets very dry and begins to crack. It is a good plan, after the vines are in full growth, to mulch the border slightly with rotten manure, such as old mushroom-bed dung. The same attention to atmospheric moisture and airing as directed for the first year's growth, of course applies to that of the second.

Instead of permitting the lateral growths to ramble as directed for the first season's growth, do not allow them to make more than two leaves, and stop the main growths as soon as they reach half-way up the rafters. This stopping causes the buds on the lower part of the vines that are to bear next year to become fuller and stronger. Allow the leader to break and grow on to the top of the house, there to be stopped finally. After this stopping allow the lateral growths, especially those on the top part of the vine, to make another leaf, to encourage root-growth. Now is the time that the most rapid thickening of the rod and the full development of its buds take place. If all be right they will swell with astonishing quickness, bursting their bark and expanding their foliage to the full. At this stage see that none of the ties by which they are supported get too tight and cut them.

Keep a constant look-out for red-spider if the weather be hot and dry; and if it appears, give a few vigorous syringings with clean tepid water. The outside border should also be watered two or three times in summer in dry seasons, and a slight mulching applied as directed for the inside border. From the daily inside sprinklings the outside border is more likely to get injuriously dry than the inside one in hot summers. When the ripening process has turned the rods brown and the laterals up to the second joint, remove the third leaf from every lateral. This will encourage still further the plumping up of the main buds at the base of the laterals, and from which the crop is to come next year. In a few weeks after, the second leaf should be removed, thus leaving one on each lateral, which, with all the foliage on the main rod, keep green and healthy as long as possible. Give more air as the ripening of the rods goes on; at the same time gradually decrease moisture in the air; and rest not satisfied until the wood is solid and well ripened. If any doubt exist on this point, in dull seasons especially, maintain the fire-heat and a circulation of dry warm air till they are brown and hard as a hazel-rod. A large, flabby, and ill-ripened growth will bring nothing but disappointment; and if this point of culture is not gained, all else will avail little. When perfectly ripened, fire-heat of course should be discontinued, and the house be as well aired as full ventilation will admit. The temporary vines need not be discussed under this head; for the management of the third and fruiting year applies to them as well as to permanent vines. Suffice it to say, that they may be allowed to bear from eight to twelve bunches, according to their strength. I have planted and grown temporary vines over and over again, from which the second year I have taken twelve bunches of grapes. A set of vines planted in 1870 out of 6-inch pots, and treated in all respects as I am directing, made each two hard solid rods the second year of their growth, many of which measured $2\frac{3}{4}$ inches in circumference. From the temporary vines I took in most cases twelve bunches averaging 2 lb. each. The temporary vines which furnish the bottom part of the roof should be cut out immediately the crop is cut the second season. Those at the top can be left to bear another season without detriment to the permanent vines.

MANAGEMENT OF VINES THE THIRD AND FRUITING YEAR.

Pruning for the First Crop.—For the first crop the vines should be fruited to little more than the extent of one-third the rafter, it being of much importance to get the buds at the bottom of the vine to start strongly and evenly the first year, to secure at once strong fruiting spurs and buds all over the rods. If the rods are left longer than this, especially if they have to be started early, the top buds are apt to break strongly, and those below are less likely to keep anything like pace with them. With this shortening back, and the cutting off of the laterals close to the bud on the rods, the pruning is complete for the first fruiting season.

Time to commence Forcing, &c.—After cleaning the vines as recommended for the previous season, the whitewashing of the walls and the thorough cleansing of everything connected with the house, the border should be pricked up with a fork, and a top-dressing of about two inches of rotten manure spread all over it. The time to start the vines of course depends on when ripe grapes are required, and whether the vines are ultimately intended for early forcing. If started last year at the 1st of February, they may this season be started three weeks earlier with fire-heat, having previously, in gardening phrase, shut up the house for fourteen days—which means that the vinery be kept close without fire-heat unless the weather be frosty, when during that fortnight the temperature should be kept ranging from 40° to 45° at night. Vines started

THE GRAPE VINE.

at the 1st of January generally ripen their crop from the middle to the end of June. The following year forcing may commence three weeks earlier, and so on, till, if required, the forcing may begin in November, to ripen the crop in April.

In starting young strong canes early, there is much more difficulty in getting them to break regularly than there is with weaker or older vines; and to prevent their breaking and growing at the top before the bottom buds start, fix the vines to the lower wires only, and bring down their tops semicircle form to near the floor of the house, where the temperature is lowest. In this position allow them to remain till they have burst into growth over their whole length.

The good old system of putting a bed of leaves on the inside border is a great assistance in getting the vines to break regularly and strong. By turning a portion of the warm leaves over at intervals, they give heat and moisture sufficient to the air for the first fortnight, and throw some warmth into the soil besides. There is much difference of opinion as to the utility of heating vine-borders from beneath by means of hot-water pipes, but for very early forcing there can be no doubt it is of great service when judiciously applied. That vines started in November or any of the winter months start earlier and more strongly in borders heated from beneath, has been abundantly proved; and where such a means exists, it should be applied to raise the temperature of the soil at the commencement of forcing to say 60°. When vines that have a portion of their roots in outside borders have to be started before March, they should be covered in October with fern-leaves or straw, so that the heat may be retained in the soil, and to throw off rain and snow; and a fortnight before forcing is commenced, a bed of leaves, as recommended for the inside border, should be laid on it, to be also protected from rains, that would wash the heat out of it.

Temperature.—Apply fire-heat sparingly for the first fortnight; give just sufficient in conjunction with the heat which escapes from the bed of leaves, to keep the night temperature at 45° in cold frosty weather, and at 50° when the weather is mild. After the first fortnight raise it by degrees to from 50° to 55°. As soon as the buds have fairly started, give 5° more by degrees, making a point of rising to 60° when the young shoots are showing their bunches. By the time they are in bloom it should be raised to 65°, which is sufficiently high as a night temperature in the earlier months of the year. Range the day temperature with sun-heat from 10° higher than the night in the early part of the season, to 15° as the natural heat increases and less fire-heat is needed to keep it up.

The temperatures which are here recommended are sufficiently high for the early months, when mostly dependent on fire-heat. But further on in summer, especially after the grapes are thinned and stoned, and a higher temperature can be kept up with a minimum of fire-heat, the night temperature may be kept at 75° till late at night. Muscats, from the time they show their bunches onwards, require 5° more than the general run of other varieties; and to set Muscats well in the months of April and May, the night temperature should be 70°. As soon as the grapes begin to colour, a slight and gradual decrease of temperature should take place; and in the case of summer-ripened grapes, entirely discontinued after they are quite ripe. I have always found that grapes that have plenty of time to colour put on the finest finish both in colour and bloom.

Moisture.—As soon as artificial heat is applied, syringe the vines three times a-day with clean water at the same temperature as the air, or rather warmer. Keep the steaming-tray full night and day. A moist atmosphere, as all early forcers of the vine are aware, is of great importance in exciting vines to start regularly and freely. It keeps the bark on the stem moist as well as the coating on the buds, and is much more favourable to a good " break " than dryness. Continue the syringing till the first young leaves are formed, then discontinue it, and do not resume it again till the grapes are cut, unless rendered necessary by the presence of red-spider. There is, perhaps, no urgent objection against constantly syringing the foliage, except when the vines are in bloom and the grapes colouring. But, unless to keep down red-spider, I could never see that it did any good; and to syringe with some waters in which there are deposits such as lime, spoils the appearance of the fruit. Moreover, syringing has the objectionable tendency to drive the foliage out of its natural position. And on bright mornings, if all the moisture is not dried up through the night, there is a risk of getting the leaves injured by the rapid evaporation of the moisture off the leaf, or what is generally termed scalding.

When syringing is discontinued, in the case of early forcing with a maximum of fire-heat, keep up a constant supply of moisture by means of the steaming apparatus and daily sprinklings. Even in the case of Black Hamburgs, and other free-setting sorts, it should not be withheld when the vines are in flower. Atmospheric moisture, however, must not be carried to excess, especially in the mornings. An over-moist atmosphere when the house cannot be regularly and freely ventilated, to a certainty produces those excrescences so often met with on the under sides of vine-leaves, in dull wet seasons especially. It is desirable to follow nature as far as possible, and the foliage of vines and all plants should be allowed to become perfectly dry, and surrounded with a comparatively dry air for a time, once in the twenty-four hours. It gives a texture and strength to the foliage which cannot be attained under the influence of too much moisture. When colouring is first noticed, avoid withdrawing the moisture suddenly, but let it be done gradually till it ceases altogether, when the grapes are nearly fully coloured. A dry air is favourable to the proper ripening of grapes which have to hang for months after being ripe, and fire-heat should be applied at intervals in fine days, when the ventilators can be opened to carry off the moisture. On damp days it is best to keep the house shut up.

It is not very easy to give definite directions how often borders should be watered. If the borders are well drained, and the soil open, vines when in full growth and bearing require a great amount of water. Before forcing commences, the border should have a good soaking, and it should never afterwards be allowed to get very dry. Whenever it shows signs of dryness or cracking in the least, give a good watering, always with water at 80°. I do not approve of allowing inside borders to get mealy dry, even after the grapes are ripe, or when they have all been cut. Even then the constitution of the vine requires that the soil be moderately moist. After vines have borne a few full crops in borders, manure-water may be freely used in a moderately strong state, always avoiding rank doses of any preparation. Sheep, deer, and cow manure, and guano, make excellent manure-water for vines.

Ventilation.—Air should be admitted daily from the time the vinery is shut up for forcing. This is necessary for the double purpose of changing the atmosphere, and preventing its rising above the maximum temperature. When the air is cold and frosty, as it frequently is early in the season, it should be admitted in small quantities at a good many points. Large volumes of air admitted at a few places cause violent cold currents, which are undesirable, and hurtful to the tender foliage. As the vines advance into leaf, and the sun gets strong, give a little air early in the morning to allow the moisture that may be about the foliage to escape before the sun comes fully on the house. The amount of air should be increased by degrees till the sun is in meridian, and again reduced as the sun declines. Unless in exceptionally stormy or cold weather, a little air should be left on all night, This is especially necessary in these days of large close-lapped panes of glass. When the grapes are colouring, give more air than at any previous stage; and when quite ripe, let a constant and more bountiful supply of air circulate about them.

It frequently occurs that vineries have to be erected against existing garden-walls; and in cases where these walls are too low to give the proper pitch to the roof, a good plan is to raise them with mullions and sashes, corresponding exactly with the front ventilating lights, the only difference being that the back lights are hinged at the bottom, and open from the top outwards. Fig. 8 represents this method of both elevating and ventilating. The roof can, in this case, be constructed of sashes in one length, and be fixed.

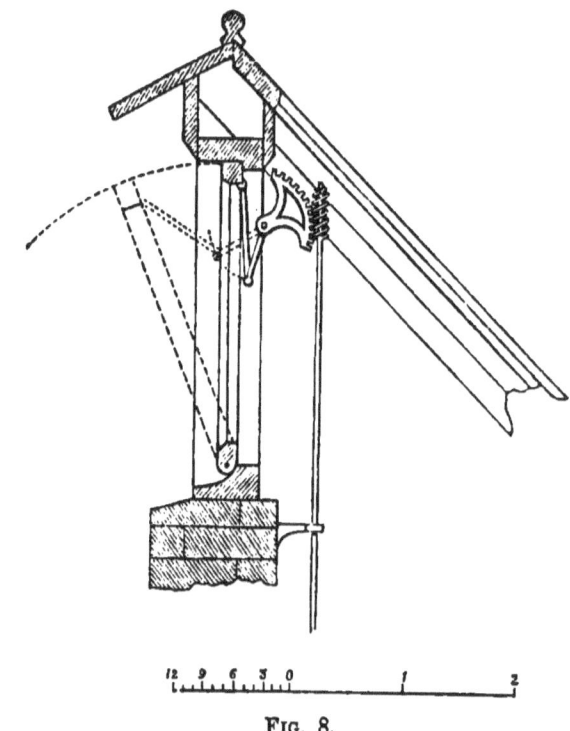

FIG. 8.

An overhanging coping to the back provides for wet-weather ventilation, by allowing the sash to open outward to a certain extent without letting wet in. Of course, this method of ventilation is not to be recommended for early forcing, as the opening is to the north; but for summer vineries it answers admirably.

WEIGHT OF CROP, THINNING, DISBUDDING, ETC.

Cropping vines too heavily is a prevailing error in grape-growing. Presuming that the rafter is, say, 24

THE GRAPE VINE.

feet long; that the young vines are to bear to a third of this length the first year, and that they show more than a bunch to each shoot:—remove them all but one to a shoot as soon as they are far enough advanced to be got hold of; and after the berries are set—presuming that the bunches are large, as they generally are on young vines—remove all but four bunches on every rod. This will leave eight bunches on a vine. Of course the largest and most shapely are generally left; and in most cases it may be presumed they will average at least 2 lb. or more. This is a crop sufficient for the first year in the case of permanent vines. None of these bunches should be left on the leading shoots, which should not be stopped this year till they reach the top of the house. When the vines are in full bearing, 1½ lb. of grapes to every foot run of the main stem of the vine may be regarded as a fair crop.

In disbudding the side growths of young vines, due regard must be had to a regular establishment of permanent fruiting points or spurs. From 18 to 20 inches apart will be close enough; and this will generally call for the removal of two buds for every one left all along the main stem. These side fruit-bearing growths should be stopped two or three joints beyond the bunch that is left. This, generally speaking, will give foliage sufficient to clothe the whole roof, when the main stems are trained 3 feet apart. If there is room for a more lengthened growth, it should be allowed to those from which the bunches are all taken off. This gives foliage enough to sustain the vines in vigour. Closer stopping has a tendency to weaken the vines in time. Allow the lateral growths which spring from the axils of the leaves of these fruit-bearing shoots to form one leaf, then stop them, and do not allow them to make more growth the whole season. A lesser number of large well-developed leaves is preferable to a greater number in a crowded condition.

As soon as the shoots can be tied down without fear of their breaking, carefully bring them down till they can be tied to the under sides of the wires. This operation must not be attempted at once. They must be brought down by degrees, beginning with them when their points have nearly touched the glass. Even when they can be tied down safely at one time, they frequently force themselves off the main stem in the course of a few hours. Shorten the laterals, on the portion of the main stem which is not bearing, to one leaf, when the wood has become brown.

In thinning off the bunches to the number directed, make a partial thinning when the shoots are tied down, and the final thinning when they are out of bloom, except in the case of Muscats, the thinning of which should be left till it can be seen which bunches have set their berries most regularly. The thinning of the berries should take place, in the case of Hamburgs and all free-setting sorts, as soon as the berries attain the size of radish-seeds. But with the shy-setting sorts it is best to delay their thinning till they are larger, and it can be seen which are properly fertilised and which are not.

SPUR-PRUNING FOR NEXT SEASON'S CROP.

It is now very generally admitted that the close-spur system of pruning is the best—*i.e.*, to cut back this season's fruit-bearing growth to within an eye or bud of the main stem. Fig. 9 will show the inexperienced at a glance what this means. In each succeeding year the pruning takes place back to the single bud at the base of last season's bearing growth. As the vines get older, a cluster of buds generally forms at the spur, notwithstanding this close pruning. Only the strongest of these that grow are left to bear fruit. This close pruning is much preferable to leaving two or three eyes. Not only can the vines be maintained for a longer time in a more manageable and sightly condition, but they yield more compact serviceable bunches, that swell their berries better than those long and looser bunches generally produced from buds further from the main stem. Prune, especially vines to be forced early, immediately they have shed all their leaves. The wounds should always be dressed with styptic to prevent any chance of bleeding. When in the course of time spurs get long and unsightly, a portion of them can be cut right back to within an inch of the main stem, and the adventitious buds there will break again and form fruit-bearing wood. By cutting back a certain number annually, they can thus be kept within bounds, or young rods can be brought

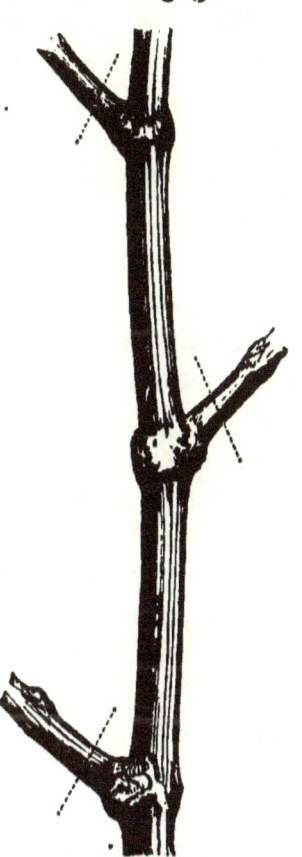

FIG. 9.

away from the bottoms of the vines, and the old ones cut out altogether.

TRAINING.

With regard to the extension system of training, by which a vine is made to fill a whole house, there can be no objection to it, provided a border extending away from the front of the vinery in proportion to the extension of the branches can be secured for that large range which an immense vine, filling it may be one large house, requires for its roots. This condition secured, there can be no objection urged against what is called the extension system. Another matter to be taken into consideration is, that a vine having its roots extending to an immense border area is less under control, especially for early forcing. All things considered, I prefer in a general way a compromise between the one-rod and the extension system; and think that a vine limited to two main rods is, in by far the majority of cases, more under the control of the cultivator, and best adapted for early forcing.

For the supply of summer and autumn grapes, there can be no objection to filling a house with a vine or two, provided that a run of border congenial to them can conveniently be provided for such large vines. In some localities where the vinery is set down in a soil naturally congenial, there is little difficulty in this respect. But in the majority of cases the border has to be artificially prepared and limited; under such circumstances, it is better to restrict the vines to two or three rods.

KEEPING GRAPES THROUGH THE WINTER.

To preserve grapes successfully on the vines through the winter months, in the first place the crop should be rather on the light than the heavy side, the berries should be more severely thinned than in the case of summer grapes, and they should be thoroughly well ripened by the end of September. Large bunches should be even more severely thinned than smaller ones, which latter generally keep better than larger ones, because the air circulates more freely through the heart of them, and consequently damp is not so likely to settle about them. It is also of much importance that the foliage should be kept healthy as long after the grapes are ripe as possible. Grapes grown in heavy damp soils are not so likely to keep well as in drier borders; and in localities where the autumn rainfall is heavy, it is advisable to protect the outside borders from rain before the grapes are quite ripe, for grapes ripened under the influence of too wet borders do not keep so well. The inside border should not be damped in any way after the grapes have commenced to colour, but a slight top-dressing of dry finely-pulverised old mushroom-bed dung should be spread over it, and allowed to become perfectly dry, and remain so all winter. Not a pot-plant requiring water should be allowed in the house. An equable temperature of from 45° to 50°, according to the weather, should be kept up by means of fire-heat when necessary. Extra heat should be put into the pipes on fine days, and air put on at top and bottom to expel damp from the house. Avoid the practice of firing with the view of drying up damp on wet or foggy days. It has the effect of drawing a stream of moisture through the house, to be condensed on the surface of the berries, and cause them to damp. When such weather occurs, rather keep the ventilators shut, and keep a very slight warmth in the pipes. Grapes are now very successfully preserved by being cut before the dead of winter, after the vines have shed their leaves, with a portion of wood attached to the bunch, which is inserted in bottles of water having a few pieces of charcoal in them, and ranged in rows in racks made for the purpose, in a dry room where the temperature can be steadily kept at about 40°. In this way they can be kept for many weeks; and where it is necessary to have plants stored in late vineries, it is far preferable to leaving the grapes to take their chance along with them. Of course, the flavour of the grape is slightly deteriorated from imbibing part of the water. But it allows the vineries to be used for other purposes, and the vines to be pruned before there is any chance of their bleeding.

GENERAL MANAGEMENT OF BORDERS.

In many cases borders do not receive that amount of attention after they are first made, necessary to keep them in good condition for a lengthened period. The management of the borders being only another term for the management of the roots, its importance is not easily overrated. I have recommended that in making borders, their completion should extend over a period of at least three years. It would, however, be greatly to the benefit of vines, if all interference with the border and roots did not end there. It is for many reasons not always convenient to keep adding to the front of the borders for an indefinite number of years. Space alone, in most instances, forbids this; and this being the case, the roots have a tendency, more especially when their outward extension is barred, to seek downwards, far from the influence of heat and air, and where the soil is constantly moist. Fortunately this tendency can be counteracted, for roots have the habit of going to points where they are fed.

In order, then, to keep the roots as near the surface as is desirable, the most successful means is to remove, at intervals of two years at least, all the inert soil that is found on the surface of the border unoccupied with roots. This should be carefully done with a fork, and sufficiently deep to lay bare some of the roots without disturbing them much. Then cover them over with a mixture of fresh loam two parts, rotten dung or horse-droppings one part, and lime-rubbish or charcoal pounded rather finely one part, with the addition of half a barrowful of bone-meal to every six barrowfuls of the mixture. Lay this over the roots to the depth of 6 or 7 inches. If this top-dressing is kept moderately moist, the roots will work upwards into it and multiply rapidly. In the heat of summer a light mulching of half-decayed stable-litter should be spread over it, to prevent moisture from evaporating and the necessity for much watering. In thus treating a border of vines that have to be forced early, the top-dressing should be put on in the autumn, before the border is covered up from cold and wet, and the heat from the fermenting material will warm the new surface-soil, and all the more encourage the roots to work upwards.

In all localities where the rainfall is great, vine-borders should be protected from excessive moisture; for unless the borders are in superexcellent order, and the roots all thoroughly ripened, a great quantity of the small fibry roots which are made in summer die off through excessive moisture, and this tells very much against the vines when they start into growth. I have first laid on the surface of the borders a layer of fresh leaves, and then thatched it with wheaten straw. This incurs much labour and litter. Wooden shutters are much better, and corrugated iron ones better still, and in the long-run the cheapest, from their durability. The water which runs off these coverings at the front of the border should be conducted by open gutters into some drain, so that it does not keep the ground in front of the border, where there are generally a mass of roots, damp.

Vine-borders should be copiously watered in the heat of dry summers; and to prevent rapid evaporation, and nourish the vines as well, they should always have a covering—or, as it is generally termed, a mulching—of farmyard manure. All cropping of the borders with vegetables or flowers is an evil, and should never be practised.

There is much difference of opinion as to whether, in the case of early-forced vines, applying a bed of fermenting material all over the surface of the outside border a short time before forcing commences, is any more effective—in the absence of any means of heating from below—than simply to cover the border to a considerable depth early in autumn with some dry material, to conserve the heat which exists in the soil at that time. I once tested a border that had been covered up early in autumn with 1 foot of leaves and then thatched with straw; and found, on plunging a thermometer in the soil to the depth of 15 inches, that in sixteen minutes it rose to 60°. I regularly cut grapes in April from the vines in this border, with all the roots outside the vinery, and never applied any other means of heating.

RENOVATING EXHAUSTED VINES.

Vines are not unfrequently injured by cropping them too heavily for a series of years. This is apparent in the weakly character of their growth and diminutive grapes. Where the border is considered in a sufficiently good condition not to require renewing, the best treatment for vines thus broken down is either to forego a year's crop altogether, or to crop them very lightly for a year or two. At the same time, the surface of the border can be dealt with as I have described at page 103, and the vines can be otherwise fed. While undergoing this process, they should be encouraged to make as much foliage as space will allow.

Exhaustion of vines from crowded training and close stopping is sometimes met with in its worst forms. As has already been referred to, the rods of vines should never be trained closer than 3 feet, and the fruit-bearing spurs not closer than 18 to 20 inches. I have seen, in conjunction with close training, the fruit-bearing wood pinched at the bunch, or just one joint beyond it. This, with anything like heavy cropping, is certain in a very few years to cripple the vines. They are in fact smothered, and worked hard into the bargain. To put fresh vigour into such vines, cut the superfluous rods out, to give those left more room, and let the laterals grow two or three joints beyond the bunch.

The premature destruction of foliage is another fertile source of injury, whether it takes place from red-spider or scorching. The evil most commonly arises from the ravages of spider. As the pulmonary arteries of the body convey the blood to the lungs, there to be exposed to the air we breathe and undergo change, and be diffused through the system for its nourishment, so is the sap in the vine sent up to the leaves, there to undergo change, and be made fit for plant-nourishment. And injury to the lungs does not more certainly lead to debility in the animal, than does the premature destruction of the foliage to the vine or any other plant.

Early forcing, especially when the roots are in a cold ill-drained border, is most injurious to vines; and when the principal cause of exhaustion is from a cold ill-drained soil, and where they are otherwise in such a condition that good results might be expected from them—if in a more congenial border—the best way is to clear away the whole soil, disentangling and saving every root that can be saved, to make the drainage effectual, and make a new border, carefully planting the vines again. The best time for this operation is in autumn after the grapes are cut, while the vines are still in leaf and able to make fresh roots. Supposing the vines have roots in both outside and inside borders, the one should be renewed one year and the other the next. When the operation commences, shade the roof with canvas; and after the roots are laid in the fresh soil, give a good watering at 120°, and cover up the border with dry litter to retain the heat. In 1856 I lifted a house of vines, as thus recommended, the first week in October —only the whole instead of half the roots were lifted—and by the end of July 1857 cut a fair crop of grapes from them. And in December of 1858 I lifted a vine after it had been three years planted, and planted it in another vinery in which I had previously commenced the forcing of pot-vines, and it ripened ten good bunches in May 1859. These instances are mentioned to show how well vines bear being carefully transplanted or lifted.

THE POT-CULTURE OF GRAPES.

Now that we have such good keeping varieties of both black and white grapes, that hang even till May, there is perhaps less necessity for forcing pot-vines for the supply of grapes in March and April than existed some years ago; still the production of grapes from pot-vines is perhaps more extensively practised now than ever it was. When certain varieties of grapes, such as Black Hamburg and other early sorts, are required in the end of March and April, I consider it better to produce the first month's supply from pot-vines than to start permanent vines in October and November to supply them. The vines in most instances ultimately succumb to the process; whereas, if started a month or six weeks later to succeed pot-vines, they are much more easily kept in fair condition, and, moreover, produce better crops. I have for many years regularly ripened a crop of grapes from pots in April, and kept up the supply by ripening a succession for May and June from permanent vines, and consider this the best method to adopt where early grapes are required.

There are other cases where pot-vines supply grapes in a most acceptable way, such as when vines and vine-borders have to be renewed; in which case a vine in pot can be fruited at intervals among the young vines, without the one injuring the other. In cases where I have had vines and borders to renew, I have ripened a crop from pots in April and May, and then planted the young vines in time to make good canes the same season, the supernumeraries of which were fruited heavily the following season—thus not losing much by the renewal of borders.

Vines in pots are also successfully dwarfed and fruited in small pots on the Chinese system for the purpose of dinner-table decoration, for which purpose they are very interesting. Mr W. Thomson, who illustrates this practice by an engraving in his 'Practical Treatise,' describes this process : " When the vines are placed in heat, a small pot is slipped over the rod, and in this pot a neatly-made stake painted green is placed, and the soil filled in round it. Through this stake a strong set of wires are run at right angles with each other, to which the branches of the vine are tied. The small pot gets filled with roots by the time the grapes are ripe, when it may be detached from the large pot and set in a small vase on the table, when the tree-like plant, with its fine pendulous bunches, looks all that can be desired."

The cultivation of grapes in pots differs in no essential way from that of permanent vines, except that they require constant watering, and feeding at the root with mulchings and manure-water. They should always, if possible, be plunged in a gentle bottom-heat—at least, till they are fairly started into growth.

INARCHING VINES.

It is now a well-established fact, that some of the more tender and much-esteemed varieties of grapes succeed better when inarched or grafted on to others of a more vigorous constitution, and the practice is now quite common. Inarching on to established vines enables the cultivator to introduce new or desirable sorts, at a time when it may not be possible to plant them out in new borders; and by the same process those who have only a very limited accommodation for vines can have any variety introduced into their collection with the greatest ease.

There are many well-known ways of inarching and grafting the vine, but there is none which I have ever seen practised that is so simple, or that makes so complete and speedy a union, as that of uniting two young green growths in the ordinary way of inarching. I have often taken a young vine struck from an eye when not more than 18 inches high, and inarched it on to the growing side shoot of a vine. The rapidity with which the two unite is wonderful. All that is necessary is to place the young vine in a position suitable for joining it to the stock, then with a sharp knife to cut a slice from its side about 2 inches long and about half through the young growth at its deepest part. Then a similar slice is cut from the stock, and the two wounds nicely adjusted to each other. First, in tying them, let the two be rather easily fixed to each other above and below the union, and then bind them sufficiently close with soft matting to cause them to fit nicely together. In fourteen days they will have so far united that the ligature may be slackened a little to give the wood room to swell. In another fortnight the union will be complete. During the process supply the young vine with water till the union is formed, and then, if the plant is not required, it may be allowed to dry off altogether; or where this is undesirable, it should be cut through below the union by degrees, and the top cut off the stock in fourteen days after, that the sap may be entirely directed to the young vine.

Were a graft of a young vine in a ripened state put into my hands that I desired to work on to another vine, I would much rather strike an eye from it, and inarch it green wood to green. The process is more simple and certain, and the union becomes more perfect in a shorter time.

After experimenting with various stocks, I have come to the conclusion that the Muscat of Alexandria and Black Hamburg are the best stocks, especially the Muscat; and such varieties as the grizzly and white Frontignacs and Muscat Hamburg, which are not so much and generally grown as their merits deserve, do best on Muscat of Alexandria. I have also found Black Hamburg the best stock for Golden Champion and Duke of Buccleuch; and the finest bunches and berries, both as regards colour, size, and flavour, of Gros Guillaume that I have ever seen, I have had from grafts grown on the Muscat of Alexandria.

SETTING UP GRAPES FOR EXHIBITION.

Grapes are very often inefficiently set up for exhibition, and are consequently not seen to the best advantage. This is especially the case at some of what may be termed country shows. I have therefore thought that fig. 10, taken from a photograph, would serve to show exactly what is generally considered by exhibitors of grapes the best way of carrying and setting up grapes for competition. The bunch, it will be observed from the figure, is resting on a slanting board. The board is first covered with a thin sheet of cotton wadding, and then with a sheet of soft white paper. The bunch is cut with rather more than an inch of the vine adhering to each side of its stem. A piece of narrow tape is fastened to the piece of vine, and passed through a hole near the top of the back perpendicular board, and securely fastened there. To keep the bunch firmly in its place, a piece of narrow

Fig. 10.

soft tape is worked with great care between the berries near the middle of the bunch with a long needle, and each end of the tape is passed through holes previously prepared on each side of the main stem of the bunch and tied underneath. The bunch is thus fixed so that it can neither slip down the slanting board nor roll about.

When more than one bunch is set up, the grapeboard must be of proportionate length. But it is not desirable to have them longer at any time than will hold three to four bunches, with sufficient space between each to let them be properly inspected.

It is always best to fix the bunches just as they are cut from the vines, laying them on their flattest side. In doing this it is never desirable to lift a bunch after it is laid on the board, for it cannot be easily done without more or less disturbing the bloom of the grape. When all are fixed in their places, fit what I shall call the exhibition platform into a square box just wide enough to take it in, and deep enough to clear the fruit when the lid is screwed on. Then put a couple of screws through the box from the outside into the back board of the platform, and they cannot move. In conveying them, care must be taken to keep the box level, and not to jolt it severely.

PACKING GRAPES.

The packing of grapes to be sent long distances by rail and other conveyances requires to be carefully managed. There are many ways of packing them. I have seen each bunch laid on a thick stiff sheet of paper and folded up sufficiently tight to prevent the bunch from moving about in the paper. They are then packed closely in boxes deep enough to admit a layer of paper-shavings under and over them, so that when the lid of the box is fastened down each parcel was held securely in its place. The stiffness of the paper is supposed to come in contact with the bunch at fewer points than when wrapped up in more flexible paper, and on that account to better preserve the bloom. There is, however, at the same time, room left for the oscillation of those berries not in immediate contact with the paper, and this is objectionable. In sending grapes to a distance I have never adopted this mode of packing, but have either wrapped each bunch in a sheet of fine tissue-paper, and packed them on a firm bed of paper-shavings as close as they would lie, with just sufficient wadding between each to fill up the irregularities of the outline of the bunches. When the box is thus filled, a sheet of wadding is spread regularly over the bunches, and over all a layer of paper-shavings; so that when the lid is shut down they are subject to as much pressure as prevents their moving. At other times, when only sending a few bunches in one compartment of a box, I have spread a sheet of paper over the shavings in the bottom of the box, and laid all the bunches as nicely fitted into each other as possible on it, then put another sheet of tissue-paper over them, then some cotton-wadding, finishing off with a layer of paper-shavings. In this way I have always found them go quite safely. When a quantity has to be sent in one box it should be divided into compartments, so that when the box happens to be set down standing on end or side, the grapes at the lower part of it cannot possibly be subject to much pressure from the top end of the box. I do not know of any way of sending them to preserve their bloom, for unless some person is sent with the box there must be packing material on the upper side of the grapes.

INSECTS TO WHICH VINES ARE SUBJECT.

Red-Spider (fig. 11).—Until the advent of the *Phylloxera*, this was the most formidable insect to which vines are generally subject. It is far more troublesome on some soils and in some seasons than others, being worst on hot gravelly soils and in dry localities, and least prevalent on moist soils. It thrives best in a hot dry atmosphere, and is far more common where hard firing has to be practised early in the season. On vines that start naturally in April and May, and that do not require much fire-heat to ripen the crop, it is generally not much to be feared. Whenever it makes its appearance on the foliage, the best way is to attack it immediately—before it spreads—with a sponge. Put as much Fowler's Insecticide into warm soft water as will colour it, and with this sponge every leaf on which it first makes its appearance. It generally appears at some particular spot near the heating apparatus; and though sponging it off may seem a slow process, yet an active hand can soon go over a great number of leaves; and, in the long-run, I have always found this to be the least laborious method. After the sponging, if clean water is easily got, give the vines a vigorous syringing for a few days in succession. Keep a look-out for the insect constantly after the first attack, and deal with it in the same way. There is no doubt that constantly syringing the vines is the best preventive, and syringing is much to be preferred to the destruction of the foliage by spider. In some waters, however, there are deposits which discolour the grapes, and it is very undesirable to use water of that description unless the sediment can be filtered out of it. Sulphur,

THE GRAPE VINE.

hot-lime, and soot in equal parts applied to the pipes, also help to keep it in check: the former does no harm to the vines, but it must not be applied till the grapes have approached the stoning period, or the result will be rusted berries.

When vines get dry at the roots, they are very subject to spider; and it is important for this cause, if for no other, to keep them regularly moist. The old loose bark should be cleanly removed from vines every year and be well scrubbed with soap and water, using a rather stiff brush. Every part of the woodwork and glass should be thoroughly scrubbed every year, and kept well painted, the walls washed with hot-lime, having a little sulphur mixed with it, the pipes painted yearly, and every crevice in which the foe can find a refuge filled up.

FIG. 11.

Thrip (fig. 12).—This is an insect which can hardly be said to be indigenous to the vine; but when plants, such as azaleas and others, are kept in vineries, thrip is very apt to get on the vines. It is very troublesome and destructive. Of course the best preventive is to keep plants which are subject to it out of vineries. Hand-sponging and fumigating with tobacco-smoke for two or three consecutive evenings are the most effectual ways of dealing with it. Like

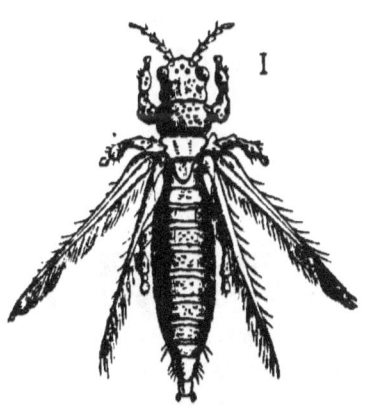

FIG. 12.

the spider, a dry warm atmosphere favours the spread of the thrip. Such soft woolly-leaved vines as Gros Colemar are apt to be injured by strong doses of tobacco-smoke, so that this cure must be cautiously administered.

Mealy Bug.—This, like thrip, will not appear on vines unless brought into the vinery on other plants. But once it gets a footing, it is one of the most troublesome of insects, and if left to have its own way, will breed with wonderful rapidity, and overrun the whole wood, foliage, and fruit. The very first appearance of it should be the signal for dealing with it as promptly and thoroughly as possible. While the vines are in leaf, the most effectual way is to pick it off with a pointed piece of stick. The summer season is the time to deal most successfully with this insect while it is moving about. The vines should be very carefully looked over each week, and every appearance of the bug destroyed. This must be followed up till the leaves drop off. After the vines are pruned, every morsel of loose bark under which it creeps must be removed, the vines thoroughly scrubbed with water, in which about the size of an egg of soft soap and a gill of tobacco-liquor to every gallon has been mixed; then fill up every crevice by applying Gishurst's Compound, at the rate of 8 ounces to a gallon of water, with a brush. The spring following examine the vines after they start every few days, and destroy any bugs that appear.

Phylloxera vastatrix.—Horticulturists have within the last few years had a most formidable addition to the host of foes with which they have to grapple in the successful cultivation of the grape vine. And it is scarcely possible to conceive of a more insidious and destructive enemy than the new invader—*Phylloxera vastatrix*—is proving itself to be. Any who have had an opportunity of watching the destructive power of this tiny insect, will not be at all surprised to know —especially when the enormous interest that France has at stake in her vineyards is taken into consideration—that the French Government are so alarmed at its appearance that they have offered a reward of £12,000 to any person who will devise a means of destroying the pest, without, at the same time, destroying the vines. But as yet no such remedy has been discovered. According to the report of E. L. Beckwith, Esq., on the wines of the Universal Exhibition at Paris in 1868, the quantity of wine manufactured annually in France amounts to 831,000,000 gallons, exclusive of 165,000,000 distilled into brandy. Taking this enormous sum at the very low average rate of 2s. 6d. per gallon, it can easily be understood why France is so much concerned and dismayed at the progress of a foe which perils the very existence of her vineyards, and how this army of insects threatens to be a more formidable enemy, in a pecuniary sense, than the squadrons of a German Emperor. It is already committing alarming ravages in some of the wine departments of France, and has spread into Spain, Portugal, and Austria.

About eight years ago the *Phylloxera* unfortunately made itself known in this country, and has proved fatal to the vines in some English vineries, crossed the Channel to Ireland and the Borders to Scotland. I have recently heard of its fatal effects in a good many of the English counties. I have no conclusive proof up to this time that it exists in any place in Scotland except Drumlanrig, although I have heard of the vines in several places in Scotland having in some cases died outright, and in others been curiously affected. Although such circumstances are suspicious, it can only be hoped that it is not the result of *Phylloxera*.

After the most careful observation, I have come to the conclusion that there does not exist in British gardens another insect that can be compared to *Phylloxera*, in the rapidity and certainty with which its work of destruction, in the case of the vine, is carried on, nor one that is so difficult to combat successfully without the most prompt and ultra means. And in the interest of British grape-growing, all who have any knowledge or experience of this destroyer should proclaim its whereabouts, and record their experience and observations; and at the same time, and above all, give it no quarter by risking its existence by any half-measures, but remorselessly stamp it out as the most formidable pest that ever found its way into a vinery. Indeed I do not know that it is not a matter quite worthy of being dealt with as the rinderpest in cattle has been dealt with by the powers that be.

It will be in the recollection of many of our readers that in the 'Gardener' of 1869 (page 202), illustrations of this insect are given, and a paper which originally appeared from the pen of M. J. E. Planchon in the 'Comptes-Rendus de l'Institut' is translated. The history and habits, as far as then known, of the pest, are thus minutely described:—

"I will here give a brief *résumé* of all I learnt about the habits of the *Phylloxera vastatrix* from a series of observations made on the spot, in three short visits to the south of France; also all I noticed with reference to the specimens which I kept in glass bottles during forty consecutive days.

"Its best-known form is that in which no trace of wings can be discovered. When the insect is about to lay its eggs (that is, in its adult female state), it forms a small ovoid mass, having its

THE GRAPE·VINE.

inferior surface flattened, its dorsal surface convex, being surrounded by a kind of fillet, which is very narrow when it touches the thoracic part of its body, which (formed by five rather indistinct rings) is hardly separated from its abdominal part of seven rings.

"Six rows of small blunt tubercles form a slight protuberance on the thoracic segments, and are found very faintly marked on the abdominal segments. The head is always concealed by the anterior protuberance of the buckler; the antennæ are almost always inactive. The abdomen, often short and contracted, becomes elongated towards laying-time, and there can be easily seen one, two, or sometimes three eggs, in a more or less mature state.

"The egg sometimes retains its yellow colour for one, two, or

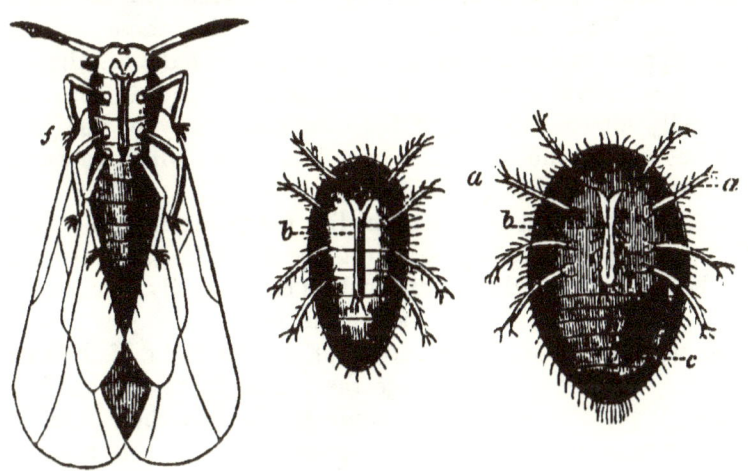

FIG. 13.

Phylloxera vastatrix (J. E. Planchon).—Female specimens and their egg. *a a*, Antennæ; *b b*, Horns or suckers; *c*, Egg plainly visible in the body of the insect; *f*, Winged form of the insect. All greatly magnified.

three days after it has been laid; more often, however, it changes to a dull-grey hue. From five to eight days generally elapse before it is hatched. The duration of this period depends a good deal on the temperature. The quantity of eggs, and the rapidity with which they are produced, are probably determined by a variety of circumstances—the health of the insect, the quantity of nourishment it is able to obtain, the weather, and perhaps other causes. A female which had produced six eggs at eight o'clock A.M. on the 20th of August, had fifteen on the 21st at four P.M.—that is, she laid nine in thirty-two hours. Other females lay one, two, or three eggs in twenty-four hours. The maximum quantity is thirty in five days. The eggs are generally piled up near the mother without any apparent order, but she sometimes changes her position so as to scatter them all around her. They have a smooth surface, and adhere lightly to each other by means of a slimy matter which attaches to them.

"Hatching takes place through an irregular and often lateral rent in the egg, the empty and crumpled membrane being found among the other eggs in different stages of hatching.

"During the first period of their active life—two, three, four, or five days, as the case may be—the insects are in an erratic state. They creep about as if they were seeking for a favourable situation. Their movements are more rapid than those of adults. They appear to inspect, as it were, with their antennæ, the surface they travel over. The movements of the antennæ are generally alternative, and, if the comparison may be pardoned, are not unlike the two sticks of a blind man, which he uses to explore the ground he is about to tread.

"After a few days of this errant life, the young insects seem to fix upon a spot to settle in. Most frequently this is a fissure in the bark of a vine, where their suckers can be easily plunged into the cellular tissue, full of saccharine matter. If you make a fresh wound on the root by cutting off a little piece of the bark, you may see the *pucerons* range themselves in rows around the wound, and, once fixed, they apply to the root their antennæ, which appear like two small divergent horns. At this period of their life, about the 13th or 14th day after their birth, they are more or less sedentary ; but they change their places if a new wound is made on the root, which promises a fresh supply of food.

"What sense is this which directs these subterraneous *pucerons* towards the place which is most suitable for them? It cannot be sight, as their eyes are merely coloured spots, and they creep as if they were blind. It cannot be hearing, because they seek no prey but a vegetable tissue. It is probably the sense of smelling ; and one may well ask if the nuclei which appear enshrined in the last articulations of the antennæ are not the organs of this function, the seat of which has been so much disputed? Among these non-adult insects, attached by their suckers to the vine-root, are seen, here and there, some of middle size. Their colour is a deeper orange, the abdomen shorter and more squarely formed. These individuals are more sedentary than the others. I have sometimes imagined they might be wingless (apterous) males of the species; but as nothing has happened to confirm this very problematical hypothesis, and as I have seen undoubted females much resembling these examples in colour and form, I incline to the belief that there are no sexual differences among them. A kind of double moult precedes the adult state. The first takes place shortly after birth, the second after laying-time. Some uncertainty, however, hangs over the number of these changes, as the cast-off skins are often found mixed up with groups of *pucerons* of different ages, and it is difficult to distinguish them. On the morbid tuberosities of the fibrous vine-roots, or on the offshoots of the roots, the *pucerons* (perhaps better nourished) seem to pass more quickly through the different phases I have described; but excepting that their colour is paler, they present no marked difference.

"The winged form of the *Phylloxera* might easily be taken for a separate species. The rare specimens which I have seen have all come from the *pucerons* nourished on the newly-attacked vine-radicles. In their infant (or it might be called their larva) state they resemble those which I have suggested may be males, but the buckler soon becomes more strongly marked than in these last; and a kind of band seems distinctly to define the separation between this and the abdomen. The sheaths of the wings, triangular-shaped and of a greyish colour, appear on both sides of the buckler. It is easy to predict the advent of a winged insect from this chrysalis. When one of these nymphæ is seen to quit its place and to crawl over the root, or up the side of the bottle where it may have been put, its transformation is near. Soon, instead of a sort of pupa, a beautiful little fly appears, whose two pairs of wings, crossed horizontally, are much larger than its body.

"It is impossible to doubt the identity of this insect with the *puceron* which formed one of the swarm on the vine-root. The details of the structure of certain organs—the antennæ, claws, tarsi, and suckers—establish their identity.

"The horizontal position of the wings completely distinguishes the *Phylloxera* from the true aphis, whose wings are always more or less inclined upwards. The two larger wings, obliquely oboval and cuniform, have a lineal areole on the larger basilary half of their outer edge; and this is enclosed in an interior 'nervure,' which answers, I suppose, to the radial muscle. One single oblique nervure (or corneous division) is detached from this last, and reaches to the inner edge. Two other lines start from the end of the wing, and, becoming narrower as they proceed, advance towards the oblique nervure, but end before reaching it. These are not, perhaps, nervures, but rather folds, for I have observed them absent.

" The inferior wings, both narrower and much shorter, have a marginal nervure running from the base to the middle, but it loses itself in a gentle protuberance, which the wing shows in this place ; a radial nervure runs parallel to the first, and disappears before it reaches the same spot.

" The eyes, black and (relatively) very large, are irregularly globular, with marked conical nipples ; their surface is granular, but a pointed depression is observed in the centre of each glandule. A round eye-shaped spot occupies the centre of the forehead.

" Among fifteen winged specimens of the *Phylloxera* which have come under my notice, not one has presented any sexual difference. Almost all of them laid two or three eggs, and their death (which happened soon after) may have been caused by their imprisonment in the bottles. Their eggs resembled those of the wingless *Phylloxera*, and though they were only two or three in number, they completely filled the abdomen of the mother. They were easily seen by placing the insect under the microscope. I do not know how long the eggs remain before they are hatched, or if they always produce the winged form of the insect. It is probable that these winged individuals serve for the transportation of this insect plague to a distance ; not that their wings would serve them for a rapid flight—they are too inactive, they move them very little, and in rising from the ground their horizontal position is preserved. My observations were, however, made under very unfavourable conditions, the insect being in a state of captivity ; but I suppose that even in a natural state the wind is the principal agent for the dispersion of the *Phylloxera*, as it is for many of the insect tribe. In any case, the discovery of this form of the *Phylloxera* provided with wings, and evidently fitted for an aerial life, is sufficient to explain the hitherto embarrassing fact of the rapid spread of this vine-plague. As to the spread of the disease from one vine to another, the wingless *pucerons* may suffice for this, as, grouped in great numbers about the lower part of unhealthy vine-stems, they might easily attack the vines nearest them, even if they be healthy. It may be asked, in what manner these insects manage to travel from one vine-stock to another, and how they contrive to reach the fibrous roots of the newly-attacked stocks? Do they burrow under the soil, or do they not rather travel along the surface of the earth under cover of the darkness and coolness of night, and then, traversing the fissures in the bark, arrive in this manner at the extremities of the roots? This conjecture is a probable one, and the following experiment supports it:—

"In a case 1 yard long I placed some garden-soil from Montpelier, a place entirely free from the *Phylloxera*. In this earth I carefully laid some pieces of vine-cane infested with wingless *pucerons*. I placed a hand-glass over each cane, and slightly raised the glass on one side in order to allow the insect to creep out. At three centimetres' distance from the pieces of cane I put some fragments of root from a healthy vine, on which I had made fresh wounds. In twelve hours the following results were obtained: Three *pucerons* had found their way from one of the vine-canes to the nearest piece of vine-root. Some days after, twenty young *pucerons* occupied the same fragment. A few insects were to be found on the other fragments. One piece of root had attracted none, but the vine-cane nearest to it had very few insects upon it which were capable of changing their places.

"A similar experiment has been made by M. Frédéric Leydier at the farm of Lancieux, near Sigondas (a part of the country already infested by the *Phylloxera*), and by another person near Sorgues. The results of these experiments have not been satisfactory; but this does not prove that, under other conditions, or with a greater amount of perseverance, they might not have been successful. It is fortunate that this new enemy to the vine attacks it (in the first instance) at the base of the stem, and not underground at the fibres. As it is, a thorough dressing of the bottom of the stem with coal-tar will probably prove an insurmountable obstacle to the progress of this destructive insect; but were the case otherwise, it would be very difficult to get down deep enough to reach an enemy so well protected by the depth of the soil."

Regarding the appearance of the insect, and the rapidity with which it multiplies and devours its prey, this writer's observations are correct; but I differ to some extent on what the writer propounds as to its mode of attack. I refer to the article in question for the entomology of this little devourer, and will now detail some of my observations as to its effects, its mode of attack, and circumstances which favour its spread, &c. I may here state that not one of the observations to which I refer has been intrusted only to one pair of eyes, and that all which I shall relate has been corroborated by two and sometimes more observers. The insect is so minute—less than a cheese-mite—that all observations have to be microscopic.

The first warning that some evil was present in a vinery erected in the autumn of 1869, and planted in 1870, was, that two vines at the end of the house, which grew with great and satisfactory vigour all through 1870 and up to the midsummer of 1871, soon after the latter date began to flag. The leaves got prematurely yellow, and dropped off. Not for a moment suspecting the real cause, I was much puzzled at the occurrence, it being entirely new in my experience. But as the effect was so limited in its extent, and the two vines being supernumeraries, and heavily cropped, the impression wore off, and no minute investigation took place. In the spring of 1872, most of the supernumeraries that bore heavily in 1871 were removed, and the whole of the permanent vines from one end of the house to the other broke with equal vigour, each shoot being literally packed at the points with fruit. All seemed to go right till the young growths were about 3 inches long, and the stored-up sap was exhausted. Then all the vines at one end of the vinery, extending to the middle of it, called a halt, and those at the opposite end bounded on their way, running out their bunches as might have been expected. The affected half "spindled away" like straws, and the bunches never ran out properly. The roots were of course instantly examined, and all the most fibry and active parts of them were found in a peculiar half-dead-looking condition. Not even then suspecting *Phylloxera* as a cause, the occurrence was a puzzle, and some application was suspected, though I knew of nothing but pure river-water and a little soap that had been used in washing the wood-work and glass. Notches or incisions were then cut in the boles of the vines, above the surface of the soil, and a little fresh loam put round them. There they soon emitted strong bunches of roots; and they made a tremendous struggle for life, and sent their leaders to the top of a long rafter, but woefully weak compared to those at the other end of the house, and the bunches were like black currants comparatively.

As time went on, galls were discovered on the under sides of the leaves at the affected end of the vinery, and this soon revealed the foe that had been carrying on its work of destruction in ambush at the roots, and on which it was found in myriads. The invader spread towards the other end of the house as steadily and regularly as a fire would progress; and each vine it attacked on its onward march drooped, and shed its leaves suddenly and prematurely. Before it got to the extreme end of the vinery, the vines there had brought to maturity a fine crop of large bunches, and were showing no signs of distress; but— and this will give some idea of the rapidity with which the work of destruction is effected—in a month afterwards some of the vines were literally dead, not having a live root, and to save the grapes they had to be cut wholesale.

In the same range, and adjoining this house, is a Muscat-house, the vines in which ripened a fine crop of grapes to a beautiful golden colour; and on two grafts of Gros Guillaume there were ten bunches, weighing from 6 to 8 lb. each. It was not till October that the presence of the *Phylloxera* was suspected here, and by the end of November the roots of the whole of these vines were literally covered with it— so much so that, looked at with the naked eye, it imparted its own colour to the roots; and viewed through a microscope, the insects were seen to be clustered on the top of each other like miniature swarms of bees, so rapidly had they spread and multiplied.

So much for the destructive ability of *Phylloxera*. I will now briefly refer to the most important of my observations regarding its habits, &c. In each gall, formed on some of the vines on the under sides of the leaves, there was generally one full-grown insect, and clustered round it, just as described by M. Planchon eight or nine eggs. The mature insect is of a yellowish-brown colour; and, examined through a powerful microscope, is so transparent that the eggs can be seen in its inside. The eggs are equally transparent, and both are very easily destroyed. The full-grown insect appears to be made of a thin transparent skin, easily broken, with a thin transparent viscid matter internally. The way into the breeding-galls is from the upper side of the leaf. I have never been able to discover any above ground, except those in the galls; and have seen only one of the insects with wings, which is supposed to be the male, and that was on the under side of a leaf, and appeared in a semi-dormant state. Underground, they breed and spread with marvellous rapidity on the roots, and cover them so densely that they impart to them their own colour. They effect the destruction of the vine by eating all the bark off the roots, and burrowing into the second coating of the young roots; and after destroying that, they seem to move on to fresh roots, for I have not in one single instance found an insect on a root after it has been peeled and begun to decay. Contrary to the French theory that it attacks the roots at the neck of the vine, and works downwards towards the more young and fibry roots, it has been invariably found that they have begun at the points of the roots, and devoured upwards towards the bole of the vine.

It is also quite evident that, like red-spider on the leaves, it thrives best in a dryish warm soil. Having decided to thoroughly stamp the pest out by removing the whole border, I did not as usual cover the outside border with wooden shutters early in October; and, owing to the enormous rainfall of the autumn, the soil was of course unusually moist and cold outside. The most careful examination of the roots outside in this cold damp medium did not lead to the discovery of an insect on the roots up to the arches of the front of the house. The pest, however, was found in swarms on the roots to the very point at which they left the protection of the stone-work, where the soil was much drier, and here there was an abrupt limit to their extension. On the same roots not one was found beyond the arch, in which case it is clear they had worked from the inside along the roots, but in any case did not advance into the damp soil, proving that the insect does not like cold and wet. Prompted by this observation, some pieces of roots literally covered with the insects were steeped in clean soft water, and they were all dead in from forty-eight to sixty hours. So that any one receiving vines who has any dread of this pest, would do well to steep them in a tank for four or five days. I also found that three hours' exposure to 4° or 6° frost effectually destroys it; and pieces of fresh roots densely covered with it were left exposed to the air in the vinery, and in two days they were all dried up and dead. Roots were also done up in brown paper without any soil, and they died in the same space of time; in fact, seemed to evaporate. A few drops of carbolic acid in a wine-glassful of water proved instant death to them, and a very weak solution of Condy's fluid had the same effect. In fact, everything that I have learned of this insect goes to prove that it is very easily killed when it can be got at.

Numerous experiments have been tried to see if it would attack or live on other fruit-trees besides the vine. A currant-bush and a fig were planted among the roots of the vines on which the insect was in legions. These fruits were allowed to remain in the vinery for weeks, and they pushed out quantities of young rootlets into the very centre of the pests' strongest hold, but not one insect could be found adhering to either the currant or the fig. A young vine planted where the insect was not considered so numerous was attacked by it in legions. Pieces of vine-roots swarming with the pest were laid on a board, and around them and touching them were placed fresh pieces of the roots of the peach, the cherry, the pear, the gooseberry, black currant, and the plum. The whole were covered with some soil, and a large bell-glass placed over them, and left for fourteen days: at the end of that time they were all examined minutely through the microscope, but not one insect had gone on to the roots of these fruits. On to a piece of vine-root that was put along with them in a clean state they did go. These experiments go to prove that *Phylloxera* does not care so much for any of these fruits as it does for the vine. On pieces of vine-roots laid upon the same board—not covered with soil, but merely covered with a bellglass—the insect was found quite shrivelled up and dead. Tobacco-smoke, however strong, does not seem to affect it; for I placed the insect in a glass vessel and filled it as full of tobacco-smoke as it could be, but it remained alive.

There can be no doubt that there are scores of decoctions that will kill this insect—such as salt, hellebore, &c.: but the difficulty to overcome lies in the depth of soil to be so acted on; for if a few insects are left, the enemy remains in possession of the field, and there can be no certainty of stamping it out in this way. I believe that to submerge the whole border and vines in clean water would destroy the insect; but what of the eggs or larvæ ? Mr Dunn, of Dalkeith Gardens, when at Powerscourt, in Ireland, got rid of it in some vineries there by' lifting and washing the roots of the vines, and merely picking all the roots out of the soil, and mixing dry soot and caustic lime with the old soil, and replanting the vines. But that process leaves some risks in the way of stamping it out; and I know of a place in England where even more radical means failed. Therefore it must be admitted that the most certain way of stamping out this destroyer is to burn the vines, remove right away all the soil, well salt the site of the border, and wash and paint everything connected with the vinery before fresh soil is put into it. This is the process that I have adopted; and I think, in the interests of grape-growing, all who have this pest in their vineries should, for their own sake and that of others, pursue the more certain course.

DISEASES TO WHICH VINES ARE SUBJECT.

Shanking.—This disease has derived its name from its being an affection of the "shanks" or stalks of the berries. Just as the berries begin to colour and ripen, their stalks shrivel up, and become hard and wiry—in fact, die. The ripening process is thus arrested, the berries ferment, become exceedingly sour, and eventually drop off the shrivelled stalks, unless they are cut off the bunch. Generally speaking, it is most inveterate in straggling bunches, the berries of which have long slender stalks, and which betoken a debilitated state of the vine. Grape-growers have differed widely as to the cause of shanking. Some have attributed its presence to the vines being in cold, wet borders; others, to the borders being too dry; others, again, have blamed heavy cropping, &c. &c. Doubtless all these, or any other conditions that have a tendency to impair the constitution of the vine, may have something to do with the malady. But my own experience leads me to believe that a cold, adhesive, wet border is the most general producer of it; and I agree with that theory of the disease which my brother was the first to propound in his 'Practical Treatise on the Vine,' and from which I quote the following passage:

THE GRAPE VINE.

"I will describe the circumstances under which shanking is most generally met with. The most frequent of these is when the roots of the vine have descended into a cold wet subsoil; but it is also met with where the roots are not down in the subsoil, but where they are growing vigorously, towards autumn especially, in a rich, and what many would term a well-made border, where they receive plenty of liquid manure, where the foliage in the house is fine, the wood strong, and the young roots, if sought for, will be found pushing along in the rich earth in September, like the points of a goose's quill. . . . I must now describe what I consider took place in the case on hand. The vines made great strong young roots in this rich soil late in autumn; they were not short, branching, fibry roots, but soft, like the roots of some bulb; and by the time the action of the leaves had ceased, these roots were anything but ripe, and they all perished during the winter rains, back to the old stem roots from which they sprang. The vines, nevertheless, have a given amount of stored-up sap in them though they have lost their active roots, and they are pruned and started, say, the following February. While this stored-up sap lasts, they grow vigorously enough, but a period arrives when it is exhausted; and the new sap comes but slowly, for the old roots that remain are just beginning, through the action of the foliage, to start into life a fresh set of young roots, that are able as yet to supply but little. This takes place when the berry is passing through the stoning period—always a crisis with fruit of any kind—and the consequence is a thorough failure of the crop from shanking, either resulting directly from want of proper nourishment at this important period, or from some other cause which springs from this want. The crop of fruit is lost as thus described, but the vines *seem* in good health, and they make strong roots towards autumn, again to share the fate of their predecessors; and so the round goes on."

Twenty-one years ago I took the management of a number of vineries, the vines in which corresponded exactly to the above description, and I renewed the whole of the borders, and planted them with young vines. On removing the old borders, they were found to consist of damp solid soil, without any portion of opening material, and all the drainage under them was a few inches of ordinary coal-ashes. I did not find a single young fibry root from one end of the range to the other at the time—midwinter—when the soil was removed. There was nothing to be seen but old, thick, brown-like roots, and it was no wonder that the grapes shanked most severely. Having shown the principal cause of shanking, the remedy can be anticipated. Vines under such circumstances must either be discarded altogether, or lifted out of the wet retentive border and planted in soil congenial to them. For this process I refer to what has been said on renovating exhausted vines, p. 105. Ample drainage, a free open soil, protecting the roots from winter rains, and a thorough ripening of the wood and roots in autumn, with moderate cropping, are the best preventives of shanking.

Mildew.—It is generally admitted that mildew is a very minute fungus, concerning the origin of which there is yet great diversity of opinion. It is, however, a very formidable enemy to the vine, and if allowed to go on unmolested, it proves very destructive in some instances. It can be easily prevented and eradicated when it does make its appearance. An over-moist, cold, and stagnant atmosphere is the condition under which it generally attacks the vines, and I am not aware that it ever appears when there is a circulation of moderately dry and sufficiently warm air.

I never had experience of it but once, and that was during a season of dull, damp weather, in a vinery considerably below the surrounding ground-level. The water was coming into the floor of the house at the foundations, and the heating apparatus was not sufficiently powerful to keep up the heat properly. The disease first made its appearance over an open cistern of water. I at once had the cistern covered up, and the house kept as dry and warm as possible. On the first fine afternoon I mixed some flower of sulphur in a potful of water, and syringed the whole of the vines with it; this left the flower of sulphur adhering to the leaves when they dried. At the same time I coated the pipes with sulphur, and aired freely. This resulted in completely arresting the mildew; and it disappeared without any injury to the fruit, and not a speck of it has appeared on the vines since. There is no doubt about sulphur being a specific for mildew. A good syringing or two brings off all the sulphur when the malady is fairly subdued. A damp, cold, stagnant atmosphere should therefore be avoided, otherwise mildew is more likely, if it be a wet sunless season, to prove troublesome.

Rust.—I do not know whether this should come under the category of diseases, as it cannot be said that it attacks the vine as a disease is understood to attack. There are many causes assigned for this disfiguration of the berries, such as handling them with greasy hands, touching them with the hair of the head while thinning them, cold currents of air when the vines are young, and overmuch moisture in the air. I have no recollection of being conscious that rust was produced by any of these causes, though I think too much moisture in the atmosphere as likely to do so as any of them, seeing that it has an effect on the leaves somewhat allied to rust on the berries. The only case of rust worth the name that ever took place in my own experience, was in a very narrow vinery, where, to keep up the heat, hard firing had to be resorted to. Red-spider under these circumstances made its appearance, and I had the pipes covered with sulphur to check the spider. The grapes were then almost ready to thin: in two or three days after the sulphuring process, the bunches all over the house were more or less blackened. As the berries grew the rusting became more apparent. Whatever else will produce rust, sulphuring hot pipes while the grapes are young will produce it. There is no cure for it after it is produced that I know of. The best thing to do when it occurs before the grapes are thinned, is not to be in a hurry to thin, and to remove the bunches and berries most affected.

Excrescence on the under sides of the leaves.—This consists of a mass of watery-like excrescences resembling small green boils or blisters, thickly set on the under sides of the leaves. They are produced by a warm atmosphere too highly charged with moisture in conjunction with too little ventilation. I have seen some very inveterate cases of it this very damp sunless season (1872), and, as editor of the 'Gardener,' have had numerous examples of it sent for inspection. It can be prevented by not allowing too much moisture in the air, and arrested in its progress by the same means; but once the excrescences are formed, I do not know of a cure.

Scalding.—This affection seems peculiar to certain varieties of grapes, and to Lady Downes's seedling in particular, just as it approaches the stoning stage. I have frequently had berries sent to me so affected. One side of the berry looks as if it had been suddenly scalded with hot water, and the part affected collapses and decays. It is caused by heat, and the only way to prevent it is to keep the vinery well ventilated and cool by opening both the top and bottom lights. When the grapes begin to swell after stoning, there is no further fear of its appearing.

THE PEACH AND NECTARINE.

THESE two fruits are classed together. They not only belong to the same genus (*Amygdalus*), but the same species (*persica*) includes them both. The nectarine differs from the peach in being somewhat less, and in having a smooth skin, the skin of the peach being downy. There have been instances of their being both found on the same branch, and single fruits have been found with the skin of the peach on one side and that of the nectarine on the other. They may each be arranged under two classes—viz., the free-stone peaches and nectarines, the flesh of which separates readily from the stone and skin; and the cling-stones, which have a firmer flesh adhering to both the stone and the skin. The cultivation required by the peach applies also to the nectarine.

There is considerable difference of opinion among botanists as to the native country of the peach. Persia has been considered by some to have been the place of its origin. "Decandolle is, however, of opinion that China is the native country of the peach. His reasons are, that if it had originally existed in Persia or Armenia, the knowledge and culture of so delicious a

THE PEACH AND NECTARINE. 137

fruit would have spread sooner into Asia Minor and Greece. The expedition of Alexander is probably what made it known to Theophrastus, B.C. 322, who speaks of it as a Persian fruit. . . . Admitting this to be the country, how can it be explained that neither the early Greeks, nor the Hebrews, nor the people who speak Sanscrit, and who have all sprung from the upper region of the Euphrates, had grown the peach-tree? On the contrary, it is very probable that the stones of a fruit-tree cultivated from all antiquity in China may have been carried across the mountains from the centre of Asia into Cashmere or Bokhara and Persia. . . . The cultivation of the peach-tree, once established at this point, would easily extend, on one side towards the west, and on the other by Cabul towards the north of India. In support of the supposition of a Chinese origin, it may be added that the peach was introduced from China into Cochin China, and that the Japanese call it by the Chinese name *Too*. The peach is mentioned in the books of Confucius, fifth century before the Christian era; and the antiquity of the knowledge of the fruit in China is further proved by the representations of it on sculpture and on porcelain. The above are some of the arguments adduced by Decandolle against the commonly received opinion that the peach originated in Persia." [1]

The peach is very extensively and well cultivated in China. In America it is grown in great abundance, and is extensively used for making peach-brandy; and in some of the States it is an important article of food in a dried state. It is cultivated as a common standard orchard-tree. The hot summers of the Western World ripen the wood sufficiently to enable it to bear with

[1] Treasury of Botany.

impunity the intense frosts of winter. The Americans raise their trees from stones, and though they grow rapidly into a bearing condition, they are not long-lived. It is not uncommon to find orchards of from 10,000 to 20,000 trees belonging to one individual. In the comparatively mild climate of Britain, the peach, even on south walls, often suffers severely from frost. This is easily accounted for by the imperfect ripening of the wood in our comparatively dull and wet summers. The peach was introduced into this country more than 200 years ago, when most likely it was brought from France, where it had been cultivated a long time before that period. In the south of France it succeeds as a common standard; but in the north it requires to be grown against walls. In Britain it succeeds outdoors only against walls with south aspects; but even under such favourable conditions, outdoor crops are very uncertain over the greater part of the kingdom. It is only under glass that good annual crops can be produced. The peach season can, by early forcing and growing it in cool houses, be extended to seven months of the year. I have for years in succession gathered ripe peaches the last week of April, and continued to do so till the last week of October.

PEACH-HOUSE FOR EARLY FORCING.

It is needless to occupy time and space with arguments to show that for the early forcing of the peach a lean-to house, similar to that recommended for the early forcing of the vine, is the best. In all respects it may be the same except in the trellis-work for training the trees to; and even in this respect the arrangement may be the same, except that the roof should be wired more closely for peaches than for vines. However, in those days of clear glass, making hothouses much lighter than they could be made in time past, I would recommend the arranging of the trees as shown in fig. 14. The curved trellis in the centre of the house, with room between it and the front of the house, gives great convenience and facility for attending in every way to the trees. At the same time, the greater part of the back wall can be covered also, thus giving a larger fruit-bearing surface than when the trees are trained closely up all the way under the roof. The arrangement shown in fig. 14 gives a greater variety of position and temperature, and consequently a longer succession of ripe fruit. The quantity of pipes for peach-forcing need scarcely be so much as for the vine. Four rows of 4-inch pipes along the front and both ends of a lean-to house 16 feet wide, will be sufficient. A steaming-tray should also be attached to the pipes.

I have ripened peaches in April in houses not more than 8 feet wide—mere glass cases; but such small houses are so very easily influenced by the fluctuations of the weather, that they should never be adopted. And a house of the dimensions of fig. 14, I consider not too large. But this is a matter that admits of modification, according to circumstances.

PEACH-HOUSE WHEN RIPE PEACHES ARE NOT REQUIRED BEFORE JULY.

When ripe peaches are not required before July, the span-roofed form of house, the same as has been recommended for late vineries, p. 58, is the best. It

140   FRUIT CULTURE UNDER GLASS.

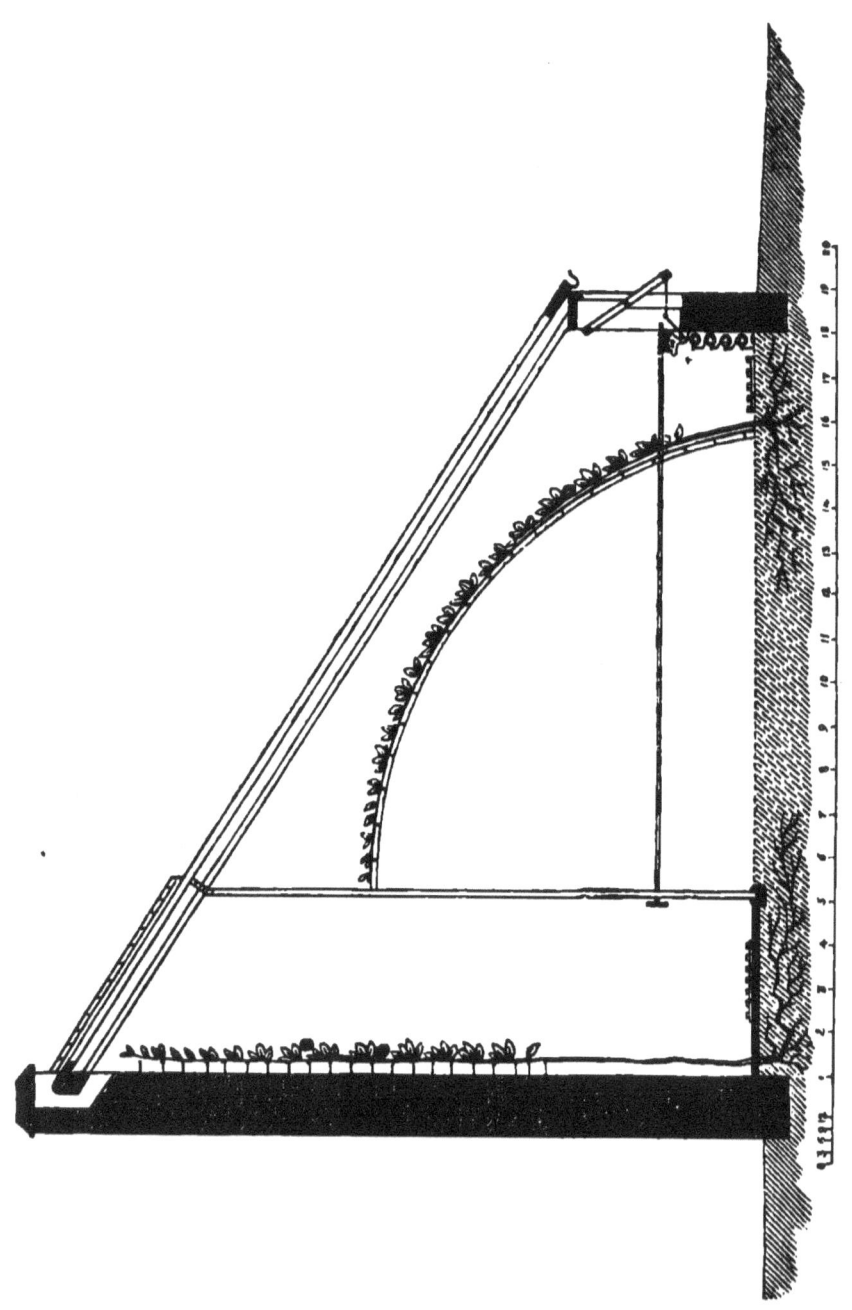

should, of course, run north and south. The span-roofed form affords a great amount of training surface, and gets the sun morning, noon, and evening. The wires should be fixed at 16 inches from the glass, and 7 inches apart. In span-roofed houses the whole surface of glass from the bottom of the front lights upwards is available for being furnished with bearing wood, as it gets ample light. For heating such houses when, say, 60 feet long by 20 feet wide, there should be at least four rows of 4-inch pipes round each side and both ends. There cannot be a greater mistake than that of under-heating with either pipes or boiler-power. It is much safer and more economical to err on the side of having too much than too little. It saves fire, and keeps up the required temperature without violently heating the pipes.

For late crops to be ripened without fire-heat, and when the object is to have peaches on to the end of October, the span-roofed form of peach-house is also best. At the same time, when an existing garden wall can be covered with a lean-to glass roof, it answers perfectly well. A house of this description—say 11 feet wide, with trees covering the whole back wall, and so far up the roof from the front as not to shade the trees on the back wall—gives great space for peaches. There should be ample ventilation at front and top, kept constantly on after all danger from frost is over. I have gathered peaches—Walburton Admirable and Sea Eagle—as late as the 24th October; while earlier varieties in the same house were ripe in the middle of August. In a house of this description there should always be a flow and return pipe, to keep frost from the trees when in blossom. I have known peach-blossom destroyed in narrow lean-to peach-houses by severe spring frosts. And with the means of keeping frost out, the floor of the house is available for flower-garden plants.

In all peach-houses ventilation should be amply provided for. In the case of very early forcing, when the crop is all gathered before the 1st of June, the top and bottom ventilation should be very abundant; indeed it is a good plan to have the roof constructed so that the lights can be partly, if not wholly, removed for two or three months in the heat of summer. At all events, the ventilation should be amply sufficient to keep the house as cool as possible. The whole of the side lights of span-roofed houses should open, and the top ventilation be made so as to open to a considerable extent. In recommending the covering of existing peach-walls with glass, I am fully convinced that this will always be found satisfactory, inasmuch as without doing anything else to the peach-trees, if in other respects they are in moderate condition, the mere covering of them with glass will not only insure crops of peaches every year, but all blistering of the foliage, and most of the other ills which beset the peach in the greater number of the gardens of this country, will be got rid of. At Archerfield I had a peach-wall covered on which the trees formerly did very little good, and after being covered with a lean-to house, they speedily became healthy and vigorous, annually bearing great quantities of fine fruit. The same applies to the peach-wall at Dalkeith, and other places that could be named.

DRAINAGE, DEPTH, AND WIDTH OF BORDER.

When the peach-house occupies a site where the soil and subsoil are uncongenial, such as poor sand, an irony gravel, or a cold stiff clay, the whole should be removed to the depth of 3 feet, and the entire site surfaced with a 3-inch layer of concrete, giving it an even slope from the back wall to the front of the outside border in the case of lean-to houses; the slope to be from the middle of span-roofed houses to the front on each side, as shown in span-roofed vinery, fig. 7. Over the concrete run tile-drains at right angles across the border, 8 feet apart, into a main drain in front, below the level of the cross drains. Over these drains and the whole concrete lay 8 or 9 inches deep of broken bricks, or coarse gravel with the sand sifted out of it, and blind the whole with finer gravel; over this lay a thin turf, grassy side downwards, and the site is ready for the soil. This leaves about $2\frac{1}{2}$ feet up to 3 inches above the front lintels or arches of the house for soil, and allowing for the necessary slope of the border, at the extremity or front it will be a little less than 2 feet. I am not an advocate for very shallow borders, when the drainage is as efficient as has been described. This matter should, however, be decided to a certain extent by the amount of rain that falls in the locality. When very wet, the borders will be deep enough at 2 feet. Their width should be regulated by the width of the house. A lean-to house 16 feet wide will require an outside border 16 feet wide, thus giving 16 feet for each of the two sets of trees, the one set on the back wall and the other on the front trellis.

Where the subsoil consists of a clean open gravel,

concreting is not necessary, and the natural drainage being good, less artificial drainage will suffice.

SOIL.

It is an established fact that all stone-fruits can be grown to the greatest perfection in strong-holding soils. This fully applies to the peach, for it is on a strong calcareous loam, resting on a dry bottom, that it thrives best. The healthiest peach-trees on open walls we have ever seen were grown in a deep strong loam, resting on an immense depth of chalk; and, generally speaking, the limestone districts of England produce the finest outdoor peaches and other stone-fruits. These facts apply with equal force to the culture of the peach under glass. To produce the most healthy, fruitful, and long-lived trees, the best soil with which to form a peach-border consists of the top spit of some old pasture-land of a calcareous nature. It should be taken to the depth of 6 inches, inclusive of the short verdure and its roots peculiar to such land. When carted in, stack it into something like large potato-pits; and if it can be allowed to lie for eight or nine months before being used, all the better. When it cannot be so arranged, it can be used as it comes from the field. Before it is wheeled into the border it should be roughly chopped up with a spade. Then add to every twelve cart-loads one of old lime-rubbish, one of charred wood, and 2 cwt. of half-inch boiled bones, and 1 cwt. of bone-meal to every 6 cubic yards of the whole. Where neither lime-rubbish nor charcoal are procurable, an equal proportion of charred soil can be substituted. These should all be well mixed together and wheeled into the border when in a dry state, making it rather firm by beating it with the back of a fork, and allowing 2 or 3 inches for subsiding. As in the case of vine-borders, I recommend that only part of the border be made at first, the rest to be added in 3 or 4 feet widths, as the roots of the trees extend. In thus making a peach-border with fresh, turfy, strong loam, I do not advise the use of any manure except the few bones, which stimulate slightly over a long series of years. Common manure, either from the stable or cow-house, is undesirable at first, on account of the natural tendency of young peach-trees to make rank, unfruitful growths. The borders can be enriched in after-years, when the trees require it, by top-dressing and watering with manure-water.

I would be sorry to convey, by these directions, the idea that very considerable success in peach-culture is not attainable except when fine fibry calcareous loam can be had from an old pasture. No doubt the character of the soil in some gardens demands that all, or nearly all, the soil for the peach-border should be exchanged for some of a very different character. Where the natural soil is very sandy, or gravelly, and shallow, satisfactory results need not be expected unless fresh soil to some considerable extent be added to it, or wholly substituted. In this case, and when strong loam cannot be had, some strong soil, of a sound clayey nature, should be mixed with the light soil; and the parings of roadsides, with the herbage and roots, will also assist in making the soil more suitable. Where, on the other hand, the natural soil is a very strong, adhesive clay, its unsuitableness in that respect can be greatly remedied by burning a third of it and mixing it with the original, and by also adding to it a portion of road-scrapings. Where the natural soil of a garden, however old, is of a loamy nature, tolerably deep, and resting on a dry healthy subsoil, and where the fine loam I have described cannot be had without great expense, I do not hesitate to say that very fair success in peach-culture is attainable by merely trenching it, and mixing in bones and lime-rubbish according to the directions given. These remarks are intended to encourage those who cannot get the turfy soil that may be considered first-rate, but without which comparatively good crops of peaches can be produced.

VARIETIES FOR EARLY FORCING.

PEACHES.

Early Beatrice ⎱ very early, but
Early Louisa ⎰ rather small.
Hale's Early—taken as a whole, the best very early variety.
Dr Hogg.

Abec.
Grosse Mignonne.
Royal George.
Violette Hative.

Were I restricted to three varieties of well-known sorts for early forcing, I would select Royal George, Violette Hative, and Hale's Early: Early Louisa and Early Beatrice are too small to be popular;—all of which are frequently ripened in April, and bear and set freely.

LATE PEACHES.

Noblesse.
Barrington.
Osprey.
Prince of Wales.

Walburton Admirable.
Sea Eagle.
Lord Palmerston.
Desse Tardive.

These varieties are arranged in their order of ripening. Besides these there are Thames Bank, Baldwin's

Late, Pride of Autumn, and Heath Cling-stone, said to be excellent late sorts that will hang till November. But were I restricted to three October peaches under glass, I would select Walburton Admirable, Sea Eagle, and Desse Tardive. In Scotland I have gathered the Admirables till 24th October in cool houses.

NECTARINES FOR EARLY FORCING.

Lord Napier.	Violette Hative.
Hunt's Early Tawny.	Balgowan.
Elruge.	Roman.

I prefer the three first-named for early forcing, though all are good, and are also fine summer nectarines, in cooler houses.

LATE NECTARINES.

Albert Victor.	Pine-Apple.
Pitmaston Orange.	Prince of Wales.
Humboldt.	Victoria—very late.

Of the early varieties, we should prefer, if only three sorts were required, Lord Napier, Hunt's Early Tawny, and Elruge; and of the late varieties, Victoria, Humboldt, Pitmaston Orange, and Pine-Apple.

PROPAGATION AND SELECTION OF TREES.

The propagation of peaches and nectarines being a process almost entirely confined to nursery-gardens, it is not my intention to enter very elaborately into the details connected with it, for very few growers or forcers of the peach are ever called upon to propagate their own trees. For the following leading particulars connected with the subject I am indebted to Mr Pitman, who for half a century has been connected with the firm of Messrs Osborne & Sons, and who for the greater portion of that period has had the management of the fruit-tree department; and all who are acquainted with the quality of his productions will accept him as an authority of the highest order in the propagation of peaches and nectarines.

The stocks used for budding the peach and nectarine on are the Mussel plum, and the Brompton or Mignonne plum. The stocks are raised by layering in the ordinary way. In preparing them for budding, they are dressed and cut to the height of about 2 feet, and planted out in autumn or early winter in lines. The following autumn they are taken up, assorted, and again planted in lines, but wider apart than the previous or first year. The succeeding summer, generally from the middle of July to the middle of August, they are budded with the desired varieties of peaches and nectarines. The following summer the buds make their first growth, and the trees are termed "dwarf maidens." In the autumn of the same year they are taken up, root-pruned, and planted in lines 4 feet apart, and 2 feet from plant to plant. Their growth, which generally consists of one strong shoot, is allowed to remain intact till the following spring.

They are then cut back more or less closely, with the view of securing the production of one central and two lateral shoots right and left; consequently not less than three buds must be left in the process of pruning. The tree is thus with its three growths termed a one-year-trained tree. In the spring of the following year each of these three shoots is cut back to from three to four buds from the base, so as to secure a tree with from 9 to 10 shoots. The tree having perfected the growth of these shoots, it is, as far as its nursery career is concerned, a full-trained tree (fig. 15), and is ready for being transferred from the nursery-rows to the peach-house trellis.

In the case of new varieties, the process of produc-

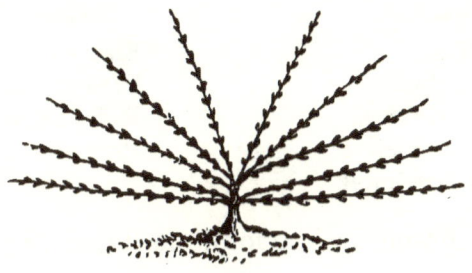

FIG. 15.

ing trained trees is hastened by pinching the top of the first year's growth from the bud after it attains a length of two or three inches. This forces the production of young laterals, which are thinned out to a central growth, and two laterals, one on each side.

In producing standard trees, the treatment of the stocks is precisely the same as that pursued in the case of dwarfs up to the time for budding, when, instead of using the peach or nectarine bud, a well-developed bud of some variety of plum is inserted at the base of the stock as close to the ground as practicable for the sake of neatness in the future stem. The following year the stock is cut back to the bud, and all growths are rubbed off, excepting the produce of the inserted bud, which under favourable circumstances rapidly attains the desired height. The following year the stems are budded with the peaches and nectarines, and in due course transplanted on walls and fences. This double budding produces a much finer and earlier growth for forming standards with stems from 4 to 5 feet high. Long observation and experience have taught Mr Pitman that certain varieties thrive and grow much better on one stock than on another. The following varieties succeed best on the Mussel plum:—

PEACHES.	NECTARINES.
Noblesse.	Elruge.
Barrington.	Violette Hative.
Royal George.	Red Roman.
Violette Hative.	Pitmaston Orange.
Late Admirable.	Hunt's Tawny.

The Brompton or Mignonne is found the best stock for—

PEACHES.	NECTARINES.
Gros Mignonne.	Balgowan.
Bellegarde.	Imperatrice.
Stirling Castle.	Tanfield's Early.
Royal Kensington.	Duc du Dutillys.
Royal Charlotte.	Malta.

The almond bears a greater affinity to the peach and nectarine than the plum; and doubtless, if our climate were more genial, it would, as in France, be the most suitable stock. As a proof of this, Mr Pitman informs me that some peach-trees raised on the almond stock, that he had to do with, succeeded admirably for a while, till an unfavourable season caused them to succumb; while the same varieties on the plum stock endured the ordeal unscathed. The French growers are also partial to the St Julien pear as a stock for peaches and nectarines.

In selecting young trees, it is always most satisfactory, both to the nurseryman and the buyer, that the latter go to the nursery and choose for himself. Avoid trees that have stood long in the nursery-rows, and that have been frequently cut hard back, and choose those having from eight to ten strong, well-ripened shoots. See that the union with the stock is perfect and free from gumming, and the stem healthy and growing-like, having no sign of being bark-bound.

PLANTING.

The border and trees being in readiness, the operation of planting is a very simple one. The first thing to decide is the distance at which the trees are to be planted. I am averse to thick planting for permanent trees. To restrict a peach-tree planted in a good peach-border is very unadvisable. They should have plenty of room to develop themselves. For a peach-house wall 36 feet long, two standard trees on the back are quite sufficient, thus planting them 9 feet from each end of the house. On the front trellis other two dwarfs are enough. Should it be an object to get as much fruit as possible in a short time, a temporary tree may be planted, one between the two permanent ones and one at each end, to be removed as the two permanent trees require the space. In the case of the front trellis, the temporary trees should be standards so as to clothe the upper part of the trellis for the time being. Before planting them, carefully examine the roots, and shorten back a little any that are gross and strong, and cut away all bruised or broken parts. Turn back the soil sufficiently to allow the roots to be stretched fully and regularly out on the surface. Place the boles of the trees so that they will be three to four inches clear of the back wall and the front trellis-work, so that they may have plenty of room to swell without pressing on the wall or trellis. Cover the roots carefully with the finer portion of the soil to the depth of 6 inches, making it rather firm.

Fix the tree loosely to the wall, and water the roots through a rose.

The season I prefer for planting is autumn, say the beginning of November or end of October, when the leaves are dropping off the trees. Planting can, however, be performed, and often is successful, from October to April. In planting peach-houses, where healthy trees exist on the open walls, it is a good plan to lift some that are of considerable size, say planted five or six years, and transfer them to the peach-house. I have done this and got a good crop the same season. Every fibre should be carefully saved in the process. By this means a peach-house can be furnished with fruit without the loss of a season or a crop.

PRUNING AND TRAINING.

Many ways of training and pruning the peach and nectarine have been practised and recommended. French horticulturists especially have been very successful in training them in several ways characterised by regularity and neatness. The single-cordon as well as the multiciple-cordon systems are favourite modes of training in France. Modifications partaking more or less of the French systems have been practised and recommended, especially by Seymour, in England. But the ordinary fan system of training is by far the most generally practised and liked. It is, especially under glass, the mode of training which the most successful forcers of the peach have adopted, and it is that which I recommend. Many grand old examples of peach-trees under glass are to be found in this country, which have all along been trained on the fan principle, and that are yet in fine bearing con-

THE PEACH AND NECTARINE. 153

dition, being well furnished from top to bottom with young bearing wood. Taking a young tree, fig. 15, which I have recommended for planting as the foundation of a fan-trained tree, different cultivators who are most in favour of this system of training would deal differently with the ten young growths with which it is furnished. Some would cut them all back again to within five or six buds of their base; others would not shorten them at all, but would let them start into growth with as many young shoots as could be tied to the trellis without crowding them. What I have practised and would recommend is a mean between these two. The two centre shoots I would shorten back to half their length, the other eight shoots to be merely topped back to solid, well-ripened wood. The cutting somewhat closely back of the two centre ones makes it certain that two or three good strong growths will start from near their base to properly fill up the centre of the tree with leaders. Each of the other eight shoots should have all their buds removed by degrees, except one near the base, and one or two at equal distances between it and the leading bud, according to the length of the shoots. Two buds to the left on the under side—if the shoots are long enough to have room for three on the upper side, the buds on the one side to alternate in position with those on the other. These lateral growths, with the leader, are enough to lay a foundation to serve for the future full-grown tree. The lateral growths should be allowed to grow without being stopped. Should the leaders show signs of growing very vigorously at the expense of the side growths, stop them whenever they show such a tendency. This will cause them to make lateral growths freely, and equally balance the growth of all the young shoots. This encouragement of lateral growths, especially on the young wood in the centre of the tree, gives sufficient to furnish the tree without having recourse to the undesirable practice of first allowing a few very strong leaders to monopolise the sap, and then to cut them down at the winter pruning. In this way much time is gained in covering a wall or trellis with bearing wood.

A young tree thus managed on what may be termed a mean between the extension and the cutting-hard-back systems, produces a comparatively large well-furnished tree the autumn after it is planted, and one which requires very little or no winter pruning before starting it into another year's growth. If the summer disbudding and pinching of the first season's growth have been properly attended to, the tree will be so thoroughly furnished with young wood that all the pruning that should be done is simply to remove any shoots that would crowd the tree. The distance between the shoots should not be less than 3 or 4 inches. In February 1878, I planted a number of young peaches and nectarines in an orchard-house. In the autumn not a single shoot was shortened back, and at the close of their second year's growth the trees thoroughly furnished in many instances spaces of 18 feet by 13 feet, and a great many of them 16 feet by 12 feet, besides bearing a good crop the season after being planted. There are some magnificent trees at Brayton Hall, which Mr Hammond, the able gardener there, managed on the extension system, and consequently filled their allotted spaces and bore grand crops in half the time in which this could have been done by the old cutting-back system.

After the trees have grown and covered the space allotted to each, the system of pruning must be directed so as to continually keep the whole tree regularly supplied with young fruit-bearing wood. With a view to this, of course the yearly removal of old wood in winter, and the laying in of a corresponding amount of young wood in summer, must be carefully attended to. Fig. 16 gives an idea of what I

Fig. 16.

mean by this, and will serve to illustrate the pruning out of old wood and laying in the new. The shoots represented by the solid lines are those which bore fruit last summer, and those shown by the dotted lines, growing from the bases of the fruit-bearing wood, are those laid in in summer to bear the following season. In pruning such a tree, the last year's wood, shown by the solid lines, is cut off close to the young wood which is to supply the next year's crop.

Some make a practice of cutting back the young bearing wood to two-thirds its length. I do not advocate this indiscriminately. Where the shoots are long and not well ripened, and the buds consequently weak, they should be shortened back to where the wood is firm, and always to a strong wood-bud. Peach-trees in a healthy condition have their buds in clusters of three—a wood-bud in the centre, and a fruit-bud on each side of it; and to such a cluster of buds they should always be cut when cut at all.

Well-established trees that have borne heavy crops regularly, and especially those that have been forced early, generally make shorter and stronger growths, well studded with strong clusters of buds. In this case it is unadvisable to shorten them back at all. A watchful eye must always be kept on the lower portion of the tree, so that it is not allowed to get bare of young fruit-bearing growths. It need scarcely be said that, from the fact that it is the young wood that bears, the tendency is for it to be in greatest abundance at the top.

The best guarantee against trees becoming bare of young bearing wood at their lowest parts, is to annually cut back a few healthy young growths to 2 or 3 eyes, and allow as many of these to bud and grow as may be required to keep up the supply of young wood. This is an indispensable necessity, from the fact that portions of old wood have annually to be removed at the top of the tree. In practice, all other things being equal, there is little difficulty experienced in thus furnishing the lower portions of the tree with bearing wood. All cutting should be effected with a sharp thin knife; and whenever it becomes necessary to remove an old limb, the wound should be painted solidly over with white paint.

I have already referred to what is termed Seymour's system of training, from its having been first adopted at Carlton Hall, in Yorkshire, by a gardener of that name. By this system a tree of great regularity and neatness is formed. It differs from the fan system of training in there being no lateral growths allowed on the lower sides of the leading branches. Fig. 17 will illustrate this mode of training. "The first step in starting a newly-planted maiden tree upon Seymour's system is to head the plant down to three eyes, each of which eyes will produce a shoot in summer: at

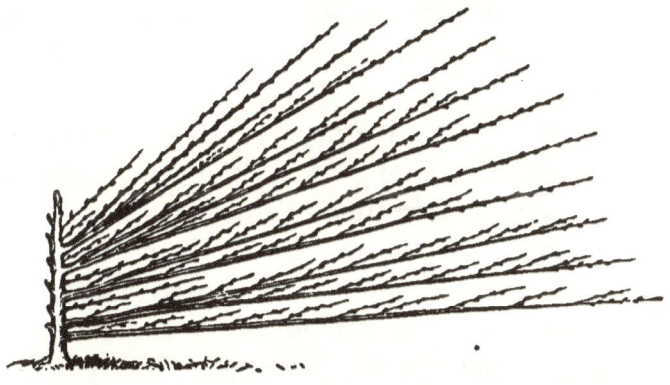

FIG. 17.

pruning-time head down the centre shoot of these to three eyes, to produce in the following summer three more shoots as before, leaving the side shoots always at full length. In spring all the buds on the lower sides of these side branches, and these from 9 to 12 inches asunder, are rubbed off, leaving those only which proceed from the upper side of the branch. When the young wood has extended to the length of 5 or 6 inches it is stopped, but the leading branches are not interfered with. Every year will produce a side shoot on each side of the tree, and the laterals that proceed from them at the distance we have stated, are at first laid in between them, but the following spring these are removed from the wall and trained up in the main side branches. By the autumn of the third year the number of laterals will be doubled on the two side branches first laid in, as a new lateral is sure to spring from the base of the one laid in the previous season, as well as one from its point. As to winter pruning in the fourth year, all the laterals of two years' growth, and which have already produced a crop of fruit, are to be removed entirely, and those of the previous summer's formation are to be unfastened from the wall and laid upon the main leading side branches in the place of those cut out."[1]

My objection to this otherwise neat and very systematic mode of training is, in the first place, that it takes a much longer time to cover a given space of trellis or wall than it requires to do so on the fan system, when the needless and objectionable close-cutting-back system is not adhered to. Then, again, when any of the leading branches give way — no uncommon thing in peach-trees — a great gap in the tree is created, which it takes longer to make up than when a gap takes place in fan training.

The time for pruning the peach under glass must be regulated by the time that forcing is commenced.

[1] Book of the Garden.

THE PEACH AND NECTARINE. 159

Generally speaking, it is best to defer pruning till the first signs of the swelling of the buds, especially in the case of the inexperienced, as then wood-buds and fruit-buds are easily distinguished. This of course refers to the shortening back of all young wood that requires it.

DISBUDDING, OR SUMMER PRUNING.

What is known by the term "disbudding" the peach, consists of the removal of all the buds while in a small state that are not required to grow into shoots, to furnish fruit-bearing wood for the following year. This operation should be begun early, as soon as the buds have started. They should not all be removed at once, but at three different intervals of time. At the first disbudding remove those which are termed by gardeners fore-right buds—that is, those that are on the front side of the shoots and that would grow at a right angle from the trellis—and those which are situated on the opposite side of the shoot, thus leaving those that are right and left. In about twelve or fourteen days after this, about the half of those left should be removed at intervals along the shoot, always leaving the best-looking two buds near the base. The trees should be examined and finally disbudded in about a week after, removing all except the most promising bud near the base, which is to form the chief growth for next year's fruiting. On short stubby growths this bottom bud and the terminal one will be enough to leave. On longer shoots one or two intermediate ones may be left if there is room enough to tie them in without crowding the tree. But always give the preference to the lowest-placed buds.

In removing the last of the superfluous buds, when they have got stronger than those taken off at the first and second disbuddings, a thin sharp knife should be used, as it makes a less and cleaner wound than when they are detached by the hand. The leading shoot, if not required to furnish the tree as in the case of young trees, should be stopped when it has grown one foot; but allow the lateral growths for next year's fruiting to grow their full length, and keep them regularly tied to the trellis as they grow—using for this purpose soft matting—taking care not to tie too tightly, but leaving room sufficient for the wood to swell.

The common error of tying in too many young growths should be avoided, as one of the greatest evils in peach-culture. It crowds the tree with wood that is not required, and prevents the sun and air from acting properly on the foliage, and the result is weak, unripened, and unfruitful wood. Whenever any given growth shows that it is going to grow much stronger than the rest, it should either be cut out altogether, or stopped, and restopped if necessary, to prevent its monopolising the sap that should go to the other parts of the tree.

After the fruit are all gathered look carefully over the trees, and untie and cut out at once those shoots from which the fruit have been gathered, and which are not necessary for another year. This gives more room to the young wood required for the ensuing crop, and concentrates the energies of the tree on their maturation. It is not easy nor necessary thus to cut out all the wood that requires to be removed; but the lessening of it leaves but little to do at the winter or early spring pruning, as the case may be, and it lets more air and light at the foliage and buds of the shoots that are left to furnish the next crop.

THINNING THE FRUIT.

All peach-trees that are vigorous and the wood of which has been well ripened, generally set a great many more fruit than are required, and therefore have to be thinned off. This operation should not be completed all at once, but gradually, and not finally till the fruit are stoned. As soon as the fruit have swollen sufficiently to burst and throw off their flowers, the first thinning should take place. Where the fruit have set in clusters of twos and threes, remove them all but the best-formed and largest fruit, those that are placed on the under sides of the shoots, and those that are very near to the wires, and that would not get room to swell if left. When the fruit have attained the size of marbles, a second thinning should take place, removing all the smallest ones, and those that are nearest the top and the bottom parts of the bearing shoot—leaving the largest about the middle of them. Although I have never experienced very much dropping of the fruit in the process of stoning, it is always best to leave considerably more at the second thinning to be removed after they have completed the formation of the stones. Then the final thinning should take place. The weight of crop must be regulated by several considerations: if the trees are young and show a tendency to make too strong a growth, then it is best to crop rather heavily, say a fruit to every 6 or 7 square inches of surface. The ratio of cropping should be graduated according to the vigour of the trees. Those which have covered a considerable allotted space, and that are in what may be termed good bearing condition, should not be taxed so heavily. If fine fruit are required, one to every 10 or 12 square inches is sufficient. Of course their distribution may be unequal, and it is desirable that on the lower branches—stretching more at a right angle with the stem—the fruit should not be so thick as on the central parts of the trees, which have a tendency to become over vigorous at the expense of the lower ones.

ROOT-PRUNING.

I am averse to root-pruning the peach and nectarine, or any stone fruits, according to the fashion recommended by some, and have never found it necessary to cut away many of their roots after they were first planted. I have never found much difficulty in subduing any tendency that young trees have had to grow too grossly by pinching the shoots when growing, and directing the energies of the tree to its other parts. I think the practice of continually cutting hard back and preventing the trees from making a more natural headway has much to do with gross shoots. Letting the young trees bear heavily, in conjunction with the training indicated above, is generally sufficient when the trees are planted in a loamy soil into which rank manures have not been introduced. However, cases do occur when the roots of some of the stronger-growing varieties have to be dealt with. Then I would recommend a trench to be taken out at a radius beyond where the roots have extended. Encroach carefully on the roots, removing all the soil —but saving every possible rootlet—close up to the bole of the tree, or as far up as the check that is desirable would demand. Unless it be some roots very much out of proportion to the others, they should not be cut back, but be all carefully laid in the border again with some sound fresh loam under and over them, making the soil all firm about them again. This operation I prefer doing just as the leaves are nearly all dropping off. If done earlier, the wood is apt to shrivel instead of ripen.

FORCING AND GENERAL MANAGEMENT.

Time to commence forcing.—The time when ripe peaches are required must, of course, regulate the time when forcing has to be commenced. As the peach and nectarine will not submit to hard forcing, especially in their earliest stages of progress, it takes about five and a half months to ripen a crop when forcing is commenced late in November. This may be termed very early forcing. On referring to my note-books, I find that trees started—by being shut up without fire-heat for the first fourteen days—on the 15th November, ripened their first dishes of fruit from the 24th to the 30th April. Those started in January and February take fourteen days less time, but the character of the season has much to do with the exact time required to produce ripe fruit. Unless where there are several peach-houses such early forcing is not desirable, and if the trees are not in good condition it should never be attempted. From the beginning to the end of January is a good time to start the earliest house, where there are, say, three peach-houses, allowing the interval of a month between the starting of each house. These early houses, with a late one in which no fire-heat is used beyond what is necessary to protect the trees from frosts or to ripen the wood in autumn, keep up a long succession of peaches when the selection of varieties is made to this end. In the case of young or newly-planted trees that have not been accustomed to early forcing, February is sufficiently early to begin to force them the first year. The second they may be started a month earlier. By beginning a few weeks earlier every year, they can be worked round to start at any time within the limits of what is practicable, much more safely than by beginning them very early the first and second years. It may be said of plants and trees in this respect that "use is second nature;" for unless violently pushed they *will* have their period of repose, and the peach most particularly should never be subject to hard forcing.

DRESSING THE TREES AND BORDERS.

Let it be supposed that the earliest trees have been pruned, and the woodwork and glass of the house thoroughly cleansed. If there has been any red-spider about the trees the previous season, let the whole of them be first washed by means of a hair-brush and soft water, in which about an ounce of soft-soap to every gallon has been mixed. After the trees are dry, coat them over with a mixture of sulphur, cow-dung, and soot, in equal proportions, and reduced to the consistency of thick paint with hot water. To a gallon of this add 2 oz. of soft-soap. In painting the trees over with this, care should be taken always to draw the brush upwards towards the points of the shoots, to prevent the prominent buds from being rubbed off. I have often started peaches without this dressing, and only consider it necessary when the trees have been attacked by red-spider the previous season. In tying the trees, care must be taken to rub off as little of the dressing as possible.

The surface-soil should be removed from the border to the depth of 2 inches, and replaced with pure fresh loam in the case of young vigorous trees in new borders. In the case of old trees that have borne heavily for a succession of years, remove the soil down to the first roots, and replace it with an equal amount of loam, with a third of horse-droppings or manure mixed with it. If the inside border is dry, give it a good soaking with tepid weak manure-water. Presuming that these operations have been attended to a fortnight before the house is to be shut up for forcing, still keep the house cool and well aired, but keep the trees dry, so that the dressing does not get washed off them. The outside border should always be protected from cold and wet at the same time by a covering of litter and leaves and a tarpauling, or other means, such as wooden shutters for throwing off drenching rains. This is supposing that forcing is begun before the end of February.

TEMPERATURE.

Unless the weather be frosty when the house is shut up, no more fire-heat should be applied than is necessary to keep the temperature from falling at any time below 45° at night. In mild weather it will necessarily range higher without fire-heat. After the house has been shut up a fortnight, firing in a regular way should commence, and the night temperature be kept at 50°, allowing it to sink a few degrees lower on very cold nights; with a day temperature 10° higher with sun. If a higher temperature be maintained at first, the trees are subject to start their wood-buds before the blossom-buds, and the blossom under such circumstances is sure to be weak, and likely to drop off before it expands. By the time the blossoms are open the night temperature should be gradually raised to 55°, with a corresponding rise by day with sun. After the fruit are set, raise the temperature by degrees to 60° at night, and with sun it may safely run to 70° or 75° by day, according to the intensity of the sunshine. Until the fruit are stoned the night temperature should not exceed this. After they are stoned it may be raised to 65°, and to 80° with sun-heat by day. In the case of early forcing, of which I am now treating, I do not recommend a higher temperature for peaches than the last named —not that there is any fear of the fruit dropping off with a higher temperature after the stoning process is past, but I have always found that the moderate rate of forcing produced finer peaches and wood than are attainable with more rapid forcing. Of course very much depends on the state of the external atmosphere, as every experienced forcer knows. With mild weather the temperature I have named may be exceeded by a few degrees with impunity, even with advantage. On the other hand, in time of very severe frost, when hard firing is necessary to keep up the proper temperature, it is wisest to let the heat decline a few degrees. After a day of bright sunshine, which more or less heats up all surfaces, the house can be shut up with a higher temperature, and

THE PEACH AND NECTARINE. 167

the heat husbanded, so that very moderate firing keeps the heat up in the fore part of the night higher than I have named, and under such circumstances there is no objection to this.

Of course when forcing is commenced later in the season, and the trees are more easily excited, and produce their blossom and young wood more strongly under the influence of increased light, the temperature may range with safety a few degrees higher. For instance, a house started in December, for which 50° with fire-heat would be sufficient, might, if not started till far on in February, with more genial warmth, and more sun by day, be started at 55° with fire-heat, after the trees are moving naturally. In bright weather, early shutting up with sun-heat should always be preferred to hard firing without sun.

VENTILATION.

The peach dislikes a close, stagnant atmosphere, and should be as freely ventilated as circumstances will admit of all through the process of forcing. If the house is kept too close and moist before the blossom expands, such conditions are sure to produce weakly blossom, and also dispose the wood-buds to too much precede the blossom, always an evil to be guarded against. Therefore give air more or less daily, as weather permits, from the time the house is first shut up; and when the blossom is open, air freely on all dry days, and leave a little on all night, but guard against currents of cold frosty air. Most early forcers of the peach will have observed that if cold gusts of frosty air have reached any part of the tree, at that particular part the process of setting has been the least satisfactory. While a circulation of dry warm air is desirable, it should be admitted in small quantities at many points, so as to prevent the blossoms from being subjected to blasts of it. In the case of early forcing, front ventilation should not be applied, unless the air can first be warmed by some such means as that recommended in the case of vines, at least until the fruit have approached the colouring and ripening stage. Like firing, ventilation must be cautiously regulated, according to the state of the weather; and when the fruit are ripe, a free circulation of warm dry air is necessary to flavour and colour them.

MOISTURE IN THE AIR AND SYRINGING.

Although the peach is a moisture-loving plant, I do not approve of heavy and too frequent syringing at midwinter before the fruit are set. As has already been said, it has a tendency to bring the foliage too much in advance of the blossoms. Notwithstanding all that has been said in favour of syringing heavily when forcing is commenced, to cause the bloom-buds to swell freely, I have never observed that, with the house kept moderately moist without syringing, the blossoms burst at all less vigorous when syringing has never been practised till the fruit are set. The floor and paths should be sprinkled at shutting-time, and on bright mornings after cold nights when extra fire-heat has been applied. As soon as the fruit are set, the syringe should be vigorously used every dry morning, and especially in the afternoon, when the house is shut up with sun-heat.

Syringing should be thus continued until the fruit shows signs of ripening. The peach is subject to red-spider, and syringing keeps that pest at bay ; and it also likes moisture about its foliage. The morning syringing should always be early, so that rapid evaporation does not take place as ventilation is increased. Clear soot-water—that is, water in which dry fresh soot has been mixed and allowed to stand and become clear— may be applied occasionally with the engine or syringe to advantage. The ammonia from the soot gives a dark healthy hue to the foliage.

SETTING THE FRUIT.

I have never found the least difficulty in getting peaches to set freely, even when they have been started in November. The only means I have ever adopted to make a good set of fruit doubly sure, is to slightly increase the temperature immediately the blooms are fully expanded, to give rather more air, and to go over the blossoms at mid-day with a camel's-hair brush, and impregnate them, taking pollen from those sorts, such as Violette Hative, which produce it more freely than others, and applying it to such as Noblesse, which produce it more sparingly.

I do not think that setting depends so much on either dryness or moisture as on a circulation of warm air, which causes the pollen to come to proper maturity. Some growers advise that the trees be syringed with tepid water when in full bloom, and practise this to set their peach-crop successfully. I have never adopted this, and never found it necessary, but it is practised by successful early forcers of the peach. There can be no difficulty in accepting what has been said in its favour, inasmuch as it can be easily understood how the particles of pollen can be separated and carried down the pistil by means of water, as well as air. It is, in as far as it can be aided, a mechanical process. I consider the chief thing is to produce a strong healthy bloom and fructifying organs, by cautious forcing, and then the setting of the fruit is almost a certainty.

WATERING.

It is difficult to lay down directions as to the time that peaches require to be watered at the roots, so much depends on circumstances, such as the nature of the soil, &c. &c. In the case of trees having their roots both in inside and outside borders, it is never necessary in early forcing to water the outside border. The inside border should be thoroughly moistened to the bottom when the house is put in order for forcing. I have an objection to peach borders becoming dusty dry at any time; for if they once become too dry, and are then copiously watered, and started soon after, they are apt to cast their bloom-buds after they begin to swell. Under ordinary circumstances, I have found a good watering when the house is about to be started, another after the fruit are set, sufficient. After this the constant syringing and damping keep the border from drying, and the watering after they are set will carry them to the stoning process. After they are stoned, two waterings will be enough till the fruit begin to ripen. Then mulch the border with short dung, and no more water should be applied till the fruit are all gathered, after which the border must be kept moist till the wood is ripe, and the leaves dropping.

Manure-water may be freely applied at all times of watering in the case of full-grown, free-bearing trees. Young trees growing vigorously should not have manure-water, as their tendency to a gross growth will be stimulated by it.

RIPENING AND GATHERING THE FRUIT.

The colour and flavour of peaches and nectarines are perhaps more dependent on given circumstances than are the same qualities in any other fruit. Unless the sun shines directly on the fruit, it will not attain its proper colour; and unless, in addition to exposure to sunshine, they are subjected to a circulation of dry warm air, the flavour is sure to be deficient. Consequently all leaves that intercept direct sunshine must be pushed aside after the fruit has begun to take its last swelling. If the leaves cannot all be laid effectually aside, it is better to remove all or half of some of the leaves than that they should shade the fruit. I have seldom found it necessary to cut the leaves or remove them entirely. When the wood is not too thickly tied in, such a necessity rarely occurs.

As directed under the head of ventilation, the peach-house should be freely opened at top and front all day, and the wet-weather ventilation left open all night. The practice of pulling down the sashes, where this can be adopted, entirely exposing the fruit to sun and air, in ripening and colouring summer and autumn peaches, is a good one. It gives high colour and flavour. Of course this should only be practised when the weather is clear and dry.

The experienced eye can tell, in the majority of sorts, when the fruit are fit to gather without handling them. When they are handled it should be with great nicety of touch, the peach being very easily blemished when ripe. The crop should be looked over every day, placing the fingers gently behind those fruits that appear the ripest, and if with a gentle pressure from the branch the fruit does not easily separate from its stalk, leave it for another day. Each fruit should be carefully laid upon its base in a basket, the bottom of which is lined with wadding covered with tissue-paper, the fruit being regulated so that one does not touch another. It is well to gather peaches and nectarines for dessert six hours before they are sent to table, and leave them in the fruit-room to cool. Nets are sometimes fixed, and the fruit allowed to drop into them, but peaches should never be allowed to drop if it can be prevented. It is, however, best to use such a precaution, to prevent any that may drop from injury.

Peaches keep a good many days after they are ripe in a cool place. In 1865 I kept such tender-fleshed varieties as Noblesse and Bellegarde for twelve days, in close tin boxes placed in an ice-house, after they were quite fit for table, and then exhibited them in Edinburgh. Nectarines keep fully longer in this way.

PACKING PEACHES TO BE SENT TO A DISTANCE.

When peaches have to be sent by railway and other conveyances, great care is necessary in packing them. The safest way is to have tin boxes divided into compartments 3¾ inches square and 4 inches deep. In the bottom of each division put a little fine paper-shavings pressed down. Wrap each fruit carefully in a piece of tissue-paper, then set it on its base on a square of cotton wadding, which fold up over the fruit, taking each corner between the fingers and thumb, and dropping it carefully into its place. There should be sufficient wadding round each to prevent oscillation. Over the whole surface of the box spread some fine paper-shavings, so that when the lid of the wooden box, into which the tin case should fit tightly, is screwed down, the shavings may press sufficiently on the wadding to keep all steady without bruising the fruit. In this way they can be sent long distances without the slightest damage. Peaches and nectarines to be sent in this way should, however, never be over-ripe. Indeed they should be gathered a day earlier than when they are sent direct to table from the garden.

INSECTS.

Red-Spider.—I have never found much difficulty in preventing red-spider from gaining much of a footing on peaches. Cleanliness in connection with the woodwork, glass, and everything else, the dressing recommended for the trees after they are pruned, and the syringing recommended throughout the forcing season, are the best preventives. When spider does make its appearance, attack it vigorously with clean tepid water from the syringe or engine. After the fruit are gathered, a handful of flower of sulphur may be mixed with the water. Peach-foliage seems to thrive under the influence of sulphur applied in this way. This insect is easily driven off the smooth surface of the peach-leaf, and vigorous syringings I have always found sufficient to master it when it did appear.

Green-Fly.—Green-fly is very easily destroyed by fumigating with tobacco, and its very first appearance, in however small numbers, should be the signal for exterminating it. I have known it destroy a crop very much when it got a footing when the fruit were setting. The trees should be dry the evening of fumigation, and the tobacco should never be allowed to burst into flame. The fumigation should not take place when the trees are in bloom.

Brown-Scale.—I never had to deal with this insect on peach-trees but once. The trees were syringed, after they dropped their leaves, with water at 145°; and though the wood was coated with the insect, I never saw more of it after the syringing.

Thrips.—This is a troublesome enemy to peaches when it attacks them. It cannot be said that the peach is subject to thrips; but when plants infested with them are placed in peach-houses—which never should be, but often is, done—they spread rapidly on the peach-foliage. Fumigation with tobacco, on which some Cayenne pepper has been dusted, for a few successive nights, destroys it. Engine the trees freely after the fumigations to wash the insects and the smell away. When the fruit are gathered, thrips can be conquered by syringing two or three times with tobacco-liquor, made by boiling at the rate of 3 oz. of tobacco to a gallon of water. This should be applied late in the evening, and the house kept close for the night, so that the liquor may hang longer about the foliage.

DISEASES.

The peach and nectarine are singularly free from disease under glass in a good border, unless it be mildew at times on some varieties. They are rarely attacked with those diseases, such as curl and canker, which are so troublesome on the open walls. Gumming occasionally causes the death of a branch, and

THE PEACH AND NECTARINE. 175

is often the result of a bruise, or a tie that has been too tight and cut into the branch. When it appears to any extent, the best plan is to remove the affected branch at once. Mildew is the effect of over-dryness, and also of too much wet. Whenever it appears, dust the affected parts with sulphur, and if the border is dry, water it sufficiently to moisten the soil. If the cause is traceable to bad drainage, it should be rectified.

THE FIG.

"THE fig of our gardens is the *Ficus Carica* of botanists, The name *Ficus*, applied to this very anciently known fruit, is most probably derived from Feg, its Hebrew name; that of *Carica* is from Caria, in Asia Minor, where fine varieties of it have long existed. According to various authors, it is a native of Western Africa, Northern Africa, and the south of Europe, including Greece and Italy. It is certainly indigenous to Asia Minor, but it may have been then introduced and naturalised in the islands of the Mediterranean and the countries near its shores, both in Europe and Africa.

"Figs have been used in the East as an article of food from time immemorial. They were amongst the fruits brought back from Canaan by the Israelites sent by Moses to report on the productions of the land. We read of a present having been made to David of 200 cakes of figs. They were probably used chiefly in the dried state. The drying is easily effected in a warm climate by exposure to the sun's rays, in the same way as those grapes are dried which are called from that circumstance raisins of the sun. Like the grape, the substance of the fig abounds in what is termed grape-sugar. In drying, some of this exudes, and forms that soft white powder which we see on the imported dried figs. They are thus preserved in their own sugar, and rendered fit for storing up as an article of food.

"Figs were considered of such necessity by the Athenians that their exportation from Attica was prohibited. The figs of Athens were celebrated for their exquisite flavour, and Xerxes was induced by them to undertake the conquest of Attica. The African figs were also much admired at Rome, although Pliny says it is not long since they began to grow figs in Africa. Cato, in order to stimulate the Roman senators to declare war against Carthage, showed them a fig brought from thence. It was fresh and in good condition, and all agreed that it must have been quite recently pulled from the tree. 'Yes,' says Cato, 'it is not yet three days since this fig was gathered at Carthage; see by it how near to the city we have a mortal enemy!' This argument determined the senate to commence the Third Punic War, the result of which was that Carthage, the rival of Rome, was utterly destroyed.

"The fig may have been introduced into Britain along with the vine by the Romans, or subsequently by the monks. But if it had, it seems to have disappeared till brought from Italy by Cardinal Pole, either when he returned from that country in 1525, or after his second residence abroad in 1548. In either case, the identical trees which he brought were planted in the garden of the archiepiscopal palace at Lambeth, and have certainly existed for more than 300 years. This proves that the fig lives to a great age, even under less favourable circumstances than it enjoys in its native country. In this country a chalk subsoil and a climate like that near the south coast appear to suit the fig best. There the tree grows and bears as standards. They are liable, however, to be killed to the ground in winters of excessive severity, but they spring up afresh from the roots. There was an orchard not exceeding three-quarters of an acre at Sarring, near Worthing, in Sussex, containing 100 standard fig-trees. About 100 dozen ripe figs were usually gathered daily from these trees during August, September, and October. By selecting similarly favoured spots, it may be fairly concluded that this country could supply itself with abundance of fresh figs. As for dry ones, they are obtained in large quantities from Turkey, the Mediterranean, and other countries, but the supply for centuries back has chiefly been from Turkey. The import has been as much as 1000 tons a-year, and now that the duty is taken off, the quantity imported will doubtless be much greater.

"The inflorescence and the fruit of the fig are very distinct in their character from other fruits. It consists of a hollow fleshy receptacle, with an orifice in the top, which is surrounded and nearly closed by a number of imbricated scales—as many as 200, according to Duhamel. The flowers, unlike those of most fruit-trees, make no outward appearance, but are concealed within the fig on its internal surface; they are male and female, the former situated near the orifice, the latter in that part of the concavity next the stalk. On cutting open a fig when it has attained little more than one-third of its size, the flowers will be seen in full development; and provided the stamens are perfect, fertilisation takes place at that stage of growth. But it often happens that the stamens are imperfect, and no seeds are formed, nevertheless the fruit swells and ripens."[1]

The fig is considered one of the most wholesome of fruits, both in a dried state and when newly gathered in a ripe condition. It being a fruit which yields ample returns for the care that it requires, it is a wonder that it is not more generally allotted a prominent place in glass houses in this country. Still its culture, both in pots and planted out in prepared borders, has been considerably extended of late years, and it is evidently a fruit rising in favour with all possessors of gardens in which it can be accommodated under glass. Its cultivation under glass has long been practised; but, strange to say, it has generally occupied the position of an interloper, and been assigned a place merely on the back wall of a vinery, or in pits under the shade of vines and peaches. Under such circumstances it never can develop its capabilities, either as to its prolific fruit-bearing character or flavour, and no wonder, therefore, that it has not been much thought of. It is now treated differently, and more in accordance with its nature and requirements; and houses entirely devoted to fig-culture either in pots or planted out, are daily becoming much more common. When its excellence as a fruit, and the fact that, unlike most other fruits, it bears two and even three crops yearly, are considered, the wonder is that it is not more thought of than it is.

[1] Lindley's Treasury of Botany.

FIG-HOUSE.

The successful cultivation of the fig does not necessitate any peculiar or special arrangements in providing a structure suitable for it, provided it has plenty of light and means of ventilation, and a moderate command of heat. It is successfully cultivated trained

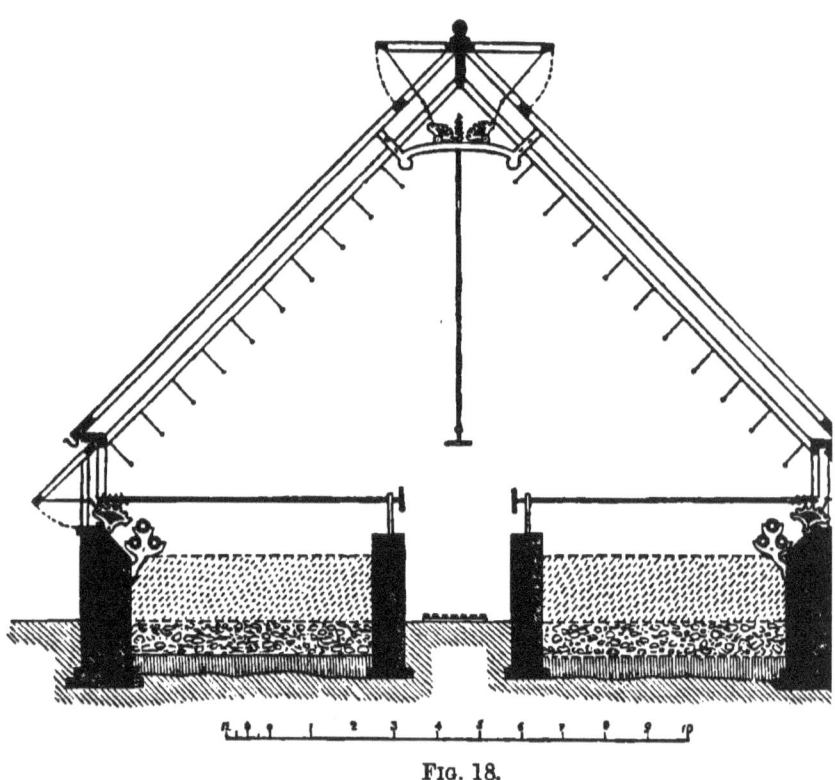

FIG. 18.

on trellises all over the roofs of houses in all respects like vineries and peach-houses, both lean-to and span-roofed in form—in narrower houses, mere glass cases, trained to the back wall like a peach—or planted out in pits of less dimensions, in bush form like a gooseberry or currant, or with its roots confined to pots of by no means large dimensions. In short, it is the most accommodating of fruits in this respect, and good crops can be produced in all these forms of erections, provided they are otherwise properly managed. As in the case of all other fruits, I recommend that for early forcing the lean-to form be adopted, and the trees trained near the glass, just like vines. For late crops the span-roofed form is to be recommended, as providing the greatest fruiting surface at least expense. Fig. 18 represents a span-roofed house well adapted for the latter, and shows also the arrangement which I consider best as to the bed for the soil or border. Over-luxuriance, and therefore unfruitfulness, must always be provided against in the culture of the fig; hence I recommend the space for the roots to be limited and perfectly under control, and in wet cold localities entirely under glass, at least for some years after the trees are planted. Should their after-condition indicate that they would be benefited by an extension of the border outwards, it can easily be carried out. Like the peach, the fig when growing likes a moist atmosphere, and a steaming-tray on the pipes should always be provided, especially when early forcing is practised. The roof should be wired the same as for vines.

SOIL AND FORMATION OF BORDER.

The fig is not by any means difficult to accommodate with soil, provided it is not rich nor resting on a damp bottom. Naturally it is a most luxuriant grower, producing in rich soils immense growth and foliage with next to no fruit. To secure well-ripened fruitful wood, this tendency has to be taken into account, and requires to be counteracted by the constituents of which the border is formed. Two parts loamy soil—such as has been recommended for vines, but lighter — and one part old lime-rubbish, without manure of any sort, forms a border sufficiently rich for several years without any assistance but water, and it forms an excellent channel for applying manure either by top-dressing or in a liquid form when such becomes necessary. These two constituents should be thoroughly mixed together, in a dry state, before being put into the bed. If loam fresh and turfy cannot be procured, common garden-soil that is not highly impregnated with manure can be substituted with success—for, as has been already remarked, the fig is not by any means fastidious.

Where the subsoil is clayey, or cold and damp, the roots should not have access to it, therefore the whole of the site should be effectually concreted. To have the individual trees entirely under control, the site for the soil should be intersected by walls formed of brick to separate the roots of each tree entirely from those of its fellows. This leaves the cultivator every chance of treating individual varieties and trees as circumstances may suggest, without interfering with any other. The width of these spaces should be determined by the length of roof or rafter. For such as is represented by fig. 18, each compartment may be from 10 to 12 feet, that being sufficient space for each tree. Immediately over the concrete two efficient tile-drains from each compartment should be led into the main drain running underneath the pathway. Over the whole bottom broken bricks or road-metal to the depth of 8 inches should be laid, and blinded with some finer material, such as coarse sandless gravel. With a turf grassy side downwards all over this drainage, the site is ready for the soil; and, to begin with, it should not be filled in more than 20 inches deep, rather firmly packed, leaving 4 inches for the addition of top-dressings when such become necessary.

VARIETIES OF FIGS.

In order to keep up a constant succession of ripe figs for a good many months of the year, as shall be treated of, not very many varieties are necessary. Taking into consideration the fruitfulness and good qualities of figs in cultivation, I do not know of any so thoroughly satisfactory as the old and well-known Brown Turkey and White Marseilles (Raby Castle). These are splendid varieties for both pot-culture and fruiting in borders. Some smaller varieties are extremely fruitful, such as Black Provence, Singleton, White Ischia, and others; but they are small, and not so desirable as those first named. Mr Barron, Garden Superintendent at the Royal Horticultural Gardens, who has had great opportunities of forming an opinion, and who has excelled in the pot-culture of the fig, in writing regarding keeping up a rich and varied supply from a house devoted to the cultivation of the fig in pots, and where the collection is limited to say fifty plants, gives the following as his selection for keeping up a continuous supply of ripe fruit from June to Christmas. The varieties he puts into groups thus, showing how they will give a supply of fruit in each month: "July—White Marseilles, De la Madeleine, Gros Monstrueuse de Lipardi, Brown Turkey. August — White Marseilles, Lee's Perpetual (Brown Turkey), De Lipardi. September—White Ischia, Grosse Violette de Bourdeaux, Black Provence, Grosse Verte, Bourjassotte Grisie, Col de

Signora Blanca, De l'Archipel, and the second crop of White Marseilles and Lee's Perpetual. October— White Ischia, Black Provence, Grosse Verte, Bourjassotte Grisie, Col de Signora Blanca, and Col de Signora Nera. November—White Ischia, Grosse Verte, Lee's Perpetual, D'Agen. December—White Ischia, D'Agen, the latest of all." Negro Largo is also a fine variety for pot-culture, but our experience of it when planted out is that it is a shy fruiter.

Where, however, space is limited so that such a collection is impracticable, I recommend as the most constantly prolific and otherwise excellent, the varieties I first named. They are medium-sized and of excellent flavour. What the Black Hamburg is among grapes, I consider Brown Turkey to be among figs; and in small gardens, where space for only one variety can be afforded, this is the most constantly prolific, and otherwise satisfactory.

PROPAGATION.

The fig is perhaps the most easily propagated of all the more tender fruit-bearing trees or bushes. Wherever a branch touches the soil in the growing season, it there very speedily throws out roots, and can therefore be very readily increased by layering. It also produces suckers freely, and these can be detached and trained into any form required. It is easily increased by eyes or cuttings in spring, much the same as is practised in vine propagation. I, however, prefer plants propagated by cuttings, for all purposes and forms of training. The cuttings should be selected and detached from the trees while in a dormant state, laid in by the heels in moist soil, where severe frost cannot affect them, and where, at the same time, they will be kept cool. The straightest, shortest-jointed, and best-ripened growths of the previous season, about 8 inches long, having a strong terminal bud, are best. In detaching them from the parent plant, take with them an inch or two of the two-year-old wood. All that is necessary in preparing them for the cutting-pots is to cut them cleanly through just at the union of the one year's growth with the other. The middle of February is a good time to put them into heat. Drain the required number of 4-inch pots efficiently, and fill them firmly with sandy loam. Make a hole in the centre of each for a single cutting, and place a little sand under their base and round them. Water them, to settle the sand firmly about them, and plunge the pots in a bottom-heat of 80° to 85° where the temperature of the air does not exceed 60° at night, and shade them during sunshine. It is desirable that the formation of roots should be as nearly as possible contemporaneous with top-growth. A rather strong bottom with a comparatively low air temperature favours this. Over-watering must be avoided, and if they are placed in a close propagating-house, pine-pit, or dung-frame, very little will be necessary to keep the soil moderately moist until the buds begin to push and leaves are formed, after which their getting once very dry may prove fatal to them. If they do not root when they have formed a leaf or two, they do so very soon after. Until they do form roots keep the foliage moist, and do not expose them to over-much air. By turning a plant or two carefully out of their pots it can easily be ascertained when they have formed roots, after which gradually dispense with shading, and air more freely.

Allow them to grow in the 4-inch pots till they have

well filled them with roots. Then shift them into 6-inch pots, draining them well, and using one-year-old turfy loam without any manurial addition. They will now grow rapidly without bottom-heat, should have as much light as possible, and be aired sufficiently to keep them from making weakly long-jointed growths. Figs are very fond of moisture, and may now be well syringed every sunny day at shutting-up time, which should be sufficiently early to cause the heat to run to 80° for a short time, but not subjecting them to a higher night temperature than 60° to 68°, according to the weather.

The description of cuttings I have recommended have generally a cluster of buds near their points; and as their training must begin with their growth, these buds must be dealt with accordingly. Whether the plants are ultimately intended for pot-culture or as bushes, or trained trees on trellises near the glass, I in all cases prefer a plant with a clean stem of from 10 to 12 inches at least. All lateral growths must therefore be removed, or rather prevented by rubbing off the buds, and the leader alone allowed to grow to the desired height, when the top bud should be pinched out. When to be planted out and trained to a trellis 2 or 3 feet below the level of the first wire, the height at which they are stopped must be regulated accordingly. I consider it of the greatest moment in the successful culture of the fig that every tree or bush for pot-culture or planting out should be trained with a clean stem. When allowed to form growths sucker-fashion near the surface of the soil, it is impossible to balance the trees with uniformly fruitful growths. As I am now treating of plants to be planted in borders, and trained near to the glass like vines, I will leave the training most desirable for pot-plants for the present, as their cultivation in pots will embrace that point also. Their natural inclination, when in a young state, to grow too rampant, makes it most desirable that plants being reared for planting in borders should be induced, if possible, to form a stubby habit of growth before being planted out. Therefore I do not recommend their being planted the year they are propagated, but to be confined to a rather small pot with poor soil. When they have formed a leading shoot to the desired height, been stopped, and have broken two or three buds at the top, shift them out of the 6-inch into 8-inch pots, and place them in a light house, where they will make short-jointed and well-ripened wood.

If, after being stopped, they break into more than three growths, rub off all except the leader and one on each side of the stem. Should any of them break with less than three, cut a nick above the one that is desired to break, and more than likely it will come away. When the leader has grown about 15 inches, stop it and the two laterals again, to cause another pair of lateral growths to break horizontally, and with another leader, thus laying the foundation for their being trained horizontally to the wires of the fig-house. They can be kept growing thus in a temperature not quite so high as for vines till the middle or end of August, after which they will require more air and a drier atmosphere, in as light a place as possible, to thoroughly ripen their growths. It is astonishing the immense bushes that can be formed the first season even from single eyes, if shifted on and pinched; but the object in the case of the plants now under consideration, as has already been stated, is not so much size the first year, as a well-compacted growth, and a proper foundation for permanent horizontally-trained trees in the fig-house border. It is questionable if it would be any loss of time, in bringing trees into a fruitful condition, to keep the plants two instead of one year in comparatively small pots, to get them into what may be termed a semi-stunted growth.

As soon as they have ripened their wood and shed their leaves, they can be stored away in any place where they will neither be exposed to severe frost nor to a temperature high enough to excite them into growth before spring, keeping them just moist at the root, but nothing more. About midwinter they should be pruned, if they require any pruning at all, after the way which I have recommended them to be stopped when growing. The trees will have a leading shoot and two pairs of horizontal growths. If the leading shoot is, however, longer than is sufficient to reach to two wires of the fig-house beyond the highest pair of laterals, cut it back to that extent; and if the lateral growths are not thoroughly ripened, shorten them back to firm wood. Remove all the buds with the point of a sharp knife from the leader, except the highest three, one of which will form the leader, and the two next to it the lateral growths to train right and left to the wires, and other two buds to break into growth, to furnish the lowest unfurnished wire: thus leaving on the leading stem of last season's growth five buds to furnish a leading, and two pairs of horizontal growths for the two lowest unfurnished wires. By pruning the trees when at rest, they do not bleed so much as when cut in spring with the sap in motion.

THE FIG.

TIME AND MANNER OF PLANTING.

The best time to plant young trees, the preparation of which has just been detailed, is in spring, when they begin to swell their buds, and are about to start into growth. If kept in a cool place, as recommended, this will take place about the end of March or early in April, according to the mildness or coldness of the season. As has already been stated, the counteraction of the fig's natural tendency to a gross unfruitful growth in the younger stages of its progress is always an important point, necessary to the speedy furnishing of a fig-house with fruitful wood. The method of planting must also be directed to this end. Perhaps a less gross growth can be had the first season by just turning the matted balls of roots out of their pots, and inserting them entire into the border, ramming the soil firmly about them. Such a mode of planting any tree is highly objectionable, and in the case of figs there will be strong roots coiled at the very bottom of the balls, which will strike deeply down into the border, leaving the surface parts of it unoccupied with roots for a long time, and consequently less under the control of the cultivator. Moreover, by planting this way there are sure to be some gross roots that will be the means of producing gross shoots in certain parts of the tree.

The best way is to entirely shake the soil from the roots, carefully disentangle them, and cut closely back all the thickest of them, leaving those only which are more fibry and close to the stem; and in the operation of planting, to spread these regularly out in the border, covering them with not more than 3 or 4 inches of soil. Before planting, presuming that the border is made of such porous material as has been recommended, and not wet, it should be trodden firmly down before the trees are planted. This prevents it from holding so much water in suspension as when in a more loose and spongy condition, and, as a consequence, assists in checking a too vigorous growth. When the trees are all planted, at from 10 to 12 feet apart, the surface of the border should be slightly higher than it is ultimately intended to be, as it will in course of time subside a little. Settle the soil about the roots with water applied through a rose. Tie the trees loosely, for the present, in their places, training the main stem straight up the roof of the house, the laterals horizontally to the wires, and they are ready for a start.

Of course, in planting a house in this way there will be ample light admitted to the body of it for a few years, to admit of a row of figs in pots being grown on each side of the passage, either plunging them in the border, or placing them on the surface. These will yield a supply of fruit till the permanent trees come well into bearing. Some plant a double quantity of trees, and remove the supernumeraries as the permanent require the space. But seeing that planted-out trees never bear very freely for several years after being planted, I recommend those in pots in preference until they become unnecessary and impracticable from the extension and bearing condition of the planted-out trees, which are far less troublesome than plants in pots, unless in the case of very early forcing perhaps.

TRAINING AND GENERAL MANAGEMENT THE FIRST YEAR.

Immediately the trees are planted, keep the night temperature at 55°, allowing it to increase 10° or 15° by day with sunshine. As soon as they have well burst their buds into growth, raise the night temperature to 60°, with a corresponding increase by day. Keep the atmosphere genially moist, and syringe the trees freely with tepid water early in the morning and when the house is shut up in the afternoon. Give more or less air every day, according to the weather. Watch the progress of the buds, and if the three terminal buds directed to be left at pruning-time start freely into growth, and the two lower ones do not show signs of also moving freely, cut a notch into the wood with a sharp knife immediately above the latter, to check the flow of sap past them, and they will grow more in proportion with those higher up.

With the syringings recommended and a moist atmosphere they will not require water applied immediately to their roots for some time—not at least till they have formed some leaves, and have begun to grow freely. Even then avoid giving them too copious a supply. Just give sufficient in conjunction with the syringings to prevent their being checked injuriously for want of it; otherwise the tendency to produce strong growths will be promoted. As the season advances and less fire-heat is required, advance the temperature to 65° and to 70° at night. As the trees grow more rapidly, give a corresponding amount of air, always in conjunction with sprinklings, to keep the air moist and the foliage free from red-spider.

Usually the leading shoot pushes away into growth with greater vigour than the lateral; advantage should be taken of this tendency to manipulate it so as to get it to throw out lateral growths right and left, instead of allowing it to push ahead without doing so, and the following season to have to cut it back to get it to break regularly. There are two ways of handling this leading growth to get it to furnish the wires with horizontal growths the first season. The one is to pinch or rather bruise the point of it a little below each wire, so as to completely check or stop its growth, and cause it to burst into growth at the axils of the leaves, one of which growths is again trained as the leader, to be again stopped for the same purpose, and the other two trained right and left to the wires. This method does not result in so straight and trim a main stem as is the case with the second method, which is to allow the leader to force on its way till it has passed three or more of the wires, then to be stopped and have a notch cut half-way through it at those buds that are best situated for furnishing the wires with what may be termed cordon shoots. This will nearly always cause these buds to swell and grow a little, especially if the leaders of the lower and stronger cordon branches are stopped at the same time. In the case of strong-growing varieties it is astonishing the extent of foundation that can thus be laid for the future tree in one season. The system of allowing great growthy leaders to extend themselves and rob the lower portion of the tree, then to be cut back perhaps to the first or second unfurnished wire in spring, is a great waste of plant force and time too; besides, it tends to the production of a few strong unfruitful growths, instead of a greater number of more fruitful ones.

The lateral growths formed the previous year, when the young plants were in pots, should be dealt with in the same way as the main stem, it being necessary that they also should be furnished with lateral shoots, to supply the fruit-bearing wood of the future.

Throughout the whole season the trees should be subject to a moist atmosphere and liberal syringings, for the fig in a growing state delights in moisture; and when not sufficiently supplied with it, red-spider is sure to infest it. This is more especially essential as they should not be over-stimulated at the root with either water or manure of any kind before they come freely into bearing. The result at the close of the first season should be as much of the formation in the way of shaping the trees as possible with moderately strong but thoroughly matured growths. At the close of the season nothing should be withheld that is necessary to thoroughly consolidate or ripen the wood. Fire-heat should be increased in October, and the air kept dry and circulating about them till this end is thoroughly attained.

PRUNING AND PINCHING.

When the trees have shed their leaves, they should be kept comparatively dry at the root all winter. What pruning is necessary should be performed in winter when they are at rest. Very little pruning will, however, suffice, if their summer growths have been produced and regulated according to the foregoing directions. There will be the main stems, with the cordon branches that were established the previous year, when the young plants were in pots,—now extending right and left to about four feet,—with their

194   FRUIT CULTURE UNDER GLASS.

lateral growths at regular intervals, and the cordon growths produced this season. My practice in pruning figs thus trained horizontally, and from which two crops are to be annually ripened, differs somewhat from that usually pursued, and may be described as a mixture of vine-pruning on the close-spur system and ordinary peach-pruning. The accompanying woodcut, fig. 19, will illustrate at a glance what I mean by this, and serve for the rule which I consider the best in fig-pruning generally. It may be explained to the tyro, that the first crop of fruit produced in fig-forcing is got from the young wood of the previous summer's

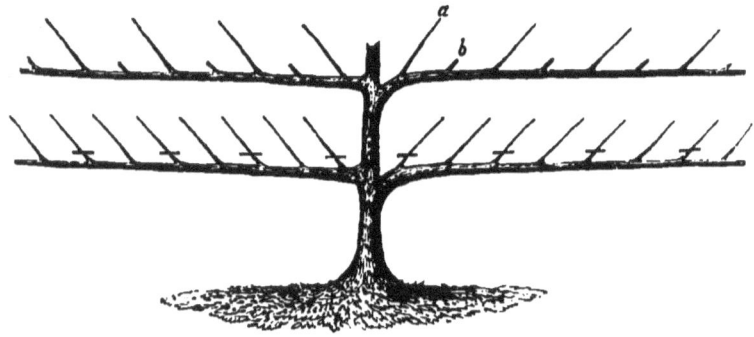

Fig. 19.

growth; and the second, which ripens generally in September and October, from the young growths of the same summer, and which are produced contemporaneously with the first crop of fruit on the previous season's growths. In order to have a regular crop over all the tree at these two seasons, this habit must be borne in mind, and the pruning performed accordingly, so that the trees may be regularly furnished with these two sets of growths. According to the illustration, there are the main, or cordon branches, furnished with a set of lateral fruit-bearing growths. I

THE FIG.

recommend that every alternate lateral be pruned back to an eye, at *b*, as is generally practised with the vine. The other shoots are left as the summer pinching is supposed to have left them, and will, if well ripened and short-jointed, produce a fig at every bud, especially those near their tops. Those cut back may form more than one eye; when this is the case, all should be rubbed off but one, to be stopped by pinching or bruising its point, when it has grown to from five to seven joints, after which stopping it very soon forces fruit from the axils of the leaves, which fruit ripens in autumn. All attempts at fresh growth beyond these autumn fruits should be rubbed off as they make their appearance. In the case of the previous year's wood, bearing the first or early crop, a couple of joints of young growth is all that should be allowed. In the case of a well-established tree, with its roots thoroughly under control, and in a fertile state, this system of pruning and summer pinching, it can easily be seen, directs the efforts of the plant to the production of fruit, and only as much young wood as is necessary for next season's crop. The young wood produced this summer is that on which next season's early crop is produced, so that the early fruit-bearing wood is that which in the winter pruning is spurred back—*i.e.*, shoot *b* is cut back this year, and shoot *a* the next.

The fig can thus be systematically pruned without the too common confusion of a lot of haphazard growths in all directions, either to be lopped off with the knife, causing unnecessary wounds and bleeding, or to be tied up in confused unmeaning bundles, serving no purpose whatever. A little trouble and attention in the way of directing the summer growths to form trees thus into cordon, or horizontal leaders, with lateral fruit-bearing growths, to be alternately spurred back, reduces the management, and yearly pruning and pinching, to as simple a routine as that of spur-pruning the vine, and has great advantages over the system of tying in three times more growths every season than are required, to be cut away in winter, sadly mutilating the trees.

Root-Pruning.—For the first few years after young figs are planted, root-pruning should be as carefully attended to as the training and pruning of the trees themselves, otherwise they will not so soon be brought into a fruitful condition. The roots should be seen to at the time of winter pruning. A trench should be taken out down to the drainage round each tree at about 3 feet from the stems, and the roots carefully disentangled, lifted back to within 20 inches of the stem, preserving all the finer fibry roots, and cutting back those that are strong. The second year the same process should be attended to, but not encroaching so near the stem. In my own experience I have found that in limited and not too rich borders, two root-prunings have been sufficient to bring the trees into free bearing, unless it be some of the more gross-growing and generally the least desirable sorts. Such free-fruiting and desirable varieties as Brown Turkey, Grosse Verte, and Raby Castle can be brought into free-bearing condition by two root-prunings, with the system of pruning and pinching the tops that has been recommended.

Before treating of the general management in forcing the fig so as to keep up a supply of fruit from May till the beginning of winter, I will now refer to figs in pots, as they form an important feature, especially in the very early forcing of the fig.

FIGS IN POTS.

There is perhaps no other fruit-bearing bush or tree that is more manageable or more productive when confined to pots than the fig. In this way it is most serviceable and easily cultivated throughout the season. But it is especially when very early forcing is required that plants in pots are to be recommended. They can also be made to bear in a very young and small state. I have struck them from eyes in February, and by shifting and pinching have formed comparatively large heads on a clear stem in 9-inch pots, with a good sprinkling of ripe fruit on them late in the autumn of the same year. This refers to Brown Turkey and one or two of the most free-fruiting varieties. For the propagation of figs to be permanently cultivated in pots, I refer to the directions already given under that head, as the process does not differ in any way from that recommended in the case of plants for planting in borders. The training of pot-plants is, however, different, inasmuch as the object desired is a plant with a bush-like head of bearing branches and twigs. As in the case of plants for borders, plants with clean single stems, about a foot high, are best for pots —such plants as may be described as dwarf standards.

Training, Pruning, &c.—Fig. 20, engraved from a photograph, represents a plant four years old from the cutting, in an 11-inch pot, bearing its second crop of fruit of the same season. It bore two heavy crops the previous year. To form such a plant, the point was pinched out of the cutting when about a foot high. When the several shoots with which it broke away into growth were long and strong enough to bear it, they were occasionally bent downwards with the hand, and when they had grown 6 or 7 inches long, they had the terminal bud pinched out of them, and these shoots started away again with generally two growths. The plants were then shifted into 8-inch pots, and encouraged to grow in a warm moist house with plenty of light and air. After being well ripened they were pruned back,

FIG. 20.

each shoot to three eyes, except some which were short and stubby enough not to require it. The following spring it was, along with several dozens of others, some larger and some less, but all the same age, shifted into 11-inch pots after they began to grow, and they bore two good crops, and have made plants that, with top-dressing and manure-watering, would continue for several years to bear fine fruit in the same pots. Still it is desirable to give them a small annual shift until they are put into 15-inch pots, which are large enough for any purpose. After they get into pots of the last-named size, and when they require stimulants in the way of fresh soil, the best way is to partially shake them out about the latter end of October, and cut back some of the strongest roots and pot them in fresh soil. By this means they can be kept in excellent bearing condition for many years.

After they begin to bear they require next to no winter pruning. It should all be done by summer pinching, removing entirely superfluous growths that would crowd the plants—pinching those that are left at every third or fourth joint. Varieties vary very much in their habit of growth; some make grosser and longer-jointed wood than others, and require to be cut back after the leaves are shed. Such varieties, as a rule, are not so useful for pot-culture as the more stubby growers, and they seldom yield a satisfactory first crop, but bear chiefly a second crop on the young wood. These varieties are of course to be avoided when early fruit is desired, and it is for early crops that pot-figs are especially valuable. Always in winter pruning, wherever it is necessary, leave untouched all short stubby growths with a cluster of buds near their tops. These are the most fruitful parts of the trees, and are freely produced by well-established trees when bearing heavy crops.

While the plants are young and being trained, it is often necessary, in order to form the heads into proper symmetry, to have recourse to staking and tying the shoots or branches in their proper places. After the plants get established, and what in pot-culture may be termed full grown, neither this nor much pruning is required beyond cutting out old wood to make room for new as occasion may require.

Soil for figs in pots.—The soil for plants in pots should be richer than has been recommended for borders. Two-thirds of rather a strong loam, with a third of horse-droppings and a little bone-meal, answers well in all pottings after the trees have arrived at a fruit-bearing condition. I have sometimes plunged the pots in borders of soil for summer and autumn fruiting, and let them root through into the border, but do not recommend the practice. I approve of plunging the pots, but not of letting the roots leave the pots, and it should always be prevented. It induces the active roots to leave the pots where they are regularly fed, and causes gross shoots to be formed at the expense of the fruit and the general growth of the other parts of the trees. This applies more particularly to young growing trees. In the case of older and free-bearing trees there is less objection to the practice.

FORCING AND GENERAL MANAGEMENT.

There is perhaps no other fruit-bearing plant that submits with greater freedom and success than the fig to early forcing, and it certainly yields under favourable treatment a very good return in the shape of two crops of fruit annually. In some cases it has been made to produce a third crop by commencing to force early, and prolonging the process late in the season; but although this is possible, it is by no means desirable—for, besides the debilitating influence on the plants, the third crop is never fine in quality.

THE FIG.

Where a regular succession of ripe figs is required from April to November, I recommend that there be a set of plants in pots, and another planted out, as has been treated of. Those in pots should be started about the new year, to ripen their first crop in April and May, and their second in July and August. Those planted out in borders, if started at the end of February or beginning of March, ripen their first crop in the end of May and June, and their second will be all gathered before the middle of October, thus keeping up the supply of ripe figs for at least six months of the year.

In beginning to force those in pots at, say, the beginning of January, it is very desirable that they be supplied with a gentle bottom-heat. Although this is not absolutely necessary, yet they start more freely into growth, the young fruit is less likely to drop off, and it swells better with bottom-heat than without. A house or pit in which figs can be thus early forced, may be, and generally is, used for other purposes besides. In some cases early strawberries are forced along with them on shelves on the back wall near the glass; in others, a pot-vine is fruited on each rafter; and in others, all these three fruits are forced in the same house. But there is no doubt that where circumstances admit of all these having compartments to themselves, they can be forced with less trouble and more success.

TEMPERATURE, WATERING, ETC.

In early forcing of every description, a lean-to light house, with a good command of both top and bottom heat, is best for figs. If oak-leaves can easily be got, it does not matter much whether the bottom-heat is wholly derived from a bed of leaves of considerable depth, say $3\frac{1}{2}$ to 4 feet, or from a lesser quantity of them in conjunction with hot water circulating below them. So long as a bottom-heat of about 75° can be maintained, it does not matter much which system is pursued.

Supposing that a set of pot-plants are at command in a well-ripened and fruitful state, and that ripe figs are required by the end of April, by the 1st of January they should be plunged to the rim in the leaves. If there has been any red-spider on them the previous year, let the shoots be well washed with a soft brush and water, and then painted with a little sulphur, soot, and clay, well mixed together in water. Remove any loose soil that may be on the surface of the balls, and replace it with loam and horse-droppings in equal proportions. In plunging them, give them sufficient room to allow the leaves and young growths to expand without crowding. Give a good watering of water at 80°. See that the bottom-heat ranges about 75°, and that the night temperature is kept steadily at 50°, with an increase of 8° or 10° by day, till they show signs of growth, and the young fruit have begun to swell. Then raise the temperature to 60° at night, with a corresponding increase by day. Give air freely on all favourable opportunities, and syringe the trees morning and evening with water a few degrees warmer than the atmosphere of the house. After the young fruit get to the size of nuts, over-syringing must be avoided, especially in dull weather, as an excess of water at the root, in conjunction with a too free use of the syringe, has a tendency to cause the fruit, especially in dull weather, to become yellow,

THE FIG.

and drop off before the setting process is past. At the same time avoid an arid atmosphere, or a check from want of water at the root. Either extreme must be avoided until it be seen that the fruit are out of danger. But with well-ripened wood and bottom-heat, the fruit are rarely lost. As soon as the young growths have made four or five joints, pinch out the terminal bud, and increase the temperature to 65° in mild weather. When the second crop has fairly shown itself, feed the plants liberally with liquid manure, as there is then a great demand on the energies of the plant. Manure-water, made from sheep's dung and soot, should be given in a weak clear state every alternate watering; or guano, at the rate of a handful to a large garden watering-pot of water, answers well.

RIPENING THE FRUIT.

Until the first crop begins to show signs of ripening, keep the atmosphere moist, and syringe at least at shutting-up time on all fine days; but as soon as they begin to ripen discontinue syringing. Give more air and just sufficient water at the root to keep the foliage and second crop of fruit healthy and free from danger, otherwise the flavour of the first crop when early will be deficient, and a badly ripened fig is a very insipid production. But I would here warn the inexperienced against an extreme of drought either at the root or in the air; for this would place the second crop in jeopardy. Circumstances must be modified to meet as much as possible the welfare of both crops.

The ripening stage is easily detected: the fruit suddenly complete their second swelling; the skin cracks longitudinally, and frequently it drops down from the neck of the fruit, becoming soft at its junction with the stalk. To gather a fig in perfection, it should be allowed to hang till the juice begins to exude from its eye or apex. Of course, if they have to be packed and sent to a distance, they should be gathered a little earlier than if just to be sent to the table.

SECOND CROP.

As soon as the first crop is all gathered, give every encouragement to the second, especially as the natural heat of the season has increased. The temperature may range a few degrees higher; syringing be resumed and practised regularly on all fine days; and more water can be given at the root. The house may be shut up in the afternoon with a temperature of 80° to 85° according to the weather, with a corresponding degree of atmospheric moisture. The fig is very fond of heat especially derived from the sun, and also of a moist atmosphere.

When the second crop begins to ripen, air liberally, and give just sufficient water to keep the system active and healthy, but no more. As soon as the fruit are all gathered, should there be any signs of redspider, syringe the foliage vigorously with water in which a little sulphur is mixed. Look over the trees, and remove entirely any growths that seem at all to crowd the bushes; and when the wood is ripened, remove the plants to the open air, plunging them in a place where they can have full sun, and keep them well watered until the leaves drop.

The routine of forcing trees planted out in borders does not differ in any essential point from the foregoing directions. They of course require less frequent watering at the root than plants in pots. Still, after the trees have thoroughly filled the border with roots and have covered the roof of the house with fruit-bearing wood, they require copious supplies of water and liberal annual top-dressing with rotten manure. When bearing heavy crops, ordinary manure, or guano-water, should be liberally supplied to them. Except when the fruit are ripening, it is not easy to over-water a limited border filled with one mass of fig-roots. In the first few years of their growth and forcing, it is, as has already been stated, undesirable to over-feed them. Old fig-trees that are properly managed sometimes show more fruit than it is desirable to have, and it is advisable to thin them slightly; for, as in the case of most other fruits, a lesser quantity of fine figs is more satisfactory than a greater number of inferior ones.

To have the first crop of fruit ripe on planted-out figs between the time that the first crop is over and the coming in of the second in pots, the time to begin forcing the former must be regulated by the time at which those in pots have been started. If they are started at the new year, the fig-house proper should be started in about eight or ten weeks after.

INSECTS AND DISEASES.

Red-spider and thrips are the chief insects that infest the foliage of the fig. The former is sure to attack the trees if they are kept too dry at the root and the syringe not freely used, but it rarely becomes formidable when they are sufficiently supplied with moisture. Thrips must be kept in check by occasional fumigations with tobacco-smoke, but never when the fruit are ripe, as they will taste of the tobacco. Mealy-bug, when it gets on to fig-trees, is very troublesome. The best way to get rid of it is to scrub the trees with soapy water, and then syringe them with paraffin at the rate of a wine-glassful to a gallon of water, syringing well with clean water a few minutes after.

The fig is comparatively free from diseases. I have seen trees affected with canker—in one instance the cause was stagnant water about the roots—for want of thorough draining.

PACKING FIGS.

To pack ripe figs to go safely to a distance requires great care. Tin boxes divided into compartments, as directed in the case of peaches, are indispensable, if the fruit are to be allowed to ripen and to be carried without mutilation. The compartments, of course, need not be so large as for peaches. Into each put some fine paper-shavings, then a layer of cotton wadding, and over the wadding a square of tissue-paper sufficiently large to come up the sides of the compartments to the top. Wrap each fruit in a tender dry vine-leaf and lay it in its place, covering it over with another leaf to keep the paper from contact with the fruit. Then double the tissue-paper over all, fill up with cotton wool, lay a little paper-shavings all over the surface of the box, and screw down as directed in the case of peaches. When figs have to be packed, it is best to gather the fruit before the juice begins to ooze out of them, but not till they rend slightly at the sides.

THE MELON.

PERSIA is the acknowledged home of the melon (*Cucumis melo*), where it has been regarded for ages not as a luxury, but as one of the necessaries of life. It is the richest of all soft fleshy fruits. The date of its culture in Europe is so remote that the time of its introduction is not capable of being recorded. The Romans, as far back as the time of Tiberius—who is said to have had a special liking for melons—cultivated them by means of artificial heat, from which it would appear that forcing was an art not unknown to the Romans. The cultivation of melons has been general in England since the middle of the sixteenth century. Although many of the varieties now in cultivation are very fine, they are not generally regarded such safe or wholesome fruits as to be liberally partaken of in this cold climate. Many, however, are passionately fond of them; and, to say the least of them, they are an interesting fruit to cultivate, and have a handsome appearance in the dessert. In too many instances, however, quality is sacrificed to external appearance; for often the more common-looking and smaller fruits are much superior in flavour to those that are large and handsome.

The varieties of melons that have been and are now in cultivation may be said to be almost innumerable. So exceedingly simple and certain—indeed so difficult of prevention where more than one variety are cultivated in the same garden—is their hybridisation, that every season is productive of fresh varieties in the majority of gardens. There are, however, three distinct types, which are known as the scarlet-fleshed, the varieties of which have sprung from the more hardy Cantaloupe; the green-fleshed, from the Egyptian green-fleshed; and the white-fleshed, from the more tender Persian varieties. The green-fleshed are the least attractive in appearance, but are generally the best flavoured in this country. The scarlets have of late years had some excellent additions to their lists. Some of the white-fleshed are thin-skinned, finely flavoured, and handsome; but to bring them to perfection requires more heat, and especially intense sunshine, than this country affords. According to the statements of travellers, there are melons in Bokhara and Turkestan which far surpass any cultivated in this country. But probably the intense sun and aridity of the atmosphere, with the attention paid to supply them liberally with water, may have more to do with their lusciousness and flavour than mere varieties; and they are, besides, more exquisitely relished in these hot dry countries than in this comparatively cold and sunless latitude, where they can only be cultivated under glass, aided with artificial heat both in the soil and air.

The chief improvement which has been effected in melon-culture during this generation may be said to consist in their being more generally cultivated in melon-houses, trained near the glass on wire trellises;

and the fruit being thus raised off the soil and suspended in the air, places them in a position more conducive to good flavour than when cultivated on the dung-bed system. And setting the fruit is more certain on the trellis system than when the plants are trained on the surface of the soil and unaided by the drier heat of hot-water pipes. Very early and late crops are less precarious and troublesome than when the heat is dependent on fermenting materials alone. Knowing that there are still plenty of gardeners and amateur growers all over the kingdom who have to raise their crops of melons by means of the old fermenting dung-bed and frames, to make these directions as comprehensive as the circumstances demand, both systems will be treated of. South of the Humber, in England, very little preparation is required to produce a crop of melons in the hottest months of the year in pits and frames, which in the earlier part of the year are generally used for hardening off flower-garden plants, without the means of applying artificial heat. In the neighbourhood of London, I have regularly grown good crops by merely putting about a foot of half-decayed leaves or stable-manure in the frame under the soil. In the north, however, seasons of such sunlight and heat as would enable this to be effected without a little artificial heat do not often occur; and in such localities it is always best to prepare accordingly, and to choose certainly not the most tender and uncertain varieties for summer culture in frames not supplied with fire-heat.

Plenty of melons have, however, been ripened in May by means of hotbeds, common garden frames and pits, but not without much care and labour. For very early and late crops this old system is not now to be recommended, in the case of any who can devote a few lights of a pit or house heated with hot water to the purpose, but can be successfully and with comparatively little trouble adopted for the intermediate crops in the hottest part of the season. Therefore, to embrace all classes of growers, I will treat of both the dung-bed and the melon-house systems.

GROWING MELONS IN DUNG-BEDS OR PITS.

The preparations necessary for constructing a seed-bed for melons being the very same as for cucumbers, in connection with which we shall detail them,—knowing that early cucumbers are more generally cultivated than very early melons,—we will not now occupy space in giving the process here, but refer our readers to the chapter on cucumber-culture. With the same appliances as for cucumbers, the same sort of pits recommended for fruiting cucumbers in answers for melons; and when they are fruited on an ordinary hotbed and frame, the heat is maintained in the same way as recommended in the case of the seed-bed for raising cucumber-plants. In fact, if melons and cucumber-plants are to be raised at the same time, the same frame answers for both.

Although melon-culture by this means has often been commenced on the 1st of January, and fruit sent to table early in May, it is a task involving the most incessant watchfulness, and is attended with more or less of uncertainty unless the spring be unusually fine. Hence I do not recommend an earlier commencement than the 1st of February, from which time even it is not for a novice to carry out the various steps in the process. Indeed it can scarcely be considered a judi-

THE MELON. 211

cious direction of means and labour to commence so early without more certain appliances than fermenting material and common frames. However, as the mode of raising and general treatment of melons started thus early will meet the case of those who do not commence till later in the season, I will suppose, in order to meet all cases, an early start, and treat accordingly.

SOWING THE SEED, AND MANAGEMENT OF YOUNG PLANTS.

If possible, choose seed not older than three or four years, of some early good-constitutioned variety, and steep the seeds in water for twelve hours before sowing them. At the same time prepare the required number of 4-inch pots, by placing one crock over the hole in their bottoms, and half-filling them with pure moderately moist yellow loam, and place them in the seed-frame to warm the soil. Sow three or four seeds in each pot, covering them with a quarter of an inch of the loam, and do not water them for the present. They should be plunged so as to get a bottom-heat of about 85°, and let the pots lean to the south, so that the young plants may get the sun when they peep through the soil. The temperature of the air should range from 72° to 75°. In the case of fermenting beds the heat at night has to be chiefly regulated by the amount of covering over the glass, and by air-giving, which latter requires to be watchfully attended to, especially in fitful weather. As soon as the young seedlings come up and expand their seed-lobes, showing which are to be the two healthiest and dwarfest plants, remove the others, and mould up the stems with warm rather dry loam, filling up the pot with two earthings after the plants have grown above the rims of the pots. Very moist soil is apt to cause damping, especially in dull weather, when more vapour of necessity collects in the frame. It is very necessary to leave a little chink of air on the frame all night, especially when mild and damp; but great care is required to prevent gusts of cold air from reaching the plants, and a screen of canvas should be suspended over the opening in cold windy weather. When the heat is more than 75° at uncovering time in the morning, increase the air, but this must not be to such an extent as will prevent an increase of heat with sun to 80° or 85° by day, and at covering-up time the amount of covering must be regulated by the temperature of the frame, and the weather. Nothing is so injurious to young melon-plants as an over-close moist atmosphere at night, with too much heat. It draws them up pale and weakly, and renders them less likely to bear exposure to sun by day, which is so desirable, except after a time of sunless weather, when a little shade is often needed on the first sunny day.

Do not give any water so long as the soil remains moist, and until it becomes manifest that they are really in need of it; in watering, do not wet the leaves. Generally speaking, the soil remains sufficiently moist till they show their rough leaves, and it is much better that such should be the case—for, with short sunless days, water would only serve to weaken them, if it did not cause them to damp off altogether; besides, in a drier soil they make a more numerous brood of active rootlets.

The application of fresh warm linings must be provided for by having a heap of fermenting material always ready. And air-giving, to keep the bed sweet and free from steam, must receive extra attention with the application of every fresh lining.

TRAINING AND STOPPING.

When the first rough leaf is expanded, and a leading shoot is formed, the training of the plants must be determined by their subsequent treatment. If they are to be grown on a trellis raised a little above the soil in a brick pit, heated by fermenting material, their leaders must not be pinched, and of course the same is applicable to those that are to be fruited in more modern melon-houses,—I may say that it also applies to what I consider the best way of planting and training them in an ordinary dung-frame. The common practice in this latter case is to pinch out the leading shoot as soon as it is formed. This forces the plants to form several growths, which, when they have grown to 5 or 6 inches, and the pots are moderately filled with roots, renders the plants ready for being planted out in the fruiting-bed—two in the centre of each light. Three shoots are trained from each plant—the shoots of one to the back, and those of the other to the front of the frame, one shoot towards each corner, and the other to the middle of the light. These shoots are stopped when within 8 or 10 inches of the side of the frame, and the laterals which they throw out produce the fruit. In this case the plants are twice stopped and of course twice checked. What I recommend in preference to this system is not to stop the plants at all, but to plant them out—as soon as their leading shoot is about 6 inches long—one pot with two plants to every two feet in length of the fruiting-bed

—the one plant to be trained due north and the other south, pinching off all attempts at lateral growth from the base of the plant at the seed-lobes, but allowing the leader to grow on unstopped, till it reaches within a foot of the side of the frame, when, if stopped, it will quickly throw out lateral growths with fruit, just the same as in the former case,—the difference in favour of the latter way of training being that the single leader reaches the desired length sooner, consequently bears stopping, and forms fruiting laterals sooner than those plants stopped young, and brought away with three growths. Of course this once-stopping system requires nearly double the number of plants to fill a frame, but in all other respects it is the best for speedy fruiting. These two systems of planting and training must determine whether the plants are to be stopped when young; and to obviate the necessity of referring again particularly to stopping, I will now explain that immediately the female blossoms with the embryo fruit appear, the lateral shoot must be stopped two joints beyond the fruit, after which the blossoms soon expand, the shoots and leaves rapidly increase in size, and it will be found that there will just be about enough of foliage thus produced to cover the whole bed. All late laterals must afterwards be pinched off, unless some be necessary to cover the surface of the soil, which is desirable; but these should not be left on the fruit-bearing lateral, provided no harm occurs to the main leaves.

SOIL AND PLANTING, ETC.

Like most other fruit-bearing plants, the melon thrives best in loamy or calcareous soil—rather adhesive than otherwise. The top 6 inches of an old pasture that has been stacked in the compost-yard for twelve months is to be preferred. For the production of early melons, in the comparative absence of sun, I do not recommend any addition of manure, especially on dung-beds, as melon-roots generally penetrate beyond the soil and feed on the manure and leaves of which the bed is composed. Neither do I recommend the soil for very early melons to be so retentive as is desirable for their summer culture. In preparing such soil for being put into the frames, the turfy portions of it should be broken up with the hand or with a spade, and the rough and fine portions well mixed together. Wire-worms are most destructive to young melon-plants; and if there be any in the soil, it should be carefully examined and the worms removed. As soon as the fruiting-bed has begun to heat, place a ridge of the soil 1 foot deep, about 2 feet wide at base, and tapering to 8 or 9 inches at top, along the centre of the frame. The ridge should be pressed firmly with the hands as it is formed, but not beaten with a mallet, as is frequently the case, especially if it is heavy. On hot-beds such as are now being considered, it is a safe plan to place thin turfs, grassy side downwards, all the length and width of the ridge of soil. It prevents the likelihood of the roots of the plants being burned by too violent a heat. All the remaining surface of the bed should then be covered with 2 inches of the loam, rather firmly pressed down, to prevent steam from escaping too freely into the frame. As soon as the temperature of the ridge of soil has risen to 80° or 85°, and the plants are ready to plant as already referred to, let them be carefully turned out of their pots, and planted two in the centre of each light, if they are such as have been stopped when young; but if not stopped, two every 2 feet apart, placing them sufficiently deep in the soil to have the seed-leaves about half an inch clear above the surface. If the loam is moderately moist, the weather dull, and less air required, it will not be necessary to water the plants when planted, nor as long as they appear to prosper satisfactorily without it. The state of the weather must, however, determine this. If the sun comes out brightly, and the plants show signs of drooping when the necessary air is on, let them be watered. Shading in all stages of melon-culture is an evil which should only be resorted to when the grower is compelled by bright sunshine after a time of dull weather,—a state of things which, early in the season, must be carefully watched, for a half-hour's neglect will destroy the plants if the frame is not properly aired and shaded—less air, of course, being required when shading is necessary. The bottom-heat, too, is apt to be dangerously increased with sunshine; and as soon as it exceeds 95°, it is a safe plan to bore a row of holes along each side of the ridge to let the heat escape.

MOULDING UP—TEMPERATURE.

After the plants fairly take with the soil and have begun to grow freely, look out for their roots at the side of the ridge. As soon as they appear, cover them with 2 inches of warm loam—this to be repeated as soon as the roots take possession of each successive layer. The original ridge, especially in the case of early melons, should be left a few inches higher than these additions of soil. The bed, by the time the final earthing-up is given, should slope to about 6 inches deep of soil at the sides of the frame. For later crops a greater depth is necessary, but for early crops this is enough.

The night temperature, after the plants are planted, should range from 72° to 75°, as near as that can be maintained. And, of course, as in the case of seed-beds, this has to be regulated and kept up by coverings, linings, and air-giving. Air-giving should be attended to by degrees, as the day progresses and sunshine strengthens; and it requires to be taken off in the same careful way in the after-part of the day, shutting up with sun-heat at a temperature of 90°, and especially while the heat of the frame is high—after it is newly put up—putting on a chink of air for the night, if they are good close frames or pits. In early spring it is seldom that much artificial moisture has to be made in the frame. This, of course, depends much on the amount of sunshine and air given; and the rule should be to prevent an arid atmosphere, or the surface of the soil from getting dry, by dewing it over with tepid water from a syringe at shutting-up time. It is seldom that much more watering than this is required with early crops until after the melons are set.

IMPREGNATION, WATERING, ETC.

The system of training and stopping already described (page 213) will have to be attended to as the plants extend themselves towards the sides of the frame. And if they are all stopped at one time, so much the better, because they are then almost sure to have the female blossoms expanded and ready for being impregnated at the same time, which is very desirable, as the frame requires to be kept dry and the plants not watered while the crop is being thus secured. As soon as the blooms are perfectly expanded, the pollen loose and powdery in the male flower, remove from the latter the corolla and apply it to the centre of the female, giving it a turn round, and leaving it resting in the centre of the bloom. This simple operation should be performed in the middle of the day, when the sun is out and air on the frames, under which circumstances the pollen is most likely to be dry and effective. They must be daily examined and attended to in this way until a full crop is set. This is easily known by the blossoms shutting up, the fruit to which they are attached becoming of a shining healthy hue, and swelling rapidly. If two plants are planted every 2 feet, as already recommended for early or indeed any crops, two fruit will be sufficient to each plant, which will yield eight fruit to every light, or 4 feet run of the frame. Of course, if more fruit are desired, they will not be so large and fine. Immediately the fruit are set, and it is evident they are swelling, the superfluous ones should be removed and the soil watered, as it generally is dry after the setting-time, and the rapidly swelling fruits make great demands on the plants. Let the water be soft rain or pond water, in all cases a few degrees warmer than the soil in the frame. It is very undesirable to be giving driblets of water at short intervals. Let each watering be thorough, so that it be the seldomer necessary. Generally two waterings after they are set are sufficient to carry the fruit to maturity, as the surface of the bed is completely shaded with foliage. No water should be given at this early season, after the fruits have ceased to increase in size, or they will be very apt to burst and be spoilt. Besides, much moisture in the soil is inimical to good flavour, and a flavourless melon is a very useless production. If they show any signs of suffering before the fruit begin to change colour, syringe the foliage and sides of the bed gently, in preference to giving a root-watering, but this must cease immediately there are the least signs of ripening. At all times avoid watering close to the collar of the plants. It is apt to cause damping and canker at the neck of the plant; and besides, the active roots are nearer the sides of the frame. As soon as the fruit are set, place a piece of tile or slate under each, to keep them off the damp soil; and, if possible, lay them on their crown, a position in which they are generally sent to table. If grown and ripened on their side, they are generally more or less disfigured. As soon as they are full grown, raise them on a pot or piece of smooth brick above the foliage, so that sun and air can play freely about them and ripen them well, taking care that they are placed so that water cannot gather about that portion of them resting on the tile.

During bright weather in April and May, a gentle sprinkling overhead, when the fruits are swelling off, at shutting-up time, is very refreshing to them, and keeps up the necessary humidity of the atmosphere. This must be discontinued immediately the fruits begin to ripen. If a fruit or two should be required as early as possible, dry some clean fine sand and cover up the fruit with it. The sun shining on this covering of sand places the fruit within it in a higher temperature, and it matures more rapidly.

When they have attained their full size, do not let the heat of the bed decline; and as they give signs of colouring and ripening, which they often do suddenly, increase the air, but do not decrease the warmth. It is easily known when they are ripe by the aroma, and more correctly by the rind cracking round the union of the stem with the fruit. They are then ready to be detached from the plant and placed in a fruit-room to cool, after which they are ready for table.

Such is the routine of melon-culture early in the season by means of dung-frames or pits. The same points of culture apply to their midsummer culture by the same means, only the conditions necessary are secured with much less attention and anxiety. More moisture in proportion to sun - heat and light is necessary, and in the heat of summer one barrow-load of well-rotted manure may be added to every five of loam. The loam itself may be somewhat heavier than for spring growth, and a depth equal to that recommended for the ridges—namely, 1 foot—put firmly all over the surface of the bed.

CULTURE IN MELON-HOUSES TRAINED ON WIRES NEAR THE GLASS—FORM OF HOUSE, DEPTH OF SOIL, ETC.

In this case the first consideration is the shape and size of houses, as well as their aspect. And as in the case of the early forcing of all fruits either in winter, early spring, or autumn, lean-to houses with a due south aspect are decidedly the best for melons. For summer culture, span-roofed houses running north and south may be considered the best. I have, however, no difficulty with summer and early autumn crops in the north aspect of houses running east and west. Indeed, the difference only consists in the desirable one, of the crop from those on the north forming a succession to those on the south aspect. This, however, only holds good in the case of those not planted before May, nor ripened after the middle of October. The best arrangement in the case of those who have only a melon-house of limited extent, and who at the same time desire to have melons continuously, say from the end of May to November, is to produce their earliest and latest crops from the melon-house, and to fill up the interval with a summer supply from dung-frames or pits, in which case I decidedly advise the lean-to form, as shown and described in connection with cucumbers, p. 264. Where a supply is required only from July till the middle of October, the span-roofed house is best, and it is desirable to have it divided into three successional compartments of equal proportions. Although I have succeeded in bringing on three successional crops in one long division perfectly well, yet these crops would be better in separate divisions, inasmuch as when the melons planted for the first and second crops are ripe, these compartments can be more successfully and conveniently used for anything else—such, for instance, as tomatoes that have been grown in pots in the open air, and many other things besides. When in more than one compartment, the heating should be arranged so as to be able to heat sufficiently all at once, or to heat each separately; and also that the bottom and top heat-supplying pipes can be worked independent of each other. Although great blunders have now and again been committed in glazing such houses with obscure glass, it need scarcely, at this period of horticulture, be necessary to warn against such glass in the case of all forcing-houses intended for tropical fruits.

It will be seen from the section of the house I recommend, that the bed for the soil is 18 inches deep. This depth may not be necessary for very early and late forcing, but for crops in the heat of summer I recommend a depth of soil of from 12 to 14 inches, according as the loam may be lighter or more adhesive in texture; and have a decided objection to laying the loam on the pavement without an intervening layer of at least 4 inches of broken bricks or stones, so as to let water escape freely from the soil, thus keeping it sweet and wholesome. I have always noticed that a body of close soil laid on smooth stone or wooden surfaces, without some material to act as drainage, becomes soured and inert next these surfaces. The side ventilators, whether they be in the form of glass upright lights or wooden ventilators in the side walls, should have perforated zinc nailed over the openings, to moderate the entrance of cold air when such is required; and the openings should be either directly under or opposite the hot-water pipes, so that the air may be heated in entering the house. Unless it be in summer weather, when the fruit are setting or ripening, I do not recommend front or side ventilation. My general aversion to very small houses, where a steady and high temperature has to be maintained, is as strong in the case of melons as in that of forcing vines and peaches; and consequently I recommend something more extensive than a place that can just be crept into, which is in every respect inconvenient and undesirable.

I have recommended a greater depth of soil for melon-houses where the plants are more fully surrounded by light and air than in a dung-bed, for the same reason it should be a little richer, and certainly not less retentive. For summer crops I have always put all the soil required in the beds before the melons were planted. In the case of early crops in melon-houses, I recommend a mean between that for which directions have been given for dung-frames—namely, to fill in the soil at three times as the roots extend.

PREPARING THE PLANTS, PLANTING, ETC.

Little need be added on preparing the plants for the melon-house trellis system of training, as the only difference between it and that recommended for the speedier fruiting in the dung-bed is, that in the melon-house they are trained to wires near the glass, and in the latter along the surface of the soil. As soon as plants in 4- or 5-inch pots (I use the smaller for spring and the larger for summer plants, having in this case a single plant in a pot) are 8 or 9 inches high, with the soil well occupied but not matted with roots, and the soil is warm in the beds, they are ready for planting. One plant every 2 feet is sufficient, but not too thick for this one-stem system of training. The plant should be put in perpendicular, with the first wire at the front or side of the house, and tied to a stake till it reaches the wire. In summer planting I always settle the soil about the balls with water at 85° to 90° immediately they are planted. The balls being moderately moist when planted, I seldom find that shading is necessary, unless it be when a continuance of dull weather is succeeded by brilliant sunshine. Then a thin shade is applied, but only till the plants can do without it. When the hot-water pipes are in front and close to the plants, it is always best to screen each plant by a thin piece of board from the drying influence of the pipes, until they are fairly established. Another precaution in planting is to keep the plant raised above the general level of the bed, by placing a ring of smooth round stones, flints, or pieces of charcoal, about 6 inches in circumference, round the plant. This I recommend as a provision against the not unfrequent cankering or damping of the stems just at the surface of the soil, which when thus elevated, and not watered within the protecting circle, is not so likely to be troublesome.

WATERING, ETC.

It is a most difficult thing in all cases to give definite rules, as far as frequency or the reverse is concerned, for watering. In this case it must depend, as in nearly all others, on the state of the weather, and to some extent on the lightness or heaviness of the soil. I make it a rule to water melon-beds as seldom, but as thoroughly when required, as possible. Suffice it to say that melon-plants should never flag from over-dryness of the soil, nor the bed be allowed to crack; otherwise the plants and crop are sure to suffer: the foliage will get yellow and sickly, and become a prey to red-spider. With bottom-heat derived from hot-water pipes, the tendency of the soil to become dry is greater than on the dung-bed;

consequently more water is required, and the necessity for thorough soakings when it is supplied is more urgent. Except perhaps in the height of summer, two or three good waterings, with the ordinary sprinklings before the fruit are set, and as many after that stage, are sufficient to bring the crop to maturity. As soon as the crop is set, I always mulch the surface of the bed with rather more than 1 inch of short manure, to prevent evaporation and the bed from cracking, and to nourish the crop. This is in all respects preferable to more frequent watering. After the fruit are all set, manure-water made of sheep or cow manure, applied alternately with guano at the rate of an ounce to every gallon of water, is beneficial.

TEMPERATURE AND SYRINGING.

The bottom-heat should range from 80° to 85°, the temperature of the air in early spring at 70° at night, and be raised to 75° when the weather becomes more genial, and less fire-heat is required to keep the temperature up. With the sun-heat by day, a rise of 10° to 15° may be allowed. The moisture of the air must be regulated according as the weather is bright or dull; when bright, with frosty nights, the moisture must be greater than when dull, and sufficient to prevent the atmosphere from feeling dry on entering the house. Except when the plants are in bloom and setting, gentle syringings are more frequently required in melon-houses than in frames; and every afternoon, when the day is bright, and a maximum of air has been admitted, a gentle syringing is very refreshing to them. In the morning the walls and paths should be damped, but not the plants themselves, as under bright sun they are apt to suffer when moisture is hanging about the foliage.

VENTILATION.

Ventilation, in the earlier stages of their growth particularly, must be very carefully managed. Sudden draughts of cold air are to be avoided, and the temperature should never be allowed to reach its maximum before air is given. It should be attended to by degrees till 12 o'clock, and gradually reduced as the sun declines in power. In dull mild weather avoid by all means keeping the house close and overmoist, under which circumstances the plants grow rapidly, with less consolidation, and therefore suffer, or require too much shading when the weather changes and becomes more bright. I am not an advocate for front or side ventilation early in the season, when there is a great difference between the internal and external temperatures. Top air under such circumstances is sufficient then to effect the change of air that is required. When the fruits are setting and ripening are the only times that I give front air, even in summer, unless the weather be exceptionally hot and calm.

IMPREGNATION, TRAINING, AND STOPPING.

The impregnation of the fruit requires the same attention in melon-houses as in frames, only the operation is less frequently a failure. Indeed there is next to no uncertainty attending it, unless in the case of very early forcing, when the setting process is not quite so free. In training and stopping the plants I generally adopt the close-stopping system—that is, to restrict the growth of the plants within the limits of the allotted space for each by pinching the growths constantly at two joints beyond the fruit, and leaving those shoots from which fruit is not taken to grow sufficiently to cover the whole of the trellis or wires with foliage without being crowded. A different system is successfully pursued by others. The plants are allowed to grow more at will, and set the first fruit irrespective of their being simultaneous, or nearly so, over the whole plant. In this way a more rambling growth is allowed, and fruit set at intervals as they show themselves; and thus fewer melons are ripened at once, but a longer succession is derived from one set of plants. In the case of those who have only a few lights to devote to melons, the practice has much to recommend it. Where there is room for succession on the more restricted system, I confess to prefer seeing a good crop coming forward at once. Even when melons in one compartment are all set within a few days, it is singular the difference there is in the time of their ripening, and the succession they on that account keep up.

VERY EARLY FORCING.

Very early forcing is much more certain with good melon-houses than with dung-beds; and in some cases the seed is sown the end of November, and the plants planted in the fruiting-house the first week of January. This, however, is not a practice to be recommended in the case of the inexperienced grower, for even with the best of appliances there is much careful balancing of circumstances required. But so early a start is an exception, not the rule. In some cases these early crops are produced in pots. January and February may be more generally named as the times at which melon-culture even in melon-houses is commenced. All other things being equal, those which are started then ripen fruit in May and June, before which time the flavour of melons is only second-rate. Later in the season they of course come to maturity in less time.

The remarks which have already been made regarding the ripening of the fruit need not be repeated here. Only I would just observe, that I do not practise the excessive drying at the root system in summer crops which is sometimes followed. I give more air, and allow the light to play freely about the fruit, but avoid starving them. Even if it did improve the flavour, such treatment would be against other fruits which have not just arrived at the finishing-point. And it is indispensable to quality in melons that the foliage be preserved intact till they perfect their crop.

When grown trained to wires thus, the fruit should be supported as soon as they show that there is an undue strain upon the stem. This is an unnatural attitude for melons, and they require support. I prefer small square pieces of common garden-net or hexagon netting with a piece of cord, or, what is better, an elastic band at each corner, so that as the fruit expands the support yields. Square pieces of porcelain have been used and recommended for this, but I have discontinued them, because moisture gathers more or less about the crown of the melon when it rests on such supports, and disfigures it. This does not apply to netting.

THE MELON.

VARIETIES.

The varieties in cultivation are so numerous, and every district has its favourite varieties more or less peculiar to itself, that there is perhaps more difference of opinion and less recognition of any standard varieties among growers of the melon than in the case of any other fruit. From my own experience in widely different localities and soils, I am inclined to think that certain kinds do better in some districts than others.

Varieties of Melons.

Colston Bassett—White-fleshed.
* Gilbert's Improved—Green-fleshed.
* Dell's Hybrid—Green-fleshed.
Golden Queen—Green-fleshed.
Heckfield Hybrid—Green-fleshed.
Cox's Golden Gem—Whitish-green-fleshed.
Bailey's Green-fleshed—Green-fleshed.
Bromham Hall—Green-fleshed.
* Golden Perfection—Green-fleshed.

These varieties are all good, but if making choice of only three, I should choose those marked thus (*).

INSECTS AND DISEASES.

Green-fly, red-spider, and thrips infest the melon. The best way to destroy them is to sponge the leaves carefully with a soft sponge moistened with weak tobacco-water, immediately either or both of these pests appear. To smoke with tobacco severely enough to destroy is very apt to injure the edges of the tender leaves. In spring the syringe should be applied occasionally in bright afternoons at shutting-up time.

Green-fly can be kept in check by the syringe also, and is easier killed than the thrip with moderate fumigations of tobacco-smoke. Melon-plants are affected with a corky-looking enlargement of the stem, generally called canker, just above the surface of the ground. Some varieties are more subject to this than others. The best preventive is to keep the soil about the collars of the plants a little higher than the bed, and to put some charcoal-dust round the stem, and not to apply water at that part.

THE STRAWBERRY.

The varieties of strawberries in cultivation have originally sprung from several species of *Fragaria*. Those known as the pine varieties have originated from *F. grandiflora*, a native of Carolina; the Hautbois have sprung from *F. eliator*, a native of England; the Scarlets from *F. Virginiana*, a native of Virginia. It was about the beginning of the sixteenth century that the scarlet varieties were introduced into this country, previous to which it is supposed our own wood or wild strawberry was the only one available.

The strawberry is a grateful and universally esteemed fruit. As a member of the dessert it is at all times most welcome, more especially in the spring of the year, when luscious fresh fruits are least plentiful and most expensive in the markets. The culture of the strawberry in pots for forcing is now very general in gardens of the most moderate pretensions, and the art of forcing it has become very perfect as compared with what I recollect it to have been. It is not now an uncommon thing, in the more extensive forcing establishments, to force from three to six thousand pots annually. The strawberry is, however, one of those fruits which can be forced more or less by all who possess a glass-house or pit, it being a fruit that can be ripened in great perfection in almost any glass structure, without any artificial heat, a little before it is fit to gather in the garden quarters.

THE BEST RUNNERS.

To be successful in forcing the strawberry early, it is of very great importance to get young fresh plants established and well matured in pots early in the season.

In the course of many years' successful practice, I have tried various ways of getting early healthy runners. Besides other methods I have allowed the parent plants to produce young runners when being forced in March, April, and May. These have been rooted under glass in small pots, hardened off, and grown on in the usual way. Very small runners have been selected from outdoor plantations in autumn, and pricked off in light rich soil, and lifted and potted about midsummer. I have left the runners on those which ripened their fruit in April and May, planted out the parent plants, carefully preserving these runners, and layering the young plants produced in this way. The last named is the best of these three methods, and plenty of first-rate plants for forcing are so produced. But the best way that I have ever adopted, either in England or Scotland, is to make a plantation of the best runners that can be had in September from those plants that were forced the previous spring. These young plants were planted expressly for the purpose of producing fine strong early runners for potting the following summer.

THE STRAWBERRY.

This autumn plantation should be made in a warm situation, in a rather light, well manured and worked soil, in lines 2 feet apart, and only 6 inches apart in the line. This close planting I adopted simply for the sake of procuring the necessary stock for potting in the smallest and most convenient space, it being much more convenient to lay and attend to them after they are laid than when scattered over a greater space. These autumn-planted runners in their turn throw out beautiful strong runners early in the season, and these are chosen for the production of plants for early forcing the following season. In ordinary seasons they are ready to lay the second week of June, which is earlier than ever I have been able to get as fine runners from plants forced and planted out in spring; and in ordinary cases older plantations of strawberries produce "spindly" runners that never make such fine plants as those produced by the method described.

PREPARING RUNNERS FOR THEIR FRUITING-POTS.

In preparing the young runners for their fruiting-pots, I have also tried various ways—such as spreading equal proportions of loam and leaf-mould between the rows, and laying them in it without pots. At other times I have crocked and filled the fruiting-pots with soil, and laid the runners at once into them. But while both these methods can be adopted with success, I prefer, as soon as the young plants begin to push out roots, to lay them in 3-inch pots firmly filled with two parts friable loam and one part of leaf-mould. These pots are plunged between the rows of strawberries, a single runner laid on each pot and gently pressed into the soil, taking care not to bury the heart of the young plant. A small stone is then laid on the stem immediately behind the young plant, to keep it firmly in its place. A peg of wood answers the same purpose, but the placing of the stone is fully more convenient, and it serves to conserve moisture in dry weather. All the runners should be stopped beyond the plant laid, and in dry weather they require to be well watered every afternoon. Managed in this way, they can be removed expeditiously, and without the least check, when well rooted and ready to be put into their fruiting-pots, which is generally in about three or four weeks after they are laid. If they are required for ripening fruit, say in the early part of March, they are most satisfactory when shifted into their fruiting-pots between the first and middle of July—a few days either earlier or later are not of much importance. The guiding-point should be the condition of the young plants. They should be well rooted, without being what gardeners called matted. A safe criterion is to shift them just as soon as they are sufficiently rooted to enable them to be potted without the ball being broken. When laid in fine soil without pots, they should be lifted and potted when sufficiently rooted to make them easily lifted with balls and without mutilating their roots.

SOIL AND POTTING, ETC.

The size of the fruiting-pots is of much importance: 5- and 6-inch pots I have always found most satisfactory. In the case of all plants from which ripe fruit are to be produced by the middle of March, 5-inch pots are to be preferred. For those to be forced later in the season, pots 1 inch or at most 2 inches larger are to be recommended. In the smaller size, when forced early they throw up their bloom-stalks more strongly, set better, and yield as large fruit as in larger sizes. The larger size is better later in the season, when the plants require much more attention in watering. I have tried experiments by selecting some of the very finest plants and shifting them into 8-inch pots, but the result was never satisfactory. For any plant to force well, it is of the first importance to have the pot thoroughly filled with roots; and in larger pots than those recommended, this condition is more difficult of attainment. . The pots should either be new from the pottery, or thoroughly washed and dry. And they should be carefully crocked; for although the strawberry requires much moisture, it never thrives in a soured soil or with stagnant water. There should be an inch of small crocks in the bottom of the pots, and over all a little of the fibry part of the soil.

The selection of soil with which to pot or shift into the fruiting-pots is of much importance. Presuming that one-third of the plants are to be put into 5-inch pots for early forcing, choose for them a friable hazelly loam, and mix with every three barrow-loads of it one of thoroughly decomposed manure, consisting of an old hot or mushroom bed in a dry state, and sifted through a $\frac{1}{2}$-inch sieve, so that it can be well incorporated with the loam. To every four barrow-loads of this add an 8-inch potful of bone-meal; mix the whole well; and instead of removing any of the fibry part of the loam, grind every morsel of it through a $\frac{3}{4}$-inch sieve, as large lumps of it become inconvenient in shifting into such small pots; moreover, the fibre gets more completely equalised and incorporated with the general compost. If a good, rather light loam cannot be procured for these early plants, a heavier loam can be lightened by adding a small portion of clean gritty sand, or, what is preferable, some finely sifted old mortar or old plaster-lime. For those intended to ripen fruit from the beginning of April onwards to the time of outdoor strawberries, 6- or 7-inch pots are to be preferred, and also a loam of a rather more holding or adhesive character, but mixed with the same manurial ingredients recommended for the early plants; a more retentive soil being more suitable for the sunnier months of April and May, when more moisture is required.

In shifting the plants, the soil should be firmly packed round the balls, so as to get as much of it into the space as possible, and also to prevent the too free escape of water between the ball and sides of the pot. Care should be taken that the hearts of the plants are not immersed in the soil; and there should be at least a quarter of an inch of the pot left unfilled up, so that the watering can be effectually done.

When shifted, they should be thoroughly watered through a rose, and allowed to stand in some position where they can escape the mid-day sun for a few days. Then remove them to some warm place where they can have the full sun all day, and at the same time be sheltered from high winds, which would lash and injure the foliage. I have generally placed the plants on a raised trellis-work, in order to prevent worms from getting into the pots, and the plants from rooting through into the ground. This precaution in the latter case is very necessary; for if placed on the ground they are sure to root through, and if left to themselves the roots will to a great extent desert the pots. In the case of the smaller pots, which

THE STRAWBERRY.

dry most rapidly, it is well to pack the space between them with half-decomposed leaves or moss. In placing them, they should be quite level, and have as much room as will allow each plant to stand quite clear of its fellow.

Watering must now be carefully attended to. The pots being efficiently drained, and the soil firmly packed in them, there is little fear of over-watering them so long as they continue in active growth. In very hot weather they may require watering morning and afternoon; and on the evenings of very warm days a syringing overhead, just as the sun is leaving them, is very refreshing to them. But the syringing must be discontinued when the dews of autumn nights set in. As soon as the roots reach the sides and bottoms of the pots, liquid manure may be given every other day. Clear soot-water, guano, sheep or deer's manure water, are all excellent for strawberries. The principal point in applying water is to make sure that the whole ball is thoroughly soaked; and in applying liquid manures, not to slop it about the foliage, on which it leaves more or less of a sediment. Should the plants break away into several weaker crowns, remove all but the strongest as soon as this tendency is observed: one good strong crown in a pot is much better than several weaker ones.

Do not allow a weed to appear in the pots; prevent every attempt at runner-making; and occasionally stir the surface of the soil, adding a light sprinkling of fine soil, in which is mixed a little Standen's manure or soot, and press all firmly down again. Under such treatment, it will be found, on turning them out of their pots by the end of September, that the balls appear literally roots, and nothing else; so much so, that they might be thrown across the garden without the ball being broken. The crowns will be firm, well developed, like the end of a man's thumb, the footstalks of the leaves strong and short, supporting broad, dark-green, leathery leaves,—sure criterions of the plants being in the best possible condition for forcing the following spring.

Should the weather be very wet in October, I would recommend that the plants be placed in cold frames, where they can be protected by glass from continuous rains, and fully exposed when the weather is fine. When this cannot be done, lay them down on their sides rather than expose them to continuous rains. By the end of October they will have completed their season's growth, and the object in regard to them now is to rest them, and protect them in a cool state from heavy rains and hard frost. Where cold frames covered with glass can be spared for them, perhaps they are best stored in them, having the pots plunged in ashes, half-decayed leaves, or sawdust. They should have plenty of air on all favourable opportunities; and during severe frost a single mat or a little dry straw thrown over the glass is protection sufficient. When cold frames or any cool place under glass could not be spared, I have kept them perfectly safe by building them into ridges, laying one row on their sides above the other, and packing between and round the pots with ashes or sawdust. In this way they escape rains, and are preserved from getting dry or excited, and in times of severe frosts are easily covered with mats of straw, easily uncovered in fine weather, and as easily got at when required for forcing. Wherever wintered, the soil should never be allowed to get dry, or the roots will suffer severely.

STRAWBERRY-HOUSE.

Having prepared strawberry-plants in pots for forcing, the next chief consideration is a suitable place in which to force them. The strawberry is in this respect, except in comparatively few garden establishments, left unprovided for in any special way, and many thousand plants are forced without what may be termed a strawberry-house. Indeed it is a subject so accommodating that it can be forced in the pit, the peach-house, the vinery, and the pinery, or by the aid of all these combined. At the same time, where there are many to be fruited annually, a house entirely devoted to themselves is not only better for them, but for the other plants and fruits with which they have so frequently to be accommodated in the same structure. Moreover, a strawberry-house can be so arranged as to answer perfectly well for other things after the season of strawberry-forcing is over. Fig. 21 is what I recommend as a very suitable and efficient strawberry-house. The bed in front, supplied with bottom-heat, is an excellent place for starting early strawberries. The back stage is supposed to be movable, if it should be considered necessary, so that, after the strawberry season is over, cucumbers, melons, and tomatoes, or young vines—in fact, many things can be grown in the back bed after the removal of the stage. In the early part of the season, the bed under the stage is available for rhubarb and seakale if necessary, or the whole house may be devoted to plant-growing throughout the summer, and until required again for strawberries. The command of such a house for strawberries allows the gardener to give them the exact treatment required. Where there are many grown, it would be best to have two divisions of such a house—the one for starting them, and the other for fruiting them in. I shall, however,

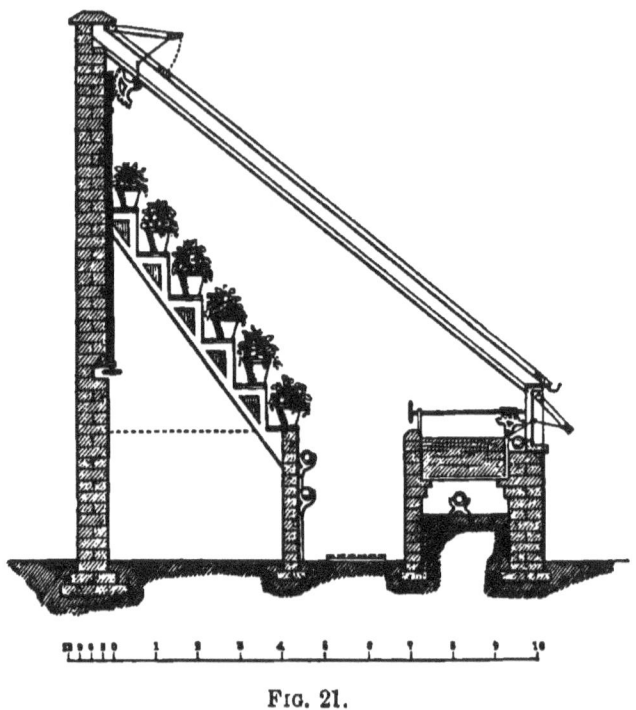

Fig. 21.

treat of strawberry-forcing in a general way, as if no such house were at command, and as being most likely to meet the case of the greatest number of readers.

FORCING.

For very early forcing, it is of much importance to aid them with a gentle bottom-heat, which can easily be effected by plunging them in a bed of leaves or tan near the glass, where the bottom-heat ranges about 75°; and when they have started into growth, they can then be moved to shelves near the glass in early

THE STRAWBERRY.

started vineries and peach-houses, where no special house for them exists, and a succession of plants can take their place in the pit.

The time when ripe strawberries are required must of course regulate the time when forcing should begin. It generally takes three months from the time the plants are started till the fruit is ripe. When forcing is commenced very early, say the middle of November, a week or 14 days more must be taken into the count. The best variety to begin with thus early is Black Prince; and plants of it introduced into heat about the 14th November will ripen their fruit the last week of February. Keen's Seedling, the next best early variety, takes 10 days more. Unless, however, there be a large stock of plants and early crops are imperative, it is not desirable to begin forcing so early. There is a degree of uncertainty and loss, generally amounting to nearly one-half the plants, in the case of those set agoing in November. A full half of the plants cannot be expected to set anything like a crop of strawberries. In fact, those that are started before the last week of December, are about the most uncertain crop that can be attempted, especially where there is no well-appointed strawberry-house. Under ordinary circumstances, I do not recommend firing to begin before January, not only on account of the uncertainty of the produce, but because strawberries ripened in comparatively sunless weather and a close atmosphere are not very well flavoured.

I will suppose the 1st of January to have arrived, the time when the earliest are, in the majority of cases, placed in heat. Let the required number of the best plants in 5-inch pots be selected, all the brown and much-spotted leaves picked off them, their pots washed clean, and if the roots appear rather bare, firmly top-dress them with a little fine loam and well-decayed cow-manure in equal parts. If, as has been already recommended, a light pit with a bed of warm leaves is at command, plunge the pots in it, so that they may get a slight degree of bottom-heat. Keep the night temperature ranging from 50° to 55°, according as the weather is cold or mild; with sun-heat, 8° or 10° more may be allowed. A close stagnant atmosphere is most antagonistic to the strawberry, consequently give more or less air every day, leaving a very little on all night when mild. Being plunged in moist leaves, watering will not be often required, but it must be attended to before the plants get too dry, so as just to keep the soil moist without being wet. As soon as ever the blooms can be discerned in the centres of the crowns, increase the heat a few degrees, but do not exceed 60° in mild weather. When the trusses are distinctly projected, remove the plants to a shelf near the glass in any structure where the night temperature ranges 60°, with 10° more by day. Avoid putting them where they will be subject to currents of cold air, or where, on the other hand, the atmosphere is close and very moist, such as a plant-stove. A peach-house or vinery is the best place, in the absence of a strawberry-house.

SETTING AND THINNING THE FRUIT, ETC.

When they begin to open their blooms, be careful not to be lavish with fire-heat should the weather be cold and harsh. Under such circumstances rather let the night temperature recede to 55°; and to prevent damp counteracting the process of fertilisation, leave a little air constantly on the house, and go over all the blooms that are ready and fertilise them with a camel-hair brush at mid-day. Those which throw their blooms up boldly above the foliage will be found to set freely; while those that do not, will not be so certain. The conditions most conducive to a successful set early in the season are,—as much light as possible, a regular supply of fresh air, a night temperature not rising above 60° nor receding below 55°, a moderately dry atmosphere, and just sufficient water at the roots to keep the plants in healthy action. Anything like stagnation of water about the roots of strawberries when in bloom is most injurious, and consequently the pots should never be placed in saucers.

When the fruit are set and about the size of peas, the chief difficulty is past. They may then have the temperature ranging from 60° to 65°, with 10° or 15° more with sun-heat. Water will be required more liberally and frequently at the roots. Unless for the later crops, when water is consumed with great rapidity, never place the pots in saucers full of water. The best way in all respects is either to cut pieces of turf and lay below them on the shelves—into them the plants root and derive nourishment—or saucers with holes in them to let the water escape, filled with half loam and half old mushroom-bed manure, can be placed under them with equally nourishing results. The finest fruit I have ever grown in pots had 6-inch pots half filled with rich fresh soil placed under them, and into these they sent their feeders *en masse*. And the pots being so far immersed in others got protection from drying currents of air and sunshine.

A close stagnant atmosphere in dull weather must be avoided after the fruit are set, otherwise they are apt to damp off or rot. A little air night and day at the highest part of the house should be constantly attended to. As the fruit swell and give every indication of a heavy crop, thin off all the smallest, leaving ten or twelve of the best-looking fruit. Every alternate time of watering give either soot, guano, or dung water till they show signs of colouring, when pure water only must be given. At all times the water should be milk-warm, and either rain or soft pond water. When practicable, I have generally moved the plants into another house where the air has been drier when the fruit were nearly ready to gather. A few days in such a place heightens the flavour and colour of the fruit, and it also makes room for bringing on a succession of plants. At all events, more and drier air should, if possible, be afforded them when colouring.

As the season advances, I need scarcely say that the precautions enforced above are not so imperative in the case of succession and late crops; still they must be adhered to, or results will be more or less uncertain. Those that ripen after the month of April can be freely removed to cooler and more airy places, in order to make them higher coloured and better flavoured. And such as ripen the end of May and June, before outdoor fruit are ripe, do well when removed to cold frames when colouring. In these they can have plenty of air by tilting the lights up back and front, or even having the frame supported up off the ground, so that a current of air can play freely about them. When the greater part of the fruit are colouring, they should not have more water than is just enough to keep the plants from drooping. The flavour is thus improved.

INSECTS TO WHICH THEY ARE SUBJECT.

Green-fly and red-spider are very apt to attack strawberry-plants when subject to fire-heat, especially in April and May; and to prevent red-spider gaining a footing, they require to be well syringed every fine afternoon after the fruit are set. And to the same end all checks for want of sufficient water must be guarded against. Green-fly is easily prevented and got rid of by fumigating with tobacco, but it must never be done when they are in bloom. It is a good plan always to smoke before the blooms open. One of the most forcible reasons against growing them in peach-houses and vineries, especially in the latter part of the season, is the frequency with which they breed red-spider, which soon extends to the peaches and vines. Many gardeners are, however, obliged to adhere to the practice, on account of the numbers of plants that have now to be reared under glass, and for want of a strawberry pit or house. That good strawberries are produced thus is beyond a question; but to ripen strawberries on the top shelves of vineries, the vines must not be allowed to run up right to the top of the house on account of the amount of shade which they throw over the strawberries, and under the influence of which they do not thrive. So that in all cases where a division of glass can be devoted to strawberries, it is much to be preferred.

STRAWBERRIES IN A GREENHOUSE OR PIT.

The amateur who pursues horticulture more as a pastime and a pleasure, and who may only possess a pit or greenhouse from which frost is excluded, can, if he fancies them, grow a few dozen strawberries on the shelves near the glass, where he can get several dishes before they can be gathered out of doors. The same can be accomplished in a cold frame, where sun-heat can be taken advantage of, by being shut up early in the afternoons in April and May, and covered at night to prevent the heat from declining so low as in uncovered frames. A well-fruited pot of strawberries makes a most pleasing dinner-table plant, with its green massive leaves and tempting fruit.

TYING UP THE FRUIT-STALKS, ETC.

Some of those varieties, such as President and British Queen, which throw up their fruit on long and more slender footstalks, require to have their trusses supported, otherwise, as the fruit become heavy, they weigh down the stem, and it not unfrequently gets bent and bruised on the edge of the pot, and the fruit is thereby hindered from swelling so well. Where they are grown in rows on shelves, a good way of supporting them is to fix short stout stakes in every fourth or sixth pot, and run a piece of thick soft twine along, on which the trusses can rest; or each truss can be tied to a slender stake.

Immediately the fruit are all gathered, the plants should be removed to cold frames or to some sheltered corner, where they can be protected from spring frosts, and hardened off preparatory to their being planted out for bearing outdoor crops, which they produce in first-rate style the following summer, and a few that same autumn.

THE STRAWBERRY. 247

PACKING RIPE STRAWBERRIES FOR CARRYING.

In these days of steam and express trains, it not unfrequently happens that forced strawberries have to be sent hundreds of miles to the dessert-table, and much of their safe and successful transit depends on the manner in which they are packed. I have been in the habit of sending them from Scotland to London three times weekly, and by the following method of packing they have been received without a bruise: They were packed in square boxes 4 inches deep, divided into four compartments. In the bottom of each division was placed a layer of fine paper-shavings, then a layer of wadding, and over the wadding a sheet of soft, pliable tissue-paper, all firmly pressed down, the one upon the other. On this foundation, with a soft, fresh strawberry-leaf beneath and between each fruit, the strawberries were laid. Over them were placed soft, young vine-leaves, then a sheet of tissue-paper, and then wadding and paper-shavings enough to fill the box as firmly as possible without bruising the fruit, as their safe carriage depends on their being packed sufficiently close and firm to prevent their moving when the box is moved. This is what may be considered an extra-careful way of packing. Generally they are packed in round or square boxes or tins, with just leaves below and above them; and with ordinary usage they carry very well. But fruits sent by rail are often roughly handled; and when fine fruit are produced after months of careful culture, careful packing must be regarded as the gardener's finishing-touch. The boxes in which they are packed should be made of thin deal or tin, in which case two or three storeys or layers of them may be packed into a stronger box.

PREPARING FRUIT FOR EXHIBITION.

In preparing fruit for exhibition, a great amount of careful and skilful generalship is required. Generally speaking, the grower who has a large number of plants to gather from on an exhibition eve, has a very great advantage over the grower with only a few scores of pots, more so than in the case of any other fruit. For with the most careful thinning, it is well known to every strawberry-forcer that each plant has generally one or two very large fruits, while the remainder are considerably less. Consequently the more numerous the plants ripening fruit at one time, the more numerous will be the monster strawberries. But size is not all on the exhibition-table; colour and flavour are also very important points, which can only be attained by free exposure to light and dry warm air. If strawberries are grown with the intention of their being prize-takers, a smaller number of fruit should be allowed to each plant. Some may require being retarded in cooler houses so as to keep back the first and largest berries; others may require a contrary treatment to bring them forward to match the retarded ones.

Most growers have their own way of setting up or dishing for exhibition. The most effective dish of strawberries I ever remember of were laid singly in a flat square basket, filled nearly to the top with wadding and covered with tissue-paper. On this surface the strawberries were laid with a small space between each. Splendid fruits of any description can never

THE STRAWBERRY. 249

have too much of each fruit seen, and in this way the eye takes in more of the individual fruits than when dished in the usual way in a semi-globular form, the fruit laid in circles with a strawberry-leaf between each, the outer row of fruits being the least and those in the centre of the basket the largest.

VARIETIES FOR FORCING.

It is not always easy to pronounce dogmatically on the varieties that are best for forcing ; I have experimented with scores of sorts, and came to the conclusion that there are not very many which possess all the qualities which fit them for forcing, and early forcing in particular. Keen's Seedling was till recently more extensively grown than any other sort, and more generally accounted the best to grow for a general crop. It, however, in some localities has proved a failure; but so far as I am aware this is the exception, not the rule. Vicomtesse Hericart de Thury is now very extensively used. It is prolific and of good quality. Black Prince is a most prolific bearer, and for very early forcing is decidedly the most certain, from its free blooming and setting qualities. I can confidently recommend for the earliest crops— *i.e.*, to ripen in early part of March—Black Prince, Underhill's Sir Harry, Keen's Seedling, Vicomtesse Hericart de Thury, and La Grosse Sucrée to succeed it. Prince of Wales is an excellent second or rather third early in the order of these three. For the latest crops nothing can equal in flavour the old British Queen; but it is not very prolific, and does not succeed well in many soils. Sir Charles Napier forces well, is large and showy, but rather acid. President is an excellent strawberry, forces well and sets remarkably free. La Marguerite and Victoria are also very showy varieties. But had I to force many thousands of plants, I would still cling to the old favourites—namely, Black Prince, Keen's Seedling, and Vicomtesse Hericart de Thury, the latter two predominating. Then for late sorts nothing can be more satisfactory than Sir Charles Napier, President, and, where it does well, British Queen. Those who may fancy a few very large fruits should grow Dr Hogg and James Veitch, but their size is about all the good quality they possess. I have, however, proved that localities, or rather soils, influence strawberries very much, some succeeding where others fail, and *vice versâ*.

THE CUCUMBER.

The cucumber (*Cucumis sativa*) is said by some horticultural writers to be a native of the East Indies. It has, however, been cultivated and esteemed in Africa from a very early period; and in the complaint of the Israelites to Moses in the wilderness, they singularly enough associated their appreciation of the cucumber with the fish, which they "freely" ate in Egypt. Fish and cucumbers are now much appreciated together. The very earliest records of English horticulture embrace the cucumber, and in Edward III.'s time it was common, but was afterwards comparatively neglected till the time of Henry VIII.; and it was the middle of the seventeenth century before its cultivation became general. In England it is very much more esteemed by the mass of the population than in Scotland. In some parts of Bedfordshire—Sandy, for instance—it is cultivated in the open air by thousand of bushels, and supplied to pickle-manufacturers for pickling.

At certain seasons of the year the cucumber is of the easiest possible cultivation, requiring next to no attention or skill. This applies to the summer months. But to supply cucumbers every day from November till June is a matter that requires great attention and care. When a supply is required the whole year round, the comparative ease and certainty with which it can be accomplished depends of course to a great extent on the appliances at command for such a purpose. When dependent for heat on the cumbrous and untidy dung-bed or linings, it is a somewhat precarious and trying task. On the other hand, with a well-constructed cucumber-house, efficiently heated with hot water, a constant supply can with certainty be maintained, and with much less labour than with dung-linings alone. Considering, however, that very many growers have yet nothing more advanced than a brick pit, heated by means of fermenting stable-litter, and, where they can be had, leaves, to supply cucumbers, my intention is to give practical directions for a supply of cucumbers, say from March till November, by such means, as well as to make some remarks on their midwinter growth in cucumber-houses heated by hot-water pipes. I may, however, remark, that it is not desired to communicate any information that might be the cause of inducing any to provide at this period of gardening practice and appliances nothing better than dung-heated pits for the growth of cucumbers from October till the end of June; for although I and many more have bridged this period of the year with cucumbers by means of fermenting materials alone, it cannot now be regarded in any other light than one of the best illustrations of being "penny wise and pound foolish."

THE SEED-BED.

It is, then, supposed that cucumbers are desired in early spring, say March. As the first step in the pro-

THE CUCUMBER.

cess, it is necessary to get a quantity of stable-litter, and, if possible, good oak-leaves, well mixed together, in the first week of December. These materials should be shaken up lightly into a compact heap. And in order to sweat or sweeten it, it will require to be turned over at intervals of four or five days, until it has parted with its rank ammoniacal vapours, and assumed a tanned colour. It is then ready to be formed into a hotbed, for which a well-sheltered site open to the south should be chosen. The bed should be 5 feet high at the back, 4 feet at front, and 2 feet longer and wider than the frame that is to be placed on it. Supposing that cucumber-plants, and perhaps a few early odds and ends, are all that are to be raised in the bed, one light box of the ordinary size will be sufficient. In building the bed, shake up the material well, lay it on in regular layers, and beat it well down with the back of the fork as the work proceeds, but do not tramp it. When of the requisite height, place the frame over it at once, and lay 6 inches of finely pounded charcoal, sifted coal-ashes, or sawdust—I prefer the first named—over the surface of the bed inside the frame. Put on the light, and protect the sides of the bed and frame itself from cold searching winds and rains, which would soon cool it, and keep the frame closed and covered up till the heat begins to rise. Then give air by day, to let any rank vapour that may arise from the manure escape.

SOWING THE SEEDS, AND TREATMENT OF THE YOUNG PLANTS.

As soon as the heat reaches 70°, and the atmosphere is sweet, soak the cucumber-seeds in water for twelve hours before sowing them. I prefer sowing the seeds in moderately drained 4-inch pots, in a compost of two parts light friable loam and one part leaf-mould. With this fill the pots half full, sow two seeds in each, covering them to the depth of half an inch; and do not give any water for the present. Plunge the pots only one-half their depth in the bed, for the bottom-heat will be strong at first. If watered and plunged deeply in the strong heat, germination is forced on too quickly, and the result is a pale and weakly seedling. In placing the pots, let them incline towards the south, so that when the sun does shine it may reach the young plants as soon as they are through the soil; and to the same end see that the glass is kept clean, for light at this season is of first-rate importance. When the weather is mild, uncover the glass the first thing in the morning, but cover up in the evening before the temperature recedes too much. Give more or less air night and day, according to the state of the weather, ranging the heat about 70°. When the air is frosty, hang a piece of canvas or woollen netting over the back of the frame when air is on, so as to prevent currents of cold air.

I have always found that the genial heat of the frame and the absence of sunshine at this season render watering unnecessary, and in fact injurious, until the plants have expanded their first rough leaves. When the young plants have expanded their seed-lobes and grown to the level of the mouth of the pots, earth them up an inch or so with the same compost in which they were sown, warmed to the temperature of the frame; and when the rough leaves are formed, fill up the pot. Into this the stems throw out greedy roots, and they are thus dwarfed and strengthened without being potted off from a seed-pan, and to some extent checked in the operation. Water will not be required, if the weather be dull and sunless, till they have rooted from their stems. Care, however, must be taken that a sudden sun-burst does not overtake them in a dry state. When watered, give as much as will wet the whole ball. Their vital action is weak, and in consequence their power of decomposition weak also; and the object being a sturdy well-proportioned plant, a stiff stem, and leaves of good substance, it is one that a superabundance of water effectually defeats. The best way is to grow with as small an amount of water as possible; a minimum rather than a maximum temperature; and to give as much fresh air daily as will dry the foliage once in the twenty-four hours. There is no surer sign that all is going on well than when, on uncovering the frame in the morning, dew-drops are studded round the edges of the leaves.

The state of the bed, after the first fortnight or three weeks, must be carefully watched, and a heap of manure and leaves, in a hot state, should be in readiness to line the bed with, whenever there is any difficulty in keeping the heat at 70°. A little should be cut off the outside of the bed all round, and holes bored into it with a stake, so as to allow the heat from the lining to act into it. The lining should not be less than two feet wide, and as carefully made up as the bed itself; and it should be covered so as to prevent rains from washing the heat out of it suddenly. In fact, great attention must be paid to the bed in this respect, to keep up a steady temperature. And as all know who have thus reared young cucumbers, constant watchfulness must be exercised in the matter of air-giving. Cold, frosty winds, with sudden sun-bursts after dull weather, make these tender plants a most precarious crop to rear successfully and well. A slight shade may sometimes be found necessary, when sudden sunshine succeeds a dull time, but the shade is a necessary evil. Damping the surface of the plunging material may be sufficient to prevent the plants from flinching or suffering under such circumstances.

After they have formed their rough leaves, and pushed their leader-shoot, they progress rapidly, and will require more water at the root; and they should be more freely supplied with it, especially if the weather be clear and dry. It is taken for granted that plants raised thus early are not intended for an ordinary cucumber-frame, to be grown on the surface of the bed, but to be grown on a trellis in a deep brick pit. They should therefore not be stopped, but allowed to grow on with one leader. If stopped, they will make two weaker shoots, instead of one stronger one, and will not be ready for the fruiting-pit nearly so soon. As they progress, and expand more leaves, do not allow them to become crowded, nor their points to touch the glass; and as they fill their pots with roots, give them a steady supply of water always of the same temperature as the frame. See that the heat is steadily kept up by turning the linings, and adding fresh warm material to them. Sometimes I have reduced the plants to one in a 4-inch pot, or when two were left, shifted the two plants into 6-inch pots if their appearance indicated that they required more nourishment, or were likely to become pot-bound.

When all has progressed favourably, they are

generally ready for planting-out in about five or six weeks after the seeds are sown. In raising cucumber-plants as has just been described, I have usually sown on or about the 1st of January, and planted them in the fruiting-pits the second week of February.

FRUITING-PITS, PLANTING-OUT, ETC.

My experience leads me to recommend much deeper fruiting-pits than are generally in use in this system of cucumber-culture. Deep pits require more fermenting material at first starting every season, but in the after-management the temperature is maintained with much less trouble. I have practised with pits of various dimensions, but found those that are 7 feet deep the most satisfactory. The pit should be sunk 3 feet below the ground-level, with the drainage so thorough that standing water is impossible. Instead of building these pits on the pigeon-hole and flue system, I would construct them of 4-inch solid brick-work, and in this way I have always found the linings as effective as with pigeon-holes; and there is no danger of the evil effects of steam, nor from mice or rats, which are sometimes very troublesome. The space for the lining should be two feet wide, enclosed all round with 9-inch brick-work, to within a foot of the level of the pit, so that the wooden shutters which cover in the linings have a good slope to throw off the wet. Linings last as long again thus enclosed and covered. The illustration, fig. 22, will best explain the pit we have described.

FRUIT CULTURE UNDER GLASS.

PREPARING THE PIT FOR THE PLANTS, SOIL, ETC.

In preparing a pit of this description for the culture of cucumbers on trellises, fill it up inside with well-sweetened stable-manure, and, when they can be had, fresh oak-leaves, previously prepared as directed for the seed-bed. In this case it is advisable that the proportion of leaves should predominate, for the heat will on that account be less violent, but more lasting.

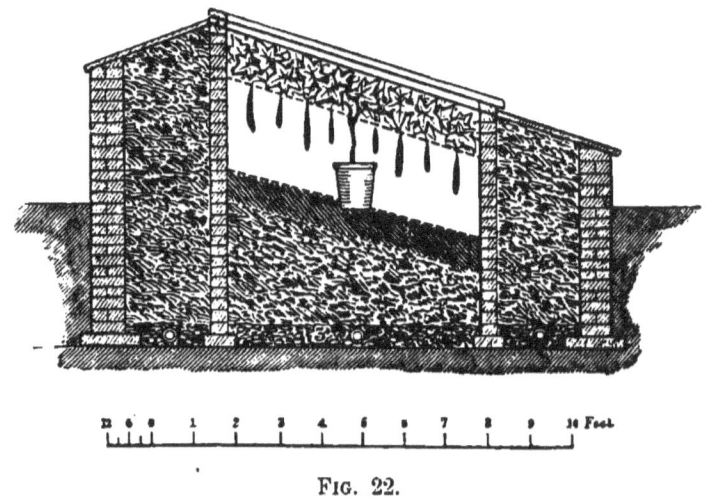

FIG. 22.
1, 1, 1, Dung and Leaves. 2 Soil.

Shake it in in layers, and tread rather firmly. This firm body of fermenting material will keep up a steady bottom-heat for a long time. The space for the lining requires to be filled with hot material at the same time; less firmly than in the inside, but quite up to the top of the pit. The soil, consisting of equal parts loam and leaf-mould, or very old hotbed manure, and a little gritty sand or charred earth, to the depth of 10 inches, should be put in the pit at once. Then knock the bottoms out of 11-inch pots, and place them on the surface of the soil, one in the centre of each light, and fill them up with soil. In these pots the plants are planted, and are thus raised nearer the light and trellis, and can consequently be got sooner into bearing than otherwise. The trellises generally used are made of light pieces of wood or strong wire-work, with meshes 4 or 5 inches square. They should not be nearer the glass than 15 inches, which gives space for the foliage, and, after the fermenting material has subsided a few inches, about 2 feet for the cucumbers to hang down.

MANAGEMENT AFTER PLANTING IN THE FRUITING-PIT.

As soon as the heat rises to 70° the pit is ready for the plants, which should be allowed to become rather dry at the root before being planted in the bottomless pots. Their stems should be covered in planting nearly to the seed-leaves, and an inch of the pots left unfilled for watering conveniently and efficiently. Fix a stake to each plant for support till they clasp the trellis with a tendril. Settle the soil about their roots with water at a temperature of 80°, through a rather fine rose; shade lightly in the middle of the day for a few days if the sun be strong. And now for a start.

The night temperature should be as near 72° as possible—say that it ranges between that and 75°, according to the state of the weather. As the heat will be strong from the fresh linings for a time, a covering over the glass of a single mat will be sufficient, except in cases of severe frost, when double mats may be necessary. Push down the lights from the top early on the afternoons of bright days, and discharge a few syringefuls of warm water round the walls and over the surface of the soil, but miss the plants. Then shut the pit entirely till covering-up time, when a chink of air should be put on for the night in case there should be any unwholesome gas from the dung, and also to prevent a weakly growth. They will commence to grow rapidly in eight or ten days after they are planted, and when uncovered in the morning dew-drops will be seen round the edges of the leaves, and white thread-like roots will soon appear on the surface of the soil in the pots. Pinch the top off each plant as soon as it gets to within 2 inches of the trellis, after which they will soon force a lateral growth at nearly every joint. These laterals should be all removed except the three at the top of each plant. As they expand their leaves and establish themselves above the trellis, remove by degrees those that are below it, and stop the three top growths at the second joint, and afterwards at every joint.

Should the middle of March prove mild, do not let the night temperature exceed 75°, with at all times a small amount of air on all night. Increase the air in the morning as soon as the heat reaches 80°, and continue to take every opportunity afforded by sunny weather of shutting up early in the afternoon with a moist atmosphere, so that the temperature may run up to 90° for an hour or two. After a sunny parching day, such practice wonderfully refreshes the plants. Always be watchful that they never receive a check from becoming too dry at the roots, for the cucumber, after it gets into full growth, with its immense surface of active leaves, requires a good supply of water. The surface of the bed in the bottom of the pot is not so

THE CUCUMBER. 261

apt to get dry, being shaded and level, but that in the pot gets dry more quickly.

I have generally cut cucumbers within six weeks after planting the plants in the fruiting-pit. When they begin to bear, it is an error to let them bear too freely at first; a few should only be left to each plant until the whole trellis is covered with foliage, by which time they require to be looked over every third day to stop, thin, and regulate the growths, so that each leaf has plenty of room to expand properly and fully perform its functions. There is no greater error than the crowding system. It ends in weakly growths, damping leaves, and malformed useless fruits. I am of course presuming that the linings have been attended to whenever signs of declining heat have been noticed. There should always be a sufficient amount of fermenting material mixed and in a hot state, ready to mix into or replace partially the linings when they cool. It is best to renew the back lining and one of the ends, and the front and other end lining alternately. April is a deceptive month to the inexperienced; and as comparatively warm is then often suddenly succeeded by very cold weather, the linings should be kept in an active condition to be able to compete with these changes, and double and single coverings used over the glass, as such weather renders it necessary.

WATERING AND STOPPING, ETC.

After the beginning of April, the foliage may be sprinkled all over through a fine rose on the afternoon of every fine day, and the pit closely shut up and aired afterwards as already directed. More frequent waterings will be required as they come into free bearing and the sun gets more powerful, rendering much more air necessary; and occasional watering with dung-water will be beneficial. Keep them always regularly stopped and thinned of all superfluous growths and leaves, but being careful never to remove the leaf from a joint where there is a fruit swelling off. Never allow the growths to run beyond one or two joints without stopping them. This treatment carefully carried out will keep them always in a vigorous and fruitful condition, and producing fine straight cucumbers beautifully covered with bloom, and the flower fresh at the end of each when ready to cut. As the season advances, and they have been in bearing for some time, remove by degrees the older growths and foliage, and train younger ones into their places. This should be diligently seen to the whole season, in order to keep the pit full of young bearing growths and healthy leaves, without which a regular supply of cucumbers cannot be maintained. Under such treatment I have invariably had these early plants as healthy and fruitful in the end of September as in May, and have seldom ever been troubled with insects or disease.

After the first week of June fresh linings are unnecessary in the southern half of England, but in more northern districts it is necessary to attend to them a little later. In the hottest weather, especially when such has been preceded by a continuation of dull days, a slight shade in the middle of the day is sometimes beneficial. When it is desired to have these plants healthy and bearing after September, it is necessary to apply fresh linings, or mildew will soon destroy them.

The foregoing directions, I trust, will be sufficient

THE CUCUMBER. 263

for those who can only command a brick pit and heat from fermenting material with which to produce spring cucumbers. Those who only grow them in summer will find them so accommodating for four or five months of the year that directions specially for that season would be a waste of words. For any one who has a frame, a little fermenting material, such as litter and short grass or leaves, and glass lights, can have little difficulty in rearing them in summer in almost any district; while in the south the ridge varieties do well in the open air the same as vegetable marrows or pumpkins. And, without adverting to the undesirableness of attempting to supply cucumbers throughout the dull winter months in dung-pits, I will now offer some remarks on their winter management in cucumber-houses or stoves heated by hot water.

WINTER CUCUMBERS.

Experienced gardeners know very well that, wherever sufficient space can be afforded in such as a fruiting pine-stove where a high temperature is necessary, there is no great difficulty in keeping a tolerably good supply of cucumbers in pots throughout the winter. I am, however, not going to recommend their being mixed up with pines or anything else: although circumstances can be modified to suit different subjects, such is not desirable. And now, where there is a demand for cucumbers all through the winter, there is generally a house or pit specially for that purpose. As in the case of the winter-forcing of the vine or any other plant in midwinter, a lean-to house facing due south, with a white back-wall and white-painted woodwork and clear sheet-glass, is the best. And the greatest amount of sun and light that can be had is perhaps of more importance in the case of winter cucumbers than any other crop.

CUCUMBER-HOUSES.

Fig. 23 represents an excellent house for winter cucumbers. Such houses are wired the same as for vines. A house 10 feet wide requires four rows of

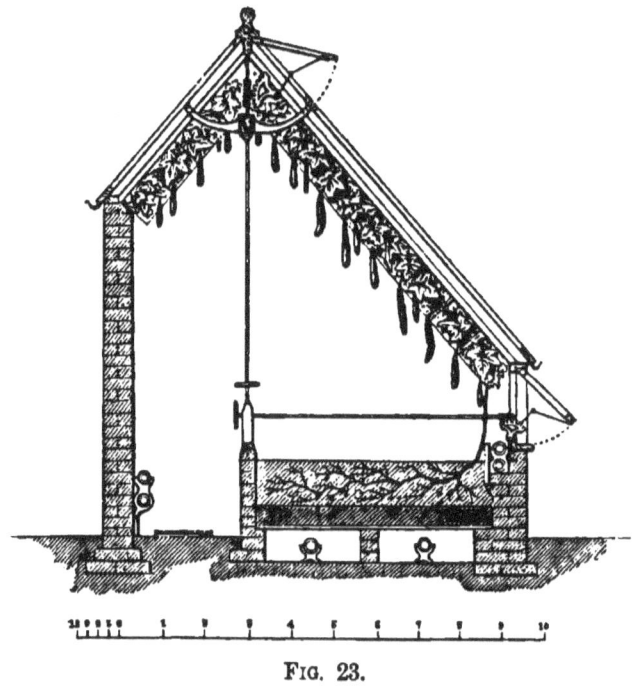

FIG. 23.

hot-water pipes for surface, and as many for bottom-heat, whether the latter be on the tank system or merely a hot-air chamber, both of which suit equally well, and the latter is the least expensive. The bed for the soil should be 16 inches deep, giving room for 6 inches of drainage or fresh leaves, and 10 inches for soil.

THE CUCUMBER.

SOIL, ETC.

In filling up this depth of soil, I do not recommend more than 8 inches at first when the cucumbers are planted, nor need the bed be filled the whole width—the other two inches to be made up with top-dressing, and the whole of the bed to be filled in after the plants come into bearing. The soil should consist of light turfy loam two parts, and one part of leaf-mould or well-decayed manure, with a sixth of the whole of coarse sand, pounded charcoal, or charred soil. A light open soil is best for winter cucumbers: soil that is likely to become solid and inert is at all times an evil in cucumber-culture, and more especially so in winter.

To have plants well established and in a strong bearing condition before winter, they should be planted out in the fruiting-house by the end of August, or very early in September. Some cultivators prefer raising plants intended for winter bearing by cuttings, which are rather more disposed to fruitfulness in their earlier stages of growth, on account of their less vigorous growth than seedlings. They are easily struck in a frame or pit with a little bottom-heat. The best way is to strike them singly in 4-inch pots, with a little sandy soil round the base and neck of each cutting. Good plants can thus be prepared in three weeks. When raised from seed, it requires to be sown in the beginning of August. I am aware that many do not sow so early, but later sowing is a mistake, as the plants should be thoroughly established and beginning to bear by the middle of October, in order to have a good supply through the winter. And by a proper selection of varieties, there is no difficulty in getting seedlings to bear well enough when sown as early as recommended, and they generally yield finer individual cucumbers.

PLANTING, TEMPERATURE, ETC.

The plants should not be planted closer than one every 2 feet, as crowding in the dull months of winter is very injurious; and throughout September and October they are all the more sturdy and hardy when grown with a liberal amount of air. A thin flimsy foliage grown in a too close moist atmosphere often becomes a prey to thrips and red-spider, two enemies which should be kept at arm's-length, and to which end the house should be thoroughly washed and fumigated before planting the plants, and no old melon or cucumber soil where these pests have had a footing should be used. When they begin to bear avoid heavy cropping, and when November arrives be more sparing with atmospheric moisture and waterings, and avoid high night temperatures, which should not range higher than from 68° to 70°. The consequences of a high night temperature, when the days are short and dull, are weakly and unfruitful growths. A covering over the glass in cold weather is much to be commended; it saves firing, and is in all respects preferable to over-heated pipes. Frigidomo is an excellent material for covering, and can be fixed to roll up and down like a shade. It is most important all winter to give a little air every day when at all practicable, and also to prevent the leaves from becoming crowded, and to stop the lateral growths at every joint.

Training, Stopping, &c.—Plants intended for winter

fruiting should not have the leading shoot stopped till it gets half-way to the top of the house, and after that, not again till it reaches near the top. The lateral growths show fruit freely when stopped regularly. It is well, too, especially in winter, to remove the male blossoms as soon as they are discerned. Impregnated cucumbers are never so equal and good as those which are unfertilised; and except for seed, no impregnation should be allowed. I cannot impress too strongly the fact, that to have a constant supply of good cucumbers over a length of time, over-cropping must be avoided by removing those not absolutely required. It is a tempting sight to have a fine display at one time. It looks well while it lasts, but the plants will rebel by resting for a season after the effort.

After they have been bearing some time and give indications that a top-dressing would be beneficial, mix two parts old mushroom-bed or old hotbed manure with one part of turfy loam, and cover the surface of the bed to the depth of 1 inch or a little more; and after the turn of the season, about the end of January, apply a similar covering to the roots that will have seized upon the first dressing. With increased daylight, they will do with increased moisture, and these top-dressings will cause them to grow more strongly, and they will go on bearing under similar treatment for a long time. It is, however, desirable, when convenience exists, to raise more plants to come into bearing in spring, and, if necessary, to introduce a new set of plants into the winter house to bear through the summer, or to allow of its being devoted to propagation or any other purpose. Not that this is absolutely necessary, although desirable, for the same plants under careful treatment often go on bearing until the house is needed for another winter set of plants.

INSECTS.

Thrips and red-spider are very apt to be troublesome on winter cucumbers, and their first appearance must be the signal for their destruction. See directions for destroying these insects at close of chapter on Melons.

DISEASES.

The cucumber-plant is subject to mildew when grown in too low a temperature, and kept too wet or too dry at the root. Whenever it appears, dust the affected parts with sulphur. Keep the bottom and top heat up to what I have recommended, and give air freely; under such conditions it will disappear. Gumming and canker, with which they are sometimes affected, is caused by the want of sufficient bottom-heat and over-watering. Whenever it appears on the fruit or plants, raise the bottom-heat, and apply less water both at the root and in the air, and dust the affected parts with newly-slaked lime. In such houses as I have recommended, and with attention to the heat and watering, neither of these diseases is likely to attack the plants. Deformed fruit are often seen on cucumbers. They are the result of general debility, and a sure sign that the plants are not sufficiently nourished, and that the temperature has been too low. To prevent malformed fruits, do not crop too heavily, top-dress the soil with rotten dung, and keep the temperature in the soil and air as has been directed.

VARIETIES.

Most growers have their favourite varieties. My own experience leads me to recommend for both summer and winter crops, Volunteer and Telegraph. These are the most generally useful cucumbers I have ever grown for both winter and summer, and I have tried scores. Sir Garnet Wolseley is a variety recently raised by Joseph Hamilton & Sons, Carlisle, and of which I have a very high opinion as a general cropper.

THE CALENDAR.

JANUARY.

Pines.—Where ripe pines are required in May and June, no time must be lost in getting the required number started into fruit. For this purpose select those Queens that have completed their growth early in autumn, and that have been rested by being comparatively dry and cool. Give them a night temperature of 65°, and a bottom-heat ranging from 85° to 90°, but never exceed the latter degree, or the roots are likely to suffer. If the soil be dry, give sufficient water at 80° to moisten it, and keep it regularly in a medium state of moisture, and gradually increase the air and moisture as the days lengthen and light increases. When the temperature exceeds 75° with sun, give a little air at the highest part of the pinery, and shut up early in the afternoon. Keep all succession stock quiet. The night temperature should range as steadily at 60° as possible. A few degrees less during hard frost or a high wind are safer than a few degrees more than 60°. 75° to 80° is sufficient bottom-heat for those. Avoid giving more water at the root than just suffices to keep the plants healthy. When the plunging material has been leaves and tan without hot-water pipes beneath them, I have frequently had pines in the most satisfactory condition without being once watered from the beginning of November to the middle or end of January. All young stock in low pits, that can be covered from dusk till dawn, should be covered in preference to firing hard to keep up the temperature; and whenever the temperature exceeds 65° by sun-heat, give a small amount of air at a number of openings, instead of much at a few.

Vines.—Give every attention to late grapes still hanging, keeping them at a steady temperature of 45° with a dry atmosphere. Instead of opening ventilators on mild foggy days, keep them shut, and embrace the opportunity afforded by clearer weather of giving a little increase of heat and air. The former practice fills the house with moist air, while the latter expels it. Go over every bunch twice a-week, and remove all decaying berries before they communicate their rottenness to others. Prune all vines from which the fruit has been cut, and that have shed their leaves. Wash every inch of inside surface, not even excepting gangways. Paint the hot-water pipes and wood and wire-work, if they require it; and if the vines have been infected with red-spider last year, wash and dress as has been directed. Remove 2 inches of the surface-soil from the inside border, and if the roots are inside the house, top-dress with 2 inches of horse-droppings or other short manure, and cover it over with an inch of loam. Early started vines will be set, and in some cases thinned. These, if required as early as possible to succeed the late grapes, may be pushed briskly along, but let the forcing be done by day principally. 65° is sufficient temperature at night, unless in very mild weather, when it may rise to 70°. Avoid an excess of moisture, especially in dull weather, and give air on all favourable opportunities, and always in the earlier part of the day, shutting up early in the afternoon. If this crop be in pots, great attention must be paid to watering, keeping the soil regularly moist. Vines in bloom require to be freely aired, avoiding cold currents as much as possible. Thin the bunches to the desired number immediately they are well set, and then the berries as soon as they attain the size of radish-seed. Stop the growths of late vines two or three joints beyond the best bunch, and carefully tie them down *by degrees* for fear of breaking the tender growths, and avoid the crowding of wood and foliage. Start succession-houses, the borders of which, it is presumed, have been well covered with leaves or litter, or both, some time ago. Begin with 45° to 50° at night, gradually increasing the heat to 60° by the time the buds have all fairly started. If they show symptoms of swelling the buds at the top much in advance of the bottom ones, bend down the tops of the vines into a cooler part of the house till the bottom buds advance. I am not an advocate for much syringing in vineries, and prefer keeping up the moisture by evaporation from steaming-troughs and floor-sprinkling. But after leaves are formed, an excess of this, with too little air, breeds wartiness on the under sides of the leaves, and checks their expansion, and impairs the whole system of the vines. Put in a sufficient number of eyes for growing into vines required for another season.

Peaches.—Should the weather be cold and dull, be cautious in the application of fire-heat, unless it be in the case of trees in full bloom, to keep up a circulation of dry air. Go over the blooms at mid-day with a camel-hair brush, and impregnate especially shy-setting sorts, such as Noblesse. Do not exceed 55° in cold weather at night till the fruit has set and begun swelling freely. On fine afternoons syringe all trees not in bloom; but when dull and cold, be content with sprinkling the floors. Prune and tie later houses, cleaning and dressing them as recommended. If the borders be dry inside, give a good soaking of water after they are top-dressed with manure. Top-dressing with manure in the case of young trees in new borders is not desirable, as they have a tendency to grow too strong. Disbud the growths early. In commencing to force, begin with a low temperature—45° during cold nights, increased to 55° when in bloom, is sufficient, with 10° more by day with sun, and give air on all favourable occasions to strengthen both wood and bloom buds.

Figs.—Where early figs are grown in pots, now is a good time to start them. They do best when plunged in a bed of warm leaves, giving a bottom-heat of 75° to 80°. The temperature of the air should be the same as that recommended for peaches. Keep them regularly moist at the root, and syringe them every fine afternoon, and otherwise keep the atmosphere moist. Should any of the plants require larger pots, shift them when put into heat. Those which have been for a few years in large pots will be the better for being turned out of them, and the crocks removed from among the roots at the bottom; the roots cut back sufficiently to allow of 3 inches fresh soil at the bottom of the pots, and top-dress the ball with horse-droppings.

Strawberries in Pots.—A number of these, according to the demand and space, should be put into heat every fortnight. Keep them near the glass, and begin with a temperature of 45° to 50° at night, increasing it to 55° by the time they show their trusses of bloom. Early-started crops now in bloom range from 55° to 60°, according to the weather. Give them a liberal supply of fresh air, but avoid currents of cold air passing over them. In all stages strawberries require to be kept moist at the root, but are best not placed in saucers till the fruit are set.

Cucumbers.—Those that have been bearing through the winter require a night temperature of 65° to 70°, according as the weather is cold or mild. If in low pits in houses, cover the glass at night in preference to hard firing. Give more or less air daily, according to the state of the weather. Keep the soil moderately moist, increasing the supply of water and the moisture of the air as the days lengthen. Do not allow the leaves and young growths to become crowded, nor the

S

plants to bear too much fruit at one time. Sow seed for succession crops in a temperature of 70°.

Melons.—Sow for early crops in the way recommended.

FEBRUARY.

Pines.—Every gardener who has to keep up an unbroken succession of ripe pines knows how desirable it is to attentively care for all pines that show fruit from October onwards throughout the winter months. All such stock may now be pushed on at an accelerated pace as the days lengthen and the sun gains in power. The temperature at night should range from 70° to 75°, according to the state of the weather, and by day with sun-heat from 80° to 85° before giving air. Shut up early in the afternoon; and where all are out of bloom, moisture should be increased in the same ratio as heat. The bottom-heat for these should be at a maximum, namely, 85° to 90°. The state of the soil must be carefully watched, and water given to keep it in a medium state of moisture, avoiding mealy dryness on the one hand and wetness on the other. Do not exceed a temperature of 70° at night in the case of those intended to start in the course of this month, unless it be in very mild weather, when a few degrees more is safe enough without hard firing. Do not be over-liberal with water till the fruit shows itself. Look over them occasionally and examine their centres; and when the fruit can be discerned emerging from amongst the leaves, see that the plants so started have sufficient weak guano-water given to moisten the soil through and through. Supposing the early batch to have shown fruit by the end of the month, increase the heat a few degrees. Let it range to 75° on mild nights. Do not much increase the air moisture till they are out of flower, and give air a few hours a-day as weather will permit. Examine succession plants in small pots, and see that they do not become too dry, and give water enough to prevent their suffering without inducing much growth yet. Let the night temperature still continue to range at 60°. If it so happens that they are strong and well rooted, or if any portion of them are such, it will be better to shift them into their fruiting-pots by the end of the month than to run the risk of their becoming pot-bound, and consequently more likely to fruit prematurely. Later plants are best not shifted till March. Take off and pot any suckers that may be on plants of winter-fruiting sorts from which the fruit is cut.

Vines.—Attend to grapes still hanging as directed last month. Prune all vines as soon as the fruit is cut from them, and dress all cuts made after this season with styptic, to prevent any chance of their being weakened by bleeding in spring. Wash and otherwise clean and dress succession vines and vineries. Remove superfluous bunches from all free-setting sorts as soon as ever it is apparent which are best to leave. Shy-setting sorts are best left till it is easily seen which are set most perfectly. Should the weather be cold, avoid hard forcing, which in dull sunless weather only debilitates and defeats the end in view. Keep vines in bloom steadily about 65° at night, with a rather dry atmosphere. Shy-setting sorts may be impregnated by drawing a dry clean hand over the bunches and tapping the vine-stems at midday, or a bunch of some free pollen-making variety may be rubbed or shaken among the blooms of shy sorts. Take advantage of forcing on bright sunny days if time is important, shutting up with sun-heat at 80°. Where the early crop is from pot-vines, and now swelling off freely, water regularly with manure-water, and the heat for such may be a few degrees more than is desirable for permanent vines. Air-giving should be carefully attended to wherever vines are started, and in all progressive stages a close stagnant atmosphere is ruinous to vines. Stop the growths as previously directed. Start succession vineries. See that all vines now started have their roots, if outside, properly protected from heavy falls of snow and rain.

Peaches.—Still continue to force with caution if the weather be cold. Do not much exceed the temperature recommended last month for the various stages. Gently syringe with tepid water when the fruit is set, giving a vigorous syringing or two to free those just set from their old blooms. Pay particular attention to inside borders, and see that they do not become too dry; and except in the case of young vigorous trees, manure-water may be given to them after the fruit is formed. Ventilate trees in bloom that require a circulation of dry air so as to prevent strong currents of frosty air, which so frequently prevail at this season, and which are fatal to the fructifying organs, and injurious to the tender young leaves. Where there is a great superabundance of young fruit formed, thin off a portion of the smallest regularly all over the trees. Prune the trees in late houses, and dress them over with the mixture recommended. Complete the planting of young trees as soon as possible if not already done. Disbud forward trees as soon as the growths are ready for it.

Figs.—Continue to put last month's directions in force, increasing the heat a few degrees as the plants begin to break freely into growth, and increase the moisture in the air as light and heat increase. Look well to the regular supply of water at the root, and keep the bottom-heat steady at 80°.

Strawberries.—In some instances fruit may be sufficiently early to be colouring by the end of the month, in which cases it is necessary to keep a dry warm atmosphere, with a circulation of air to secure good flavour. Cease giving manure-water at the root as soon as the first signs of colouring are noticed. Where fruit are swelling, and it is desirable to have them ripe as early as possible, the night temperature may be kept at 65° to 70° with impunity, and 10° more with sun-heat by day. Start succession plants. Do not expose any very early plants, from which the fruit may be gathered at the end of the month, suddenly to cold; but harden them off and otherwise care for them till they can be planted out. They will yield fine early runners for potting for early forcing, and make fine stools for cropping outdoors next year.

Cucumbers.—Those that were sown last will be ready to plant out by the middle of this month. Water always with water at 80° to 85°, and keep the night temperature at 70°, giving more or less air daily to prevent spindly growths. Sow for succession crops.

Melons.—Plant out those plants sown last month as soon as they are ready; keep them at 70° with a steady bottom-heat. Sow for succession crops.

MARCH.

Pines.—Continue to apply the directions of last month to those that are starting, and that have shown their fruit distinctly. Keep the soil about their roots moderately moist, especially avoiding a state of mealy dryness at any time—a condition which, now that the sun has more power, and that air has to be more liberally admitted, will check and stunt the young fruit. With increased light, the temperature may safely be advanced to 70° at night, and to 85° for a short time at shutting-up time, with sun-heat. More moisture in the air is also necessary as light and heat increase. When the fruit are done flowering, give a very light dewing overhead with tepid water through a very fine rose. Where there are any pines that are farther advanced, and which it is a desideratum to ripen early, these may now be pushed on with a few degrees more heat than is named above, especially when shut up with sun on fine afternoons. Very hard forcing, requiring highly-heated pipes during cold parching winds, should be avoided, and the milder weather as it occurs should be taken advantage of for pushing them rapidly on. Colour the water with Peruvian guano for every watering, and pour a little of it into the steaming-troughs. Later-fruiting stock, that are intended first to make a growth and then start, should now be kept moderately and steadily moist at the root, and air-moisture increased in proportion with a temperature of 65° at night. Generally speaking, this is the month when the majority of autumn-potted suckers require to be shifted into their fruiting-pots. If the suckers show plenty of young healthy roots round the sides of the balls, they are ready to shift. If they are not in this condition, and the soil is in a proper state, leave them till they are. My own practice is to shift any time—into pots a size larger —in October, November, December, or January, rather than run the risk of a matted ball and stunted plant that is worthless after being wintered. For Queens I consider 11-inch pots sufficiently large. For Cayennes, Charlotte Rothschild, and other large-growing sorts, I would not exceed a 12-inch pot. 11 and 12 inch pots give better returns than larger sizes. These sizes will produce Queens from 5 to 6 lb., and Cayennes from 8 to 11 lb.—weights sufficient to satisfy any requirements. Crock with ½-inch crocks to the depth of 1½ inch, and cover the crocks with a thin even layer of the fibre from the loam, and then dust with a little fresh soot to keep worms at bay. In plunging them in their growing quarters, avoid crowding. Queens should not be closer than 22 inches each way, and larger sorts 24 inches. The bottom-heat should range from 80° to 85°, not higher. Avoid shading much after shifting, unless the weather be very bright, and then only shade for two hours in the middle of the day. During cold March weather, 60° is heat sufficient for a maximum at night; when mild it may range to 65° till 10 P.M., but allow it to sink 5° before daylight. Give air in moderate quantity for the first fourteen days after shifting ; afterwards increase it, as the plants begin to grow more freely. Avoid in all pine-houses cold draughts as much as possible.

Vines.—Early crops that have finished the stoning process, and that are required to ripen as early as possible, may be encouraged forward more freely with an advance of temperature to 70° in mild weather; but if cold east winds prevail, and the days be sunless, it is better to force more gently, taking advantage of bright suns to shut up early, and husband heat for the night with the least possible amount of fire-heat compatible with the temperature required. As soon as colouring begins, give air a little more freely and decrease the moisture. The increase and decrease of these elements should never be sudden, but gradual. A small amount of air left on at night is favourable to good colour. If the early crop is from vines in pots, a constant watch must be kept to prevent their suffering from either a deficiency or superabundance of water. Discontinue watering with manure-water when colouring commences. Attend to all vines in late stages, by timely stopping, thinning, and tying down shoots. Examine inside borders, and keep them moderately moist with water at a temperature 8° or 10° more than that of the atmosphere. Where there are still late grapes hanging in small quantities, it is desirable, for many reasons, to cut them, and keep them in a dry fruit-room. As soon as they are all cut, lose no time in pruning and dressing the vines. Then the house can be kept cool and well aired for a month at least before they begin to grow. This is a good time to complete making new vine-borders and planting young vines, though it can be successfully done till midsummer.

Peaches.—If the weather be cold and sunless, force with the same caution recommended last month. To force peaches at a high temperature by dint of hard forcing is never safe, far less so till after the stoning stage. Do not exceed 55° to 60° at night, until they begin to take their second swelling; then, if the fruit are required early, the heat may range to

60° in cold, and 65° in mild weather, especially when the house can be shut up early with sun-heat. See that inside borders are kept properly moist, and syringe all houses where the fruit are set in fine days. Keep a sharp look-out for green-fly, and never let it get a footing: more especially is this pest dangerous to trees just budding into leaf and full bloom. All trees under glass, where there is no command of fire-heat, should be retarded and kept as late as possible; for if kept close and forwarded early into bloom, a risk of losing the crop by late frosts is incurred.

Figs.—Where the fruit are swelling, increase the night temperature to 60° with 10° more by day. Figs like a moist atmosphere, and should be syringed every afternoon, and the air should never be otherwise than moist, except when fruit are ripening. Give careful attention to the matter of watering, especially if they are in pots; for if allowed to become over-dry, they will cast their crop; and stagnant water about their roots will produce the same effect. Give air regularly, more or less, according to the weather, to prevent the young growths from becoming weak and the foliage thin and tender. As soon as the growths grow to five or six joints, pinch the points out of them, or squeeze them firmly between the finger and thumb to stop growth, without causing them to bleed. Start later trees.

Strawberries.—If all has gone on well, these will now be an interesting crop, and one that will be most acceptable at table, as a companion dish to late grapes and early pineapples. Attend carefully to what was said about crops that are swelling off and colouring. Where they are coming into bloom, on the shelves of pine-stoves or cucumber-houses, where a high temperature and moist atmosphere are requisite for pines and cucumbers, it is a good plan to move the strawberries into a peach-house or vinery, where the night heat does not range above 55° to 60°. Strawberries set more certainly at that temperature than with 10° higher; and when set, they can be moved back into their warmer quarters. After they are set, put successional lots of plants into peach-houses and vineries that are being started with fire-heat. Green-fly and red-spider must never be allowed a footing.

Melons.—Those planted last month will be growing freely now. Train them carefully as they advance. Water sparingly at the roots, and supply only a moderate amount of moisture to the air. The night temperature should not range more than 70°. Give air on all favourable opportunities. To grow melons in spring with a very high temperature, and much moisture and little air, ruins them, by causing them to make weak growths with thin sickly foliage. Plant out succession crops as previously directed, and sow more seed both at the beginning and end of the month.

Cucumbers.—Do not exceed 70° at night for the present. Cucumbers require more moisture at the root and in the air than melons, and soon suffer if they are allowed to become dry at the root. If sudden bright sunshine succeeds a few days of dull weather, they will flag, and should not be allowed to do so; and some thin material, such as tiffany, is best for shading with under such circumstances. Stop the lateral growths, and they will show fruit at every joint; but do not allow them to bear too freely when young. Sow and plant for succession crops.

APRIL.

Pines.—Those that started into fruit in the early part of winter will this month ripen and be found very useful when other fruits are generally scarce. As soon as they have begun to colour, give no more water at the root; and if there happen to be a few plants considerably in advance of the rest, it is best to remove them, if possible, to another compartment where they can have more air and a dry atmosphere. As April is generally a changeable month with cold nights, I do not recommend much increase of temperature over that recommended for March; 75° when the nights are mild, and 70° when cold, is sufficient. The forcing should be accelerated by day with sun-heat. They should be shut up soon after three o'clock, and get a gentle dewing overhead through a fine rose—avoid heavy syringings, which keep the soil in an unhealthy puddle. The temperature may rise to 90° for an hour or two. The fires, which should be low during day, require to be quickened early in the afternoon, so as to keep the heat from falling below the points named at 10 P.M. Although the sun has now considerable power, it is not desirable to give a great increase of air. Instead of this, it is better to frequently sprinkle the paths and walls, and keep the steaming-trays full. Watering must be carefully attended to, aiming at just keeping the soil moist but not wet. As soon as suckers appear, remove them all except two on each plant; and if gills or suckers appear on the fruit-stalk, remove them all at once. If bottom-heat is supplied to succession stock shifted in March from tan and leaves, keep a watchful eye on the ground thermometer; and if it goes above 90°, give each pot a shake from side to side, so as to leave an opening all round the pots for the escape of the heat. Towards the middle of the month it is generally necessary to water these, as the roots will be taking possession of the fresh soil, which will be getting dry. As they show signs of growth give more air, and always early in the day, so that sun-heat can be husbanded for the early part of the night instead of violent firing. Do not increase the night temperature much over that recommended for March—70° at 10 P.M., to drop to 65° in the morning. Keep the steaming-trays supplied with water; but unless once or twice a-week in bright weather, do not syringe overhead this month. Any young stock that were not found sufficiently rooted to shift in March will require to be attended to now, and shifted when moderately well rooted.

Vines.—Where the earliest crop of grapes is the produce of vines in pots, they will in many cases be ripe this month; and will not—especially if the pots are plunged—require so much water, as neither the fruit nor matured foliage can make use of so much. They require just sufficient to keep the fruit "plump" and the foliage healthy—a superabundance will give watery grapes. Keep the house cooler and drier than when they were being forced on; and while cold currents of air must still be avoided, a little air must be left on all night, in amount sufficient to prevent moisture condensing on the fruit. Crops that have arrived at the colouring point should have a decreasing supply of moisture in the air, and an increasing amount of air as the colouring and ripening processes go on. It often occurs that red-spider appears on early-forced vines just at the time of colouring, and this pest must be sharply watched and vigorously put down. Succession-houses that have been thinned, and in various stages between that and colouring, may now be pushed on with much less fire-heat than in the dull short days of very early spring, and may therefore be kept somewhat warmer: 70° during mild weather, and 65° when very cold at night, should be aimed at in the case of Hamburgs and vineries with a mixed assortment of vines. Look over the vines twice a-week, and remove all lateral growths as soon as they appear. Thin the bunches and berries in succession-houses. Muscats coming into bloom may have the heat raised to 75° during mild weather at night until fairly set. Where the borders of late houses have been kept dry inside, let them have a good soaking of tepid water,—the surface being first stirred up and left somewhat rough, or water will not penetrate freely nor regularly. See that newly-planted vines do not suffer for want of water, and rub off superfluous buds as they break.

Peaches and Nectarines.—Crops that have passed the stoning stage may be forced on more freely, and the night temperature raised to 60° and 65°, according to the state of the weather. Make the most of sunny days by shutting up with sun-heat early in the afternoon, giving the trees a syringing with water at 80°. Do not allow the trees to bring a killing crop to maturity. Water the inside borders with manure-water made from cow or sheep's manure. Tie in the young wood regularly all over the tree. Disbud trees in late houses. Keep a sharp look-out for green-fly, and keep it down, or rather never let it get a footing at all. Syringe trees in all houses where there is fire-heat applied every fine afternoon. Should mildew make its appearance, put a little sulphur in the water, and increase the heat and air. In late houses, where the fruit is all set, give a vigorous syringing to free the fruit of old blooms. Thin partially when about the size of peas, and finally those that are stoned.

Figs.—If the early crop be from trees in pots, great watchfulness is necessary in the case of watering. If they are ever allowed to become over-dry, the chances are that the fruit will fall off. Water two or three times a-week, alternately with guano or dung water, and syringe freely at shutting-up time, and keep the air regularly moist. Stop the young growths at the fourth or fifth leaf. Where fig-trees are planted in shallow inside borders, mulch with rotten dung, and keep the soil regularly in a medium state of moisture. Do not allow the trees to carry too many fruit at a time.

Strawberries.—Immediately the fruit is all picked from the earliest plants, remove them into cold pits to be hardened properly before exposure. Continue to put former directions in force in the case of those swelling their fruit, and in bloom, as well as in the case of those ripening their crop. Put the remainder of the stock of plants into cold frames, and into such structures as cold pits and late peach-houses, so as to keep up the supply of fruit till the earliest in the open ground ripen.

Melons.—Carefully impregnate the fruit-blossoms about

the middle of fine days, and stop the fruit-bearing growths one joint beyond the fruit. Till a full crop be set keep the air drier, give more air, and less water at the root. After a sufficient number of fruit are set and begun to swell, give a heavy root-watering and increase the air moisture again; and unless where there are good melon-pits with the plants trained to trellises, do not syringe overhead. With superior appliances the syringe may be used on fine afternoons, but not till after the fruit are as large as hens' eggs. Range the temperature from 70° to 75° at night. Plant out succession crops, and sow approved sorts for later crops.

Cucumbers. — Increase the temperature to 75° on mild nights when sun-heat can be taken advantage of in the afternoon. The early planted plants will now be bearing freely. Do not allow them to bear too many at a time, or some of the freer sorts, such as Volunteer and Sion House, will exhaust themselves. The disposition to ramble and grow will decrease as they come in a full-bearing state. Mulch them with rotten manure, and maintain a moist atmosphere; and, above all, see that they do not suffer for lack of water, if in shallow borders with hot-water pipes under them. Plant out later-raised plants as soon as they are established in 5-inch pots, and train as described. Sow for succession in later crops.

MAY.

Pines.—Early started fruit will now be swelling rapidly towards mature size. When it is an object to get them ripe as soon as possible, they may now be pushed on with a high temperature, but let it be principally derived from sun-heat, to run it up to about 100° for an hour or two after 4 P.M. There must be a corresponding amount of moisture supplied to the air, sprinkling the plants and fruit; but syringing must not be carried to excess, or the result will be tall unsightly crowns. When the fruit begin to change colour, withhold water at the root, and keep the air drier. Plants just showing fruit require careful attention in the way of watering, and must not be allowed to get too dry at the root, otherwise a serious check will be the result. See that they are supplied as steadily as possible with a bottom-heat of 85° to 90°. Smooth Cayennes, and other winter-fruiting varieties that have been encouraged to grow since the early part of March and that are now strong, and having well filled their pots with roots, may, towards the end of May, be kept cooler and slightly drier to mature their growth and rest them for a time before starting them. By the middle of the month, succession stock shifted two or three months ago will be growing freely, and will require great attention. Increase the moisture in the air in proportion to the increased light and progress of the plants; but avoid heavy syringings, which have a tendency to induce a soft weakly growth, as well as to keep the soil in a puddle. The soil should be carefully watched and kept moist, but not wet. Do not allow the temperature to run up too high before putting air on in the morning. In bright mornings put on a little air at 7 o'clock, and gradually increase it with the rising of the sun till 12 o'clock. Let the shutting up be gradual too—reducing the air early instead of leaving it full on till later in the day. Keep the fires low on sunny days. Hot pipes and a scorching sun should never go together in pine-culture. In a general way, shading succession pines is not desirable. It is sometimes necessary, especially in the case of Cayennes when growing fast; and after a continuance of dull weather, it is better to shade lightly for an hour or two than to allow the leaves to get browned and wiry.

Vines.—In early houses where the grapes are ripe, the atmosphere should be dry and cool. It is however possible, for the wellbeing of the vines, to carry the drying process too far, especially when most of the roots are inside. The border should be examined, and, if becoming too dry, water it in the early part of the day after the full air is on, so that moisture may not condense on the bunches. After watering, mulch with some loose dry dung, such as an old mushroom-bed. Look sharply after red-spider. In later vineries, where grapes are swelling off, keep up the temperature with as little fire-heat as possible. Shut up early in the afternoon to make the most of sun-heat, instead of leaving the vinery open later in the day, and then have recourse to violent firing to maintain the maximum night temperature. Under such circumstances as I am recommending, the night temperature can be kept to 70° till far on in the evening without heating the pipes much in the early part of it; and with such treatment, Muscats, in bright weather, may range as high as 75° at 9 P.M., falling to 70° in the morning. With increased light, and the more liberal ventilation necessary, moisture, from sprinkling the border and paths, must also increase in all cases, except where the grapes are colouring and ripe. As soon as succession-houses are set, and have their berries about the size of radish-seed, lose no time in getting them all thinned. Avoid heavy cropping as perhaps the greatest evil that can be perpetrated on the vine: it defeats its end in all ways. The grapes cannot be so fine, and it is the surest way of breaking down the constitution of the vines. Disbud, stop, and tie down late vines. Vines planted in March and April will require careful attention, as their roots have not yet much hold of the border. See that they do not get too dry at the root, especially if planted near the hot-water pipes. Tie their young growths carefully to the wires. If there are temporary vines planted among those that are to be permanent, the former require to be differently managed, as directed.

Peaches.—Peaches now ripening require a free circulation of air, or flavour will be deficient. Put aside all leaves that shade the fruit, so that the sun can lay on that mellow rich colour which is peculiar to the peach, and without which they look insipid. Syringe freely on fine afternoons later crops that are swelling off, and pay great attention to the state of the border where it is principally inside. Give heavy waterings of manure-water when required, and mulch with a light coating of finely disintegrated manure. Tie in the wood in late houses. Thin the fruit by degrees. Keep green-fly and red-spider from gaining a footing. Pinch any shoots that make rampant growths in young trees, or they will rob the weaker ones of sap, and destroy the balance of growth which is so desirable. Trees that have been planted two or three years in new borders are apt to grow undesirably strong. A good way of counteracting this tendency is to crop them rather heavily.

Figs.—These will be swelling their crop rapidly, and require to be well supplied with manure-water, especially if they are old plants with their roots limited either to pots or borders of comparatively small dimensions. Syringe freely every fine afternoon, and frequently sprinkle the paths and surface of the border through the day; but gradually withhold moisture from the air as the fruit show signs of ripening, and increase the ventilation. When the second crop is forming in early houses, thin them out in time. A fair crop of large well-swelled fruit is worth twice the quantity of small skinny produce. Attend to stopping and tying down shoots in later houses, and avoid crowding in too much wood and foliage.

Melons.—Sow and plant out for succession crops both at the beginning and end of the month. Attend carefully to the tying and stopping of those planted in April, and impregnate the blooms. The depth of soil for melons should now be more than for early crops, as it is very undesirable to be obliged to water often when the fruit is swelling. As soon as the fruit begin to ripen give more air, and no more water at the root.

Cucumbers.—Plant out for late summer and autumn supplies. Those now in full bearing will require copious supplies of water, and if from long-continued bearing they should show signs of flagging energy, top-dress the bed with well-decayed manure. Keep thrip, green-fly, and red-spider at bay by the prescribed preventives and remedies. Those that have been in bearing all winter may, if others are sufficiently advanced to keep up the supply, be torn out and their place occupied with melons, or, if required, planted again for cucumbers.

Strawberries.—Those will now be very troublesome with red-spider should the weather be hot, and particularly if the plants are standing on shelves, and, except when ripening, will require to be regularly syringed on fine afternoons. All plants that are now done bearing may, after being properly hardened, be planted out in well trenched and manured soil, to give runners for another year's supply, and also to bear outdoors next year, for which they are invaluable.

JUNE.

Pines.—Succession stock will now have well taken with their shift, and made rapid progress, and will require careful management to prevent them from making a soft watery growth on the one hand, and on the other from a wiry weakly growth. Give just enough of water to keep the soil regularly moist without being sloppy ; and instead of syringing the plants heavily overhead and about their centres, rather damp the surface of the plunging material, and just dew the plants gently overhead through a fine rose. They may now be more freely aired, opening the ventilators and shutting them gradually. The fires may be allowed to go out, or nearly so, in steady hot weather, but always kindle or set them agoing in time to prevent the thermometer from falling

T

below 70° at 10 P.M. Where bottom-heat is dependent on leaves and tan, see that the material does not shrink away from the sides of the pots. Plants intended to yield an autumn supply of fruit should show fruit this month; and if they have been grown in light pits, and are stocky, and have their pots well filled with roots, there will be little difficulty in getting them to do so. They should have a bottom-heat of from 85° to 90°, and a moist atmosphere and higher temperature applied to them immediately. Such conditions will cause them to throw up their fruit, if all others be favourable. Keep stock intended for winter supply rather cooler and drier, to cause them to rest for a few weeks previously to their being forced into fruiting a month hence. Encourage those that are swelling off their fruit with a high temperature and a plentiful supply of moisture, both in the soil and in the air. Shut them up as early in the afternoon of fine days as it is safe to do so, running up the heat from 90° to 100° for a short time. See last month's directions regarding those that are colouring and ripe. Look over all plants that are in fruit, and which are throwing up suckers, and remove them all but two or three on each plant; and wherever gills are discovered on the fruit-stems, remove them at once. Liquid manure, in the way of guano, soot, or dung water, may now be applied in a weak state every time pines are watered.

Vines.—Where established vines are now swelling off full crops, pay careful attention to the state of the borders, particularly inside. Mulch them lightly with old mushroom-bed dung, and give a heavy watering of soft tepid water about the time they are stoning, and again just as they show the first signs of colouring. The outside border, if the season be dry and hot, should be treated in the same way. In calm hot weather it will now be necessary to give front ventilation to all vines, but not to such an extent as to create violent draughts on windy days. Leave a little air on all night;

and increase the ventilation by degrees to the maximum by 12 o'clock. Let vines from which the fruit is all cut be kept cool, and their foliage well syringed occasionally, to keep them free from red-spider, and their foliage in health as long as possible. Thin all grapes immediately they are fit for the scissors, as fruit advance so quickly at this season that they soon get larger and thicker than they ought to be when thinned. If not already done, pot-vines intended for fruiting early next year should be shifted into their fruiting-pots.

Peaches.—Where the early crop is all gathered, give the trees a thorough washing with clean water through the engine, and continue to syringe or engine them two or three times a-week, to keep the foliage fresh and free from insects throughout the heat of summer. If the border is dry, let it also have a good watering, and keep everything connected with the trees tidy and clean. The starving of early-forced trees with the idea of ripening them is injurious. Keep them cool by giving an abundant supply of air at front and top. Where fruit are swelling off, continue to syringe the trees on the afternoons of fine days, shutting them up early and keeping the temperature to 65°, as a minimum, with as little fire-heat as possible. Tie in the growths and thin the fruit of later houses; and wherever fire-heat is applied, keep up atmospheric moisture in proportion.

Figs.—So soon as the first crop is gathered from early trees, give them a heavy watering with liquid manure, and mulch with short dung, so as to support the second crop now showing. Syringe freely on fine afternoons, and sprinkle the border and paths frequently in course of bright days, for figs delight in a moist atmosphere. Top-dress those in pots now swelling their second crop, and water freely with guano-water, and syringe the trees vigorously to keep down red-spider.

Melons.—Plant out a quantity for August supply. Give them a good depth of soil; a heavy loam with a very little old cow-manure mixed with it is best, especially after this season. Make the bed of soil firm, but not too smooth on the surface, or it will become caked, and not easily penetrated with water when it is applied. Stop them when they reach within 8 or 9 inches of the side of the frame, and the lateral growths will show fruit. Stop the laterals one joint beyond the fruit, and avoid overcrowding with wood and foliage. Sprinkle advancing crops on fine afternoons at shutting-up time, except where the fruit are setting. Keep those that are ripening dry, and give plenty of air, so as to get the fruit as high-flavoured as possible. Sow at the beginning and end of the month for successional and late crops.

Cucumbers.—Now is a good time to plant out a quantity of plants for late summer and autumn supply. In England they do well enough in frames after bedding-plants are turned out; but in Scotland it is necessary to have them where there is a command of artificial heat, or mildew will ruin them.

Strawberries in Pots.—These will now be nearly over, and any that are yet to ripen may be removed to cold pits and frames, where they can stand on a cool bottom, otherwise red-spider will not be easily kept in check. As soon as runners can be had, lay the necessary stock for another year's forcing. For early forcing, make a point of having them shifted into their fruiting-pots the first week of July.

JULY.

Pines.—Should the weather be such as horticulturists like and generally expect in July, the necessity for using fire-heat, to keep temperatures sufficiently high for pines in all stages of growth, will be in some localities superseded by the more natural and invigorating heat of the sun. At the same time, if a period of dull, wet, and comparatively cold weather should occur, careful attention must be paid to the atmosphere of all pine-pits. The pipes should be heated so as to keep the atmosphere from becoming stagnant, and from sinking much below the maximum temperature. Succession plants now in their fruiting-pots and growing rapidly require to be very carefully supplied with air, so as to prevent a weak and sappy growth. The state of the weather at this season generally admits of a more liberal supply of air being given. Those intended for early fruiting next year should, by the end of the month, be large plants, with their pots well filled with roots, and requiring careful attention in the matter of watering. On the afternoons of fine days these and all succession stock should be syringed through a fine rose, to moisten the surface of the leaves without causing much water to accumulate about their axils, producing a tendency to throw up suckers, and diverting their energies from the centres. The night temperature should range at $75°$, and when the nights are cold it may drop to $70°$ at 6 A.M. Early-started Queens will now be all cut, and the suckers they have produced ready to be potted. 6 and 7 inch pots will be sufficiently large for these. In plunging these, give them plenty of room, and keep them near the glass. Shade when bright till they make roots 2 inches long. When they begin to grow freely, give plenty of air to keep them stocky. If fruiting plants for another year be scarce, some of the finest of these early suckers may be potted into their fruiting-pots by-and-by, and successfully fruited next summer. Where a quantity of fruit is ripe at one time, remove the plants to a cool fruit-room. Fruit swelling off may be pushed on if necessary with a high temperature from sun-heat by shutting up early. The thermometer may rise from $95°$ to $100°$ for a while, with a corresponding amount of moisture. Water them liberally with manure-water, and syringe them overhead every fine afternoon. If a stock of fresh soil for next year is not already stored, now is a good time to do it.

Grapes.—As houses get cleared of the fruit, keep the foliage healthy and active as long as possible. Red-spider must be prevented by keeping the house cool and by frequent vigorous syringings, and by preventing the borders from becoming too dry. Grapes intended to hang through the winter should be carefully examined, and if the berries are at all likely to be too thick when they attain their full size, thin them a little more. Muscats, even in the most favoured localities, should still be fired at night, to keep the minimum night heat from falling below 75°, and the atmosphere from becoming stagnant and unwholesome. Leave a little air on all vineries throughout the night, especially as soon as the grapes show the first signs of colouring. Remove all fresh lateral growths as they appear. Stop young vines intended to bear next year, when they reach the top of the house, and their lateral growth confined to two leaves from each joint, one of which may be removed when the wood begins to get brown. It is not yet too late to plant vines struck from eyes this spring. If borders can be prepared for them any time this month, they will run the whole length of the roof, and make fine vines next year. If pot-vines have been forwarded as directed, they will now be strong canes, with full buds, and their wood changing to a brownish hue. Give them an increased circulation of air: do not allow them to make any fresh lateral growths, and see that they are fully exposed to the sun; for unless their growth be thoroughly hard and well ripened, no great success can be counted on in the way of fruit from them next year.

Peaches.—Give fruit that are colouring abundance of air night and day, and see that none of them are shaded with leaves. Copiously water with manure-water, and mulch the surface of the borders of those swelling off their fruit, and syringe them freely on fine afternoons till they begin to change colour, after which syringe no more till the fruit are all gathered. Let no amount of care and trouble be considered too much in order to keep the foliage of the early trees from which the fruit are all gathered healthy and clean. Keep them cool, and mix a little flower of sulphur in the water with which they are syringed. This is an excellent preventive of red-spider, and peaches seem to like sulphur about their leaves. Attend to the borders, and see that they do not become too dry and crack. Attend carefully to the growths of young growing trees, and tie them in their proper places, avoiding crowding them.

Figs.—Where fruit are ripening cease syringing, and give a free circulation of warm dry air. Where the first crop is all gathered, and the second advancing, see that the trees are well fed. Give the border a mulching of rich manure, and water copiously. The syringe must be used freely every fine afternoon to prevent red-spider, except, of course, where fruit are ripening.

Melons.—Melons, especially those now swelling their fruit, require much more water than is good for them when the days are shorter, and the sun less powerful. But at the same time avoid frequent driblets, and give a few thorough soakings instead. Keep the surface of the soil fresh, and prevent its cracking. A final watering should be given before the fruit begins to ripen, putting a thin layer of mushroom-dung over the surface of the bed. Remove all superfluous growths, and slightly syringe the foliage on fine afternoons up till the time the fruit begins to ripen, then keep the house or pit dry, give more air, and expose the fruit to the sun. Plant out for a late crop about the middle of the month. Melons may be planted later, and ripened late in autumn, but they are seldom much worth, and it is not generally done.

Cucumbers.—Water those in full bearing copiously with

manure-water. Remove all old and tarnished foliage and unproductive wood as fast as they can be replaced with that which is young and healthy. Syringe regularly on fine afternoons, and shut up with strong sun-heat, so as to do with as little fire-heat as possible. In the south they do well at this season in cold frames, but in Scotland they are precarious and short-lived without more or less fire-heat.

Strawberries in Pots.—All should be in their fruiting-pots by the middle of this month at the latest—earlier if possible. Place them where worms cannot molest them. Give them plenty of room. Remove all runners as they appear, and see that they never suffer from want of water. Syringe or water them overhead through a rose-pot every evening when the weather is hot and dry.

AUGUST.

Vines.—That portion of the stock which are intended for early summer supply next year, should, by the end of this month, have their pots well filled with roots, and be of a stocky well-matured growth. If kept growing late into the autumn, there is little certainty of getting them to start in time to yield ripe fruit next May and June. Care must be taken, while inducing a stubby well-matured growth and a pot full of roots, that the plants do not suffer from dryness at root and an arid atmosphere; and though towards the end of the month moisture requires to be decreased, avoid by all means the "drying-off" system. Those intended to start, after making a growth in spring, must still be encouraged to grow, and be managed as directed for succession plants last month. Smooth Cayennes, and other late varieties now out of bloom and swelling off, encourage with waterings of guano-water, a moist atmosphere, and a high temperature in the afternoon and evening when sun-heat can be stored. Fruit colouring and ripe, see former "Calendar." Suckers from those plants that have fruited up to this time will now be ready to pot. Shade them from the sun during the hottest part of the day for ten or fourteen days, by which time they will be making roots. Syringe them lightly in the afternoon at shutting-up time, and when they have made roots about 2 inches long, water them with water at 85°. After this they soon begin to grow freely, and should have an abundant supply of air to keep them stocky.

Grapes.—Early houses, where the wood is thoroughly ripened, may now have the lights removed off them where such are movable, if the wood require painting and other repairs; these, and all alterations in the way of heating, should also be carried out forthwith. Should the weather be dry, late grapes that are swelling off and about the colouring-point copiously water with manure-water, and slightly mulch if it has not been done before. Apply a little fire-heat on damp dull days, and always at night during such weather, with a little air on all night. Take every precaution to keep wasps and flies from preying on ripe grapes. Keep a constant eye to vines in all stages, and see that red-spider does not get a footing. Where the fruit are all cut, an occasional syringing and a free circulation of air night and day will keep the foliage clean. If any of the vines from which fruit has just been cut have their roots further from the surface of the border than is desirable, treat them as has been directed. Pot-vines intended to fruit early next season should by this time have their wood as brown and hard as a cane. Expose them to full sun and a free circulation of air. Should they show any disposition to make young lateral growths, remove them at once, inducing them to maturity and rest as soon as possible. Avoid exposing them outdoors in windy positions; which destroys the foliage before it has fully done its work.

Peaches.—Look carefully over all trees from which fruit has been gathered, and if there are many shoots that will not be required for next season's bearing, remove them at once, so that all light and air may play about the trees freely. If there be any red-spider about them, syringe them with sulphured water till not one remains; and otherwise give every possible attention that is necessary to retain the foliage to the last in a healthy state, so that well-developed buds and matured wood may be the result. Expose fruit that are ripening to all light and air possible. Late crops in cool houses in their last swelling should be well supplied with water at the root till they begin to colour.

Figs.—Early trees from which the second crop is all gathered must not be neglected. If in pots, keep them well supplied with water, and free from insects by frequent syringing. Should they have more wood about them than is necessary for next season, remove it, and expose them to full light and air. Where fruit are ripening, the atmosphere must be comparatively dry, with a free circulation of air, or the fruit will be deficient in flavour. Supply trees swelling off their crop with manure-water at the root—a moist atmosphere and frequent syringing are necessary to keep the foliage healthy.

Melons.—Attend to the impregnation of late crops, and avoid overcrowding with shoots and foliage. Give those swelling off full crops occasional heavy waterings with manure-water. If grown in houses on trellises, cover the surface of the bed with a coating of rotten manure 1 inch or so in thickness. Expose ripening fruit fully to the sun, and to a circulation of warm air.

Cucumbers.—Those that have been in bearing all summer may now be partially cut in, all fruit removed, be top-dressed with rotten manure, and kept at 75° at night, and they will soon make young wood and begin bearing, and give a supply till late in autumn. See that those in full bearing do not want for water at the roots, and syringe them freely on fine afternoons. About the middle of the month is a good time to sow for winter-bearing plants, or they may be produced from cuttings at the end of the month. It is desirable to get them well established while the days are yet long, and less fire-heat required.

Strawberries in Pots.—These, if shifted into their fruiting-pots last month, will now be growing rapidly, and filling their pots with roots. Give them a liberal supply of water, and occasional watering with dung-water as they get well established in their pots. See that they are not standing too closely together, preventing a free circulation of air and light about them. They should be placed in an open airy situation. If any portion of the required stock still remain unshifted, not a day should be lost in getting them into their fruiting-pots. The great point is to obtain well-ripened crowns, and pots as full of roots as they can hold. If they are disposed to root through the pots, lift them occasionally to prevent this. It is best, for this reason, to have them standing on boards or trellis-work, to prevent the roots leaving the pots.

SEPTEMBER.

Pines.—Smooth Cayennes, and other varieties that are most suitable for autumn and winter supply, will now be swelling rapidly, and should have every encouragement and attention. A top-dressing of horse-droppings will assist in stimulating them, and in keeping them uniformly moist at the root. Water them with weak guano-water every time they require watering, and keep the atmosphere moist. Shut up early in the afternoon, with sun-heat to a temperature of 90° for a time, allowing it to fall to 75° by 10 o'clock P.M. Syringe them overhead at shutting-up time, when the weather is bright, but avoid the crowns as much as possible with the syringe. Give late Queens that are colouring a free circulation of warm dry air about them, and keep them dry at the root. Should more ripen at one time than are required, remove the plants to a cool dry room, where they will keep in good condition for two or three weeks, and so keep up a succession of fruit. Now is a good time to put in a second lot of suckers, from plants which have ripened and are ripening their fruit. Plunge them in a bottom-heat of 85°, and keep the air at about 70°. If the soil is moist when they are potted, water will not be necessary till they have formed roots an inch long. Dew them lightly overhead every fine day when shut up, and give air more liberally after they have rooted and commenced to grow, and avoid crowding them in the bed. The stock of plants that are intended to start into fruit at the commencement of the year will now require careful management. No more water should be given than is sufficient to keep them from suffering either from aridity of atmosphere or over-dryness of soil. Give a liberal supply of air on fine days. By the end of the month they should be in as complete a state of rest as is possible. 65° will be a night temperature sufficiently high to begin October with, and it should be gradually lowered to this as the nights lengthen and become more cold. Those plants that are intended to start next spring, as a succession to those just referred to, and that are not now so forward, require to be encouraged to grow more freely for another month at least, and consequently require to be kept more moist, and be shut up with more heat on the afternoons of fine clear days. Avoid as much as possible a forcing-heat on dull days and at night, and take advantage of sun-heat when it can be had. All syringing of growing stock overhead should now cease.

Grapes.—Late grapes intended to hang through the winter should be quite ripe by the end of the month. In keeping grapes successfully, it is of great importance that the foliage be healthy as long as possible. And if there be any red-spider about the vines in patches, as is not unfrequent, get rid of it at once. In wet localities, where heavy autumn rains prevail, cover the outside border with shutters or tarpauling so as to throw off the superabundant wet. And as it is now desirable to keep the inside of the vineries drier, let the surface of the border be gently forked up, and a sprinkling of old mushroom-bed manure be scattered over it to the depth of an inch, first sifting it rather finely. Look over ripe crops, and cut out all berries that show any signs of decay. Keep the vines free from lateral growths, and the main foliage healthy to the last. The early part of this month is a good time to remove the inert surface-soil from borders down to the roots, replacing it with fresh turfy loam mixed with horse-droppings, and a little old lime-rubbish or charcoal. Vines from which fruit was cut in April and May will be ready to prune by the end of the month; and if intended for early forcing again, it should be no longer delayed. After pruning keep them as cool as possible. All repairs or painting requisite should be done before the weather becomes unfavourable for such work. Young vigorous-growing vines that were planted last and this year, fire and keep warm till the wood is perfectly brown and matured. Remove all young growths as they appear, and if they have been allowed to make anything of a rambling lateral growth, remove as much of it as will admit a free play of light and air about all the foliage and wood. See last month's directions regarding pot-vines.

Peaches.—Give trees that are strong, and have their wood not so solid and ripe as is desirable, fire-heat and a circulation of air in order to ripen them. If any vestige of red-spider remains or appears about them, give them a few vigorous washings on fine afternoons with the engine. Late crops in cool houses will now be ripening, and will require to be carefully guarded from flies and wasps. Push aside all leaves that in any way interfere with a full exposure of every part to sun and air.

Figs.—Encourage trees that are swelling off a crop with

waterings of liquid manure, and keep a circulation of air about them as the fruit ripens. Give those from which the crops are all gathered an occasional syringing, so as to keep the foliage healthy until it has properly performed its functions, and drops off naturally. Plants in pots from which all fruit are gathered, may be placed in any warm place outdoors where they will get full sun, and be sheltered from high winds, which would tarnish their leaves.

Melons.—Keep fruit that have got to the ripening stage dry, and well exposed to light and air. The night temperature should range about 70°. Be careful not to water crops that are nearly fully swollen, or the chances are that they will burst and be spoilt. The best way is to mulch the surface of the soil with a little leaf-mould or rotten manure to prevent the surface of the bed from becoming too dry, and from cracking. Late crops that are swelling rapidly should be kept warm, and now that the nights are longer and cooler, should have fires put on to prevent the temperature from sinking below 70° to 75°, according to the state of the weather.

Cucumbers.—Plants raised from seed sown about the middle of August will soon be ready to plant out. A light moderately rich soil is best for winter cucumbers. Grow them on with as much light and air as possible, in order to get them strong and healthy before shorter and duller days arrive. Plants still in bearing should be watered occasionally with liquid manure. Keep the temperature from 70° to 75° at night. If a low temperature is allowed at this season, mildew is sure to attack and destroy them. All symptoms of it should be checked by dusting the affected parts with flower of sulphur.

Strawberries in Pots.—If former directions have been carried out, these will now have well filled their pots with roots; and should the weather be hot and dry, give them frequent supplies of dung or guano water. It is best to water them in the morning after this season, as the drier they are at night, the less likely are they to be affected with spot in their leaves. Keep them free from runners and weeds, and give them plenty of room.

OCTOBER.

Pines.—Suckers potted in August and early part of September will now grow freely, and will require to be well aired to prevent their drawing. After the middle of this month range the night temperature from 60° to 65°, according as the nights are cold or mild. Lower the bottom-heat to from 75° to 80°. Should there be any fear of the largest and earliest of them becoming pot-bound before spring, it is better to give them a small shift, and a little more room between plants, than to allow them to be cramped in small pots. With the decline of sunshine and heat, the amount of moisture, both in the soil and air, requires to be gradually reduced. Succession plants, intended to fruit early next season, will now have well filled their pots with roots, and in other respects be in a well-matured condition, and must be kept in a state of comparative rest for the next three months. Drop the temperature to 60° at night by the end of the month; and the bottom-heat should be proportionately low—75° to 80° is quite sufficient to keep the roots in good condition. When with sun-heat the day temperature exceeds 70°, give air to prevent it rising to an exciting degree. If the pots are plunged firmly to the rim, they will require very little water through the winter. Keep a moist atmosphere in pits or houses where fruit are swelling, and range the night temperature from 70° to 75°, according as the weather is mild or cold. Shut up the house early on the afternoons of fine days, running the temperature up to 85° for a time. Gently sprinkle the plants overhead every other day when the weather is bright. See that no check is allowed from want of water at the root. Keep the bottom-heat at 85°. Suckers of Smooth Cayennes and other autumn and winter fruiting sorts can be taken off and potted as they become large enough. They will root and establish themselves before winter, and will not be so likely to become drawn as when left to grow on the parent plant.

Vines.—Look over all grapes that have been ripe for some time two or three times a-week, and wherever a mouldy berry appears remove it at once, •before it taints others. Keep everything about them as dry as possible by occasional fires, and a free circulation of air on fine days. Keep vines from which the fruit is all cut cool and well aired, unless in cases where the wood is not perfectly ripened, which should be fired till it is perfectly brown and hard. Vines planted this year, and that have continued to grow till now, should be ripened forthwith by the application of a little extra fire-heat, and, if at all crowded, by the removal of some of the lateral growth, to allow a free play of light and air about all their parts. Vines from which grapes are to be ripened early next year should be pruned immediately. Remove all loose bark from their stems, but avoid the "scraping-to-the-quick" system. If there has been any spider on them this season, scrub them with a hard brush and water, and then coat them with the mixture recommended. Thoroughly clean all the wood and glass, remove the surface-soil, and replace it with fresh, so that all may be in readiness to start forcing next month. If pot-vines have been standing outdoors, remove them to some place where their roots can be protected from heavy rains. Where very early grapes are required, the earliest of these may be started towards the middle or end of the month; and if they can be plunged in bottom-heat, they will start into growth sooner. If they have been cut or pruned in any way, dress the wounds twice over with styptic, or they will be apt to bleed. Put a few more into heat than are required for the space, in case any of them fail to show well. It is useless to start thus early with any but early and well-ripened vines, and they require to have a higher temperature to excite them than two months hence— 55° at night will be necessary.

Peaches.—Where new borders and fresh plantations of trees are contemplated, this is an excellent time to transplant the trees, just as they are beginning to shed their leaves. Trees planted a season or two ago, and that have grown too grossly, may now be carefully lifted and replanted. Keep trees that are well ripened well aired and cool; but where the wood is rather green, a little fire-heat will much assist their ripening.

Melons.—Late crops will now require more assistance from fire-heat. The night temperature should not be less than 70°, and when ripening, warmth and dryness are indispensable to anything like good flavour. Melons can now be kept longer, after being ripe, in the fruit-room than in warmer weather.

Cucumbers.—Keep up a genial growing atmosphere, not allowing the temperature to sink much below 70° at night. Give air in the early part of the day, and shut up early with sun-heat. Lessen the moisture in the soil and atmosphere as the season becomes more dull and sunless; but where the roots are near the hot pipes, see that over-dryness of soil is not allowed. Stop them at every joint, and do not allow them to become over-crowded, which produces a thin weakly foliage, that is much more apt to damp off as the weather becomes more damp and sunless. Do not allow them to bear too much fruit at one time.

Figs. — Generally speaking, all figs are gathered by the middle of this month, and the trees may be kept drier at the roots and the house cool, but see that extreme dryness of soil is not allowed. All wood not required to furnish the trees for next season had better be removed at once.

U

Early plants in pots should now be protected from heavy rains.

Strawberries in Pots. — If former directions have been attended to, these should now be ready to burst their pots with roots, and have large well-ripened crowns. During heavy rains, lay the pots on their sides, if they cannot be placed in cold pits or frames. When plants are late, place them in pits or frames, in a warm light place, and put glass over them to induce them to mature their growth better than if left in the open air.

NOVEMBER.

Pines.—Those suckers potted in early autumn will now be well rooted and established, and will require cautious treatment, so as to rest them without stinting them. After the middle of the month the night temperature should never exceed 60° in mild weather, and a few degrees less when the weather is cold and calls for extra firing. A little air should be given every fine day when the temperature exceeds 65°. Keep the bottom-heat steadily at 75°, and the atmosphere dry rather than otherwise, but not by any means parching. Very little or no water at the root will be required if they are growing in a bed of leaves and tan. Where the bottom-heat is supplied entirely by hot-water pipes, and the plunging material is shallow, an occasional watering will be necessary. Recently-potted suckers should be kept 5° warmer till they are tolerably well rooted; and if in very light pits, may be kept growing gently through the winter, especially if the condition of the stock of young plants makes this desirable. Keep all plants intended to be started into fruit soon after the turn of the day at 60° at night, with a few degrees more bottom-heat than has been recommended for suckers. These will require the same treatment with regard to watering as has been directed for suckers. Plants intended to fruit in succession to these will do with exactly the same treatment recommended for suckers, only be very watchful that they do not get such a drying as is likely to cause them to fruit prematurely when increased moisture and temperature are given to them by-and-by. Keep smooth Cayennes, and other winter varieties that are swelling off their fruit, steadily moist at the root, with a night temperature of 70° and 80°, or 10° more by day, and the bottom-heat 85°. Avoid syringing overhead after the beginning of the month, but maintain a moist genial atmosphere more by sprinkling the floors and surface of the bed than from the steaming apparatus. An over-moist atmosphere at this season is productive of large crowns, which are a great disfigurement to pines. Take good care of all fruit that may chance to show this month. These kept in a temperature of 70° all winter, will come in very acceptably in spring, when pines are generally scarce and much appreciated. Get coverings ready for pits during severe weather, which is much to be preferred to keeping up temperature by hard firing. Frigidomo is excellent for this purpose.

Grapes.—November is perhaps the most critical month for grapes of the whole keeping season. Look carefully over the bunches at least three times weekly, and remove every berry that shows the least signs of decay. Hamburgs especially require this care. Make fires sufficient to warm the pipes slightly on the mornings of fine days, giving air at the same time, so as to expel the damp. When frost occurs, keep the temperature about 45°. There should not be a plant requiring water in vineries where fruit is hanging in winter. Prune all vines that have cast their leaves, remove all the loose bark and dress them, and otherwise clean the vineries as directed. Presuming that the early vinery has been pruned and otherwise prepared for starting this month, a quantity of leaves mixed with a little stable-litter should now be formed into a bed or ridge in the centre of the house.

This will soon ferment and heat, and a portion of it should be turned over every day so as to give a little heat and moisture. This body of warm material will, in ordinary weather, keep the temperature sufficiently high with little or no fire-heat. The outside border should be thoroughly covered up with 2 feet of leaves and litter, and either thatched or covered with shutters to throw off the rains. Sling down the vines from the rafters, so that the top part of them be brought into the same temperature as the lower parts. Syringe them gently twice a-day with tepid water. Pot-vines started last month may still be kept at 55° at night until they break, when they will require 5° more heat. In their case make the most of every ray of sunshine that occurs—the less artificial heat used to keep up a given temperature the better. Examine the outlet or main drains from all vine-borders, and see that they are acting properly. See that all heating apparatus is in tight repair and acting properly before severe weather sets in.

Peaches.—Lose no time in getting those that are intended to be started next month pruned and tied. If there has been any red-spider about them last season, dress them as directed; remove the surface-soil from the border, top-dress with rotten manure, and cover over with an inch or two of soil. If the border is dry, give a good soaking of water, and towards the end of the month shut up the house, and keep the temperature from falling below 40°. Treat the outside as directed for vines.

Figs.—Prune and tie as soon as all the leaves have fallen. If, however, a proper system of summer pinching and thinning has been adopted, there will now be very little surplus wood to prune away. Remove the surface-soil of the border, and replace it with fresh turfy loam and rotten manure in equal proportions. Keep the house cool all through the month. Those in pots can be stored away in any cool pit or shed for the present.

Cucumbers.—We have now long damp nights and dull sunless days, conditions very trying to cucumbers. The temperature should range from 65° at night to 70° by day, with a few degrees more when the sun shines. Water at the root and moisture in the air must be more sparingly applied. Give a little air on all favourable occasions. Keep young growths regularly stopped, and do not allow any crowding of foliage. If green-fly attack them, destroy it by two moderate smokings with tobacco on two consecutive nights.

Strawberries in Pots.—These should now be plunged in cold frames, or removed to cold late peach-houses, where they will be sheltered from rains. Or where no such protection can be made available for them, build them into stacks, laying the pots on their sides with the plants outwards, and fill up the space between them with ashes or sawdust. Put up in this way, they can readily be protected from severe frost by throwing mats or litter over them.

DECEMBER.

Pines.—Early autumn-potted suckers that are well rooted, and wintering in dry light pits or houses, with bottom-heat supplied by hot-water pipes, will require to be carefully examined at intervals, and watered before they become "dusty" dry. This must be guarded against by watering those that require it at intervals. This applies most forcibly to a time of cold weather, when more firing is required to keep up the proper temperature, which should now be at its minimum, the days being generally sunless and short. Young stock winter with the best results at a temperature not exceeding 55° for at least six weeks at the dullest part of the year. At this season, when autumn fruit has been mostly cut, more room can generally be given to young stock. Where early pines are an object, a number of the earliest and most likely to start should now be subjected to a temperature of 70° at night, with 8° or 10° more when there is a blink of sun by day, the bottom-heat to be kept ranging from 85° to 90°. They will be dry at the root, and require to be watered, after being a few days in the temperature named. Keep the atmosphere generally moist, but not to such an extent as will cause condensed moisture to fall into the centre of the plants. The remainder of the next season's fruiting-plants may still be kept rather dry, and at a temperature ranging from 55° to 60° for the present. Continue to supply to those swelling their fruit a rather moist atmosphere, a temperature of 70° in the air and 85° at the root. Examine the individual plants weekly, and water those that require it, so as to keep the soil in a moderately moist condition. Pot suckers on stools from which the fruit have recently been cut, and plunge in a brisk bottom-heat and temperature of 65°, in a light pit; they will soon root, and make fine plants for shifting as a succession to those potted six or seven weeks ago. If these are strong, and potted now into 6 and 7 inch well-drained pots, according to their size, they will grow in these till May, and can then be shifted at once into their fruiting-pots. Where there are what I shall term half-sized plants—that is, plants in 8-inch pots—well rooted, I would have no hesitation in shifting them after the middle of the month into 11-inch pots; and pushing them on, plunged thinly in a light place, with the view of fruiting them next year.

Grapes.—Continue to keep a strict watch on all grapes that are still hanging. As soon as the early-started vines fairly burst their buds, raise the temperature a few degrees, and when the young growths are half an inch long raise the night temperature to 60°, and that of the day to 65° in mild weather. Pot-vines that are required very early may have a degree or two more, but it is far safest not to force too hurriedly, while the days are so short, cold, and dull; but to get well under way, and be ready for more rapid work when there are longer days and more heat from the sun.

Peaches.—The early house prepared as directed last month may now have fire-heat regularly applied, keeping the temperature about 50° in mild weather, and a few degrees lower when cold. Proceed with caution for the first few weeks. Syringe the trees morning and afternoon with tepid water, give a little air early every fine day, and husband every gleam of sun-heat that can be had. Prune, dress, and tie succession-houses.

Figs.—Where early figs are required, a place should be got in readiness, where those in pots can be started after the middle of the month. Bottom-heat is of great advantage thus early: it obviates the necessity of much artificial heat for a while at first if a bed of oak-leaves can be made up, in which the pots can be plunged in a bottom-heat of about 75°, with a night temperature of 50° to begin with. They not only break more freely and strongly into growth, but young fruit formed in autumn are not so likely to drop off as when forcing is commenced without bottom-heat. Syringe the plants on fine days, and just give fire-heat enough till they break to keep the temperature at 50°; and when water at the roots is required, let it be given at a temperature of 80°. If the plants have been grown several years in the same pot, top-dress them with something rich, and water with guano or sheep-dung water.

Cucumbers.—Avoid hard forcing in very cold sunless weather, or the leaves will become thin, and the whole plants weakened. When the weather is severe, it is very desirable to cover the surface of the glass, and fire more moderately.

Strawberries in Pots.—Put a quantity of these into heat according to the number of plants and available room. The early peach-house, or a shelf near the glass, is a good place to start them, as they do not do well with much heat thus early. If they can be set on a fermenting bed of leaves in a pit near the glass, it will be a great advantage to them. The mild bottom-heat will start them more kindly. Before putting them in heat, remove all decayed leaves, turn every plant out of its pot to see that the drainage is not deranged, and water them with clear lime-water to kill all worms, which, if not got rid of, will begin their injurious work immediately they are put into heat.

A FEW OBSERVATIONS ON HEATING BY HOT WATER.

THIS being a subject that is very intimately connected with the cultivation and forcing of fruits under glass, it has been considered advisable to append a few observations on the principles of heating by hot water; for, notwithstanding all the elaborate essays that have from time to time appeared in the horticultural press on heating hothouses with hot water—not to say anything of the stirring controversies that have taken place on the subject—I have the best reasons for believing that many whom the matter intimately concerns have still but very vague and erroneous ideas regarding the principles upon which the proper adjustment of hot-water boilers and pipes depend. And from some cause or other, it is a notion very prevalent that the easiest and shortest way to get deeply immersed in the disagreeable and undefined difficulty figuratively termed "hot water," is to plunge into this heating question, in which are involved furnaces, boilers, pipes, fire, and water, beside that unfortunate being who has to control the elements and conditions of combustion so as to have half-a-dozen thermometer-needles in as many hothouses standing at certain hair-like marks at half-a-dozen different times in the four-and-twenty hours.

It is my belief that, if those who have to do with fixing pipes and boilers were to make themselves acquainted with the effects of heat and the power of gravitation on water, it would be next to impossible to commit the blunders, and resort to the unnecessary and expensive precautionary measures, one so often meets with and has to deal with. It is no part of my intention to pretend to deal with that imponderable and powerful agent called by men of science caloric, but which I shall call heat—hypothetically regarded as a subtle fluid, the particles of which are to each other repellent, but attractive to all substances, though in various degrees. But the effect of heat upon water, an element composed of minute and distinct particles that are supposed not to have the quality or power of transmitting heat the one to the other, as in the case of solid bodies, is one of the matters concerning which some knowledge is indispensable in the case of all who have anything to do with heating by means of heated water circulating in pipes.

The particles of which water consists, it need scarcely be said, have a capacity for heat from different sources, but most manifestly so to us in this case from combustion in the fireplace. Now the expansion of bodies is one of the most universal effects of increasing their heat. This expansion takes place to a greater degree in some bodies than in others. Liquids expand much more by the same increase of heat than solid bodies, and air more than either. With the expansion of the individual particles of water, their specific gravity becomes less; in other words, they become lighter in proportion to their size. Here lies the whole secret of hot-water circulation in pipes and boilers, and the well-known law which should regulate their relative positions. The heated particles of water bound upwards, and, as "nature abhors a vacuum," their place is taken up by a rush of colder and heavier particles. It is of very little practical use to cavil about the question as to whether heat or the greater specific gravity of the cold water which jostles up the warmer and lighter plays the greater part in sending up and away the stream of hot water. Both have a hand in it, no doubt. This influence of heat upon water can be very manifestly shown by filling a tumbler with cold water, and mixing with it some coloured particles of matter, and then immersing the tumbler in a vessel filled with hot water. It will at once be seen, by the motion of the particles of coloured matter, that at the sides of the tumbler there is an upward current of heated, and in the centre a downward current of colder, water. This goes on until the whole is of the same temperature. A glass of warm water immersed in cold has the current reversed in its course—upwards in the centre, and downwards at the sides, where the water is being cooled. Here is the whole secret of the motion and course of heated water in the boiler and pipes of a properly adjusted heating apparatus. And one would suppose that the simple understanding of this would prevent any from making mistakes. Yet, strange to say, some who undertake hothouse-heating are entirely ignorant of these simple and well-established facts.

Wherever the heat generated by combustion in the furnace acts most directly and powerfully, from that surface bound upwards the particles of water, and to that spot, simultaneously, drop the colder particles of water, to be in their turn sent bounding on their errand of warmth. Anything that attempts to contravene this law of gravitation will be rebelled against by the elements concerned with unmistakable violence and persistency. Clearly, then, the outlet for the water, thus lightened and charged with its freight of heat, should be at the highest part of the boiler; and that by which the cold water is to run in and down, to take its place, should be at the lowest point. Boiler inventors and manufacturers recognise this important part of the matter, and always place the flow-pipe at the highest, and the return-pipe at the lowest, point of boilers.

Great importance has been attached by many to the necessity, or at least the great desirability, of having the boiler fixed at a very much lower level than the pipes; and also to the necessity of laying all the flow-pipes on the incline the whole length of the house to be heated. The importance, too, of having the return-pipes on a considerable decline, has, in my opinion, been very much over-estimated. It is entirely unnecessary to form deep, damp stoke-holes, in order to sink the boiler to a level much below the main body of the pipes, as is so very frequently met with. And as to having the pipes running at an incline, after starting from so high a level, I consider it entirely unnecessary. Indeed, one of the most efficient heating apparatus I ever superintended, started from about a foot above the level of the boiler, and ran down a gradual decline into the boiler. Immediately the water enters a hothouse it begins to part with the heat absorbed from the fire, gets colder, increases in specific gravity as it speeds in its way back to the boiler again, and a downhill career is most natural to it as soon as it leaves the highest point of action, where its heat is the greatest. Practically I have never found much difference when the pipes went the whole length of the house on an incline, or on a dead level all the way round till it came near to, and dropped into, the return-opening of the boiler. Indeed there is little fear of a good circulation, provided the pipes do not at any point descend and rise suddenly, and most especially that at any point they do not dip below the level of the return-opening into the boiler. I have had the working of apparatus where pipes, descending perpendicularly, crossed under a walk and rose again perpendicularly to heat another range of 80 feet of glass; but at none of the points were the pipes lower than two feet above the level of the return-opening into the boiler. This undesirable arrangement worked pretty well until hard firing became necessary; then the water was thrown out in plunges at the supply cistern. Such an arrangement should always be avoided.

HEATING BY HOT WATER. 317

There is another error frequently committed in arranging the route of the water. Suppose, for instance, a boiler fixed at one end of a house of, say, 80 or 100 feet long, as part of the work allotted to it. As in the case of span-roofed houses, it may be desirable to have three or four rows of pipes all round the house. Now it is not uncommon to find two rows called the flow-pipes taken all round the house to near the boiler, and there to start back with other two on the same route into the return-opening of the boiler. This is giving the water a long journey, and the return-pipes will be found comparatively cold by the time the water gets to the boiler. Now, if instead of this the whole four pipes be connected with the flow-pipe, and go round the front and end of the house nearly on a level, and start along the back down a decline to the boiler, and there plunge down the drop-pipe into the return-opening of the boiler, it will be found that while any portion of the pipes may not be quite so hot as the beginning of the two flow-pipes in the former case, there will not be any portion of them nearly so cold as the last portion of the return. I do not say that this is the best way to conduct the water; but I have proved from experience that the arrangement indicated is the better of the two named, when the pipes are, from any necessary conditions, laid all round the house in this way.

The supply of waste-water to the boiler and pipes is often placed anywhere that looks most convenient; but the proper place is to attach the supply-cistern to the return-pipe somewhere near the boiler. Fixed to the flow, the water will be frequently plunged out by the upward tendency of the hottest water. It is also very undesirable to leave the supply-cistern to be kept full either by pouring in water from a pot or by turning a tap, which is often neglected. There should always be a cistern supplied by the action of a ball-cock, and then the anxiety connected with the neglect of supply does not exist.

Regarding boilers, it is difficult to say which among many good ones are best. The upright tubulars are powerful, but expensive, and require deep stoke-holes and good fuel. Some of the improved forms of the old saddle-boiler are excellent; so are the cruciforms, which, like the saddles, burn any sort of fuel, and are easily set. For amateurs requiring to heat only one small house, the smallest form of Meiklejon's retort is excellent and cheap.

INDEX.

CALENDAR, THE.
  January, 270.
  February, 274.
  March, 277.
  April, 281.
  May, 285.
  June, 289.
  July, 292.
  August, 296.
  September, 299.
  October, 303.
  November, 306.
  December, 309.

CUCUMBER, THE.
  Its natural history, 251.
  Difficulties of early forcing by dung-beds, 252.
  Preparing the seed-bed, 252.
  Sowing, and treatment of young plants, 253.
  Application of linings, 255.
  Fruiting-pits, planting-out, &c., 257.
  Preparing the pit for the plants, soil, &c., 258.
  Management after planting in the fruiting-pit, 259.
  Watering, stopping, &c., 261.
  Renewal of linings, 262.
  Winter forcing, 263.
  House for it, 264.
  Soil, &c., 265.
  Planting, temperature, &c., 266.
  Training, stopping, &c., 266.
  Insects to which subject—thrip and red-spider, 268.
  Diseases, 268.
  List of varieties, 269.

FIG, THE.
  Its natural history, 176.
  Its introduction into Britain, 177.
  House for its cultivation, 180.
  Soil and formation of border, 181.
  List of varieties, 183.
  Propagation, 184.
  Time and manner of planting, 189.
  Training and general management the first year, 191.
  Pruning and pinching, 193.
  Root-pruning, 196.
  Plants in pots, 197.
  Training, pruning, &c., 197.
  Soil for these, 200.
  Forcing and general management, 200.
  Temperature, watering, &c., 201.
  Ripening the fruit, 203.
  The second crop, 204.
  Insects and diseases to which subject, 205.
  Packing the fruit, 206.

GRAPE VINE, THE.
  Its natural history, 50.
  Its native country, 51.
  Extent of its former culture in England, 51.
  Sites for vineries, 52.
  Vinery for early forcing, 53.
  The "lean-to" vinery, 53.
  Heated borders for this, 55.
  Ventilation, 55.
  Vinery for late grapes, 56.
  Span-roofed vinery, 57.
  Aerated borders, 57.
  Drainage, 59.
  Composition of borders, 61.
  Varieties of grapes, 68.
  Selection for planting, 70.
  Preparation of young vines for planting, 71.
  Time and manner of planting, 77.
  Treatment the season they are planted, 81.

INDEX.

Their management the second season, 86.
Their management the third and fruiting year, 90.
Pruning for the first crop, 90.
Time to commence forcing, 90.
Temperature, 92.
Moisture, 93.
Ventilation, 95.
Form for vinery against garden wall, 96.
Weight of crop, thinning, disbudding, &c., 96.
Spur-pruning for next season's crop, 98.
Training, 100.
Keeping grapes through the winter, 101.
General management of borders, 102.
Their partial renewal, 103.
Shelter from excessive rains, 103.
Mulching, 104.
Covering well-fermenting material and otherwise conserving heat, 104.
Renovating exhausted vines, 105.
Pot-culture of grapes, 107.
Inarching vines, 108.
Setting up grapes for exhibition, 110.
Packing them, 112.
Insects to which subject—red-spider, 114.
Thrip, 115.
Mealy bug, 116.
Phylloxera vastatrix, 116.
Remarks by M. Planchon on, 118.
First appearance of, 124.
Its destructive ability, 126.
Preventives against it, 128.
Diseases—shanking, 130.
Mildew, 132.
Rust, 133.
Excrescences on under sides of leaves, 134.
Scalding, 135.

HEATING BY HOT WATER, A FEW OBSERVATIONS ON, 313.

MELON, THE.
Its native country, natural history, &c., 207.
Growing it in dung-beds or pits, 210.
Sowing the seed and management of the young plants, 211.

Training and stopping, 213.
Soil and planting, 214.
Moulding up, temperature, 216.
Impregnation, watering, &c., 217.
Culture in houses, trained on wires near the glass, form of house, depth of soil, &c., 220.
Preparing the plants, planting, &c., 223.
Watering, &c., 224.
Temperature and syringing, 225.
Ventilation, 226.
Impregnation, training, and stopping, 226.
Very early forcing, 227.
List of varieties, 229.
Insects and diseases to which subject, 229.

NECTARINE, see Peach and Nectarine.

OBSERVATIONS ON HEATING BY HOT WATER, 313.

PEACH AND NECTARINE.
Their natural history, native country, &c., 136.
House for early forcing, 138.
House when they are not required before July, 139.
Drainage, depth and width of border, 143.
Soil, 144.
Varieties of peaches, 146.
Of nectarines, 147.
Propagation and selection of trees, 147.
Best stocks for different varieties, 150.
Planting, 151.
Pruning and training, 152.
Fan-training, 152.
Seymour's system of training, 157.
Disbudding or summer pruning, 159.
Thinning the fruit, 161.
Root-pruning, 162.
Forcing and general management, time to commence forcing, 163.
Dressing the trees and borders, 164.
Temperature, 165.
Ventilation, 167.
Moisture in the air and syringing, 168.
Setting the fruit, 169.
Watering, 170.

INDEX.

Ripening and gathering the fruit, 171.
Packing to be sent to a distance, 172.
Insects to which subject—red-spider, 173.
Green-fly, 173.
Brown scale, 174.
Thrip, 174.
Diseases, 174.

PINE-APPLE.
Its natural history, 1.
Houses for its cultivation, 2.
Those for summer growth, 3.
For winter growth, 4.
Pits for suckers, 5.
Situation of the houses, 5.
Amount of heat and hot-water pipes, 6.
Objections to flat-roofed houses, 6.
Steaming apparatus, 7.
Arrangement of pipes, 7.
Provision for watering, 8.
Arrangement of plants, 8.
Advantages of the tan and leaf bed, 8.
Varieties, 9.
The Queen, 9.
Smooth-leaved Cayenne, 10.
Black Jamaica, 10.
White Providence, 10.
Charlotte Rothschild, 11.
Prince Albert, 11.
Lambton Castle Seedling, 11.
Soil and its preparation, 13.
Propagation, 15.
Suckers, 16.
Potting of these, 16.
Subsequent treatment, 17.

Succession plants — their spring treatment, 20.
Their summer and autumn treatment, 27.
Fruiting plants, 35.
Selecting, arranging, and plunging them, 36.
Retarding and keeping them after they are ripe, 40.
How to keep a succession of ripe fruit all through the year, 42.
Treatment of plants that miss fruiting, 45.
The planting-out system, 46.
Insects to which subject—white scale, 47.
Brown scale and mealy bug, 48.

STRAWBERRY, THE.
Its natural history, 231.
How to secure the best runners for forcing, 232.
Preparing these for their fruiting-pots, 233.
Soil and potting, &c., 234.
Watering, 237.
Protecting and resting, 238.
House for forcing, 239.
Forcing, 240.
Setting and thinning the fruit, 242.
Insects to which subject, 245.
Forcing in a greenhouse or pit, 245.
Tying up the fruit-stalks, 246.
Packing them when ripe, 247.
Preparing them for exhibition, 248.
Best varieties for forcing, 249.

VINE, THE, see Grape Vine.

THE END.

PRINTED BY WILLIAM BLACKWOOD AND SONS.

www.ingramcontent.com/pod-product-compliance
Lightning Source LLC
Chambersburg PA
CBHW030005240426
43672CB00007B/834